Black-o-knowledge
"Stuff we need to know"

Another
Mind-Opening Book
By
James Clingman

Milligan Books   California

Published and Distributed by
Milligan Books, Inc.

Drawing Title "Listen to the Elders" by
George Williams, artist
Cincinnati, Ohio

Cover design by
A3Arts.com Gary Scott

Formatting by
Alpha Desktop Publishing

First printing, May 2004
10987654321

ISBN 0-9753504-4-7

Milligan Books, Inc.
1425 W. Manchester Ave., Suite C
Los Angeles, California 90047
www.milliganbooks.com
(323) 750-3592

Dedication

To all of the men and women who selflessly put their resources, their talents, their time, and even their lives on the line for economic empowerment for Black people in America and beyond.

To those who "Died on their way to freedom" and to those who are still fighting on the economic empowerment battlefield. Thank you, my brothers and sisters.

"How long will ye love simplicity? And fools hate knowledge?
Proverbs 1:22

"My people are destroyed for lack of knowledge: because you have rejected knowledge, I will also reject you..."
Hosea 4:6

Contents

Black-o-Knowledgements   15
Introduction   21

Section I   28
What Price Freedom?

Still Running for Freedom at Aspen Grove   29
Freedom Ain't Free!   32
Economic Lessons of the Past   35
What Price Would you Pay for a Profit?   38
Using Our Resources to Help Others. A TALL Order.   40
Reparation Preparation   42
What Did You Do On The 4th of U-Lie?   45
Juneteenth – Are we really free in 2003?   48
The Economic Legacy of Ken Bridges   51
If I Should Die On My Way To Freedom   54

Section II   56
Consciousness – or the lack thereof

Being Black When No One is Looking   57
Use Me 'Til You Use Me Up   59
Where is DuBois' Guiding Hundredth?   61
Tree Shakers and Fruit Gatherers   64
Throw-away People   67
Condo for Sale – Bushes Included   70
All Money Ain't Good Money   73
The Correct Psychological Moment   76
Internal Reparations – Repairing Ourselves
from the Inside Out   79
No Deposit, No Return   81

Section III   84
Politricks and
Other Games of No-Chance

Two Wings on the Same Bird   85
Wanted: Maynard Jackson Politics – Part One   88
Wanted: Maynard Jackson Politics – Part Two   91
Had Enough Yet?   94
Can You Hear Me Now?   97
You Asked For It   100
Standing in the Door of No Return   103
Eureka, Eureka! – I've found it!   106
The Arrogance of Power   109
Let's Take the Politics Out of Politicians   111

Section IV   114
Larceny in High Places

Politricksters, Corporate Thieves, and Hypocrites   117
Wall Street Implosion   120
Give And Take   123
Red, White, and Blue Trumped by the Green   125
Enron's End-Run   128
Martha's Stewardship   131
It's the Iraqi Economy, Stupid!   134
Peace Profits   137
How Much Money Do You Need Anyway?   140
Blackout Keeping Us in the Dark   143
Rush "From" Judgment   146

Section V   149
The Games People Play – On Us

This Racism Thing   150
We Have Been Programmed by Programs   153
"Minority" Programs Keep Us Fighting Over 15%   156
Booker T. and W.E.B. – Two Schools of Thought   159
Sibling Rivalry? I hope not.   162

The Minority Majority   165

Somebody's Calling You Out of Your Name   168

Are you a Certified Black Person?   171

Section VI   174
Puleeeeeeze! – Let's Get Serious!

We Need a Plan!   175

Kwanzaa – *Celebration or Practice?*   178

Is a Flag More Important Than a Life?   181

Another "Victory" for Black Folks?   184

The New Pepsi Challenge   187

The Shortest Boycott in History   190

What would we do without white folks?   193

Yo! Let's keep it real   195

Is the "Black Economy" an Oxymoron?   198

Section VII   201
It's the Doing That Counts

Hearing But Not Doing   202

Revolution or Evolution?   205

NOBCChE – The Secret is Out   208

Black Talk Radio – Is it talk without action?   211

Well Done Beats Well Said Every Time   214

MATAH – Taking it to the Next Level   217

The Black Capital Network   220

Kwanzaa 2003 – What do you have to celebrate?   223

Section VIII   226
What Is Your Money Saying?

Spend, Spend, Spend!   227

Let's Set Some Economic Goals   230

Another Year, Another $700 Billion   233

Money Talks – Especially Black Money   235

Let's Stop the Bleeding   238

The Power of Wealth versus the Power of Income   241

Wealth-Building Takes Backbone   244

Use Our Spending Power to Empower Ourselves   247
Turkeys' Day   250

Section IX   253
Education and Entrepreneurship

Wanted: Entrepreneurship High Schools   254
Demopublicans, Republicrats, and Entrepreneurs   256
A Grand Time with Granville and Other Friends   259
Smart Bombs and Dumb Children   262
Rebuilding the Entrepreneurial Spirit   265
Somewhere Lorraine Hansberry is smiling   267
Bill Gates – The Real Education Czar   270
Piney Woods School – Changing America ...One
student at a time.   273

Section X   276
The Business of Doing Business

Business Owners, Take Care of Your Business!   277
If You Can't Beat 'Em, Buy 'Em   280
Should Black Business Owners Sell Out?   283
A New "WB" – DBWB. Now, Profile This!   286
Four! Or Is It "Fore"?   289
Why Borrow Your Own Money?   292
I got mine, you got yours. Now what?   294
Business in the Black   297
Miami Nice! *The Power of Economic Sanctions*   299
Release Yourself!   302

Section XI   305
Home Cookin'

Cincinnati – A Real-Life Cartoon   309
Irony of Ironies   312
Tale of Two Timothy's   314
Grand Slam   317

Economic Terrorism   320
Cincinnati in Black, White, and Green   323
Diversity or Adversity? That is the question.   326
The $30 Million Rip-off   329
Boycott Bustin' Black Folks   332
Does Marvin Lewis have the power to heal?   335
Susan Taylor – "Tailor-Made" for Cincinnati   338
"Politricks" – It's that time again.   341

Section XII   344
Action-Based Solutions
It's Time to Move Forward

Economic Solutions   345
Abundance or Scarcity?   348
The Collective Banking Group   351
Distribution is the Question –
    MATAH is the Answer (Part One)   354
Distribution is the Question –
    MATAH is the Answer (Part Two)   357
Getting Our Dollars to Make More Sense.   360

Section XIII   365
The Source of Our Resources

Stewardship   366
Room at the Inn   369
The Business of the Black Church   372
Let the Churches Say, Amen. Please!   374
Black Churches Funding Black Colleges   377
Let Pharaoh Go!   380
Stand! And Move Your "S" to the Front.   384

Epilogue   386

"I may not get there with you..."
Martin Luther King, Jr.

"All of us may not live to see the higher accomplishments of an African empire, so strong and powerful as to compel the respect of mankind, but we in our lifetime can so work and act as to make the dream a possibility within another generation."
Marcus Garvey

"...you will not bring this community into the land I give them."
God speaking to Moses

Black-o-Knowledgements

Eavesdropping on the Elders

Late one evening, while I was working on this book, I inadvertently overheard a conversation among some of our elders. I didn't mean to be discourteous by listening to their conversation, but I just couldn't help myself when I heard who was doing the talking. The more I listened the more I knew their ruminations were really meant for me to hear; they actually wanted to get their message out to their children and had no other way to do it except through me. So I listened intently and even took notes in an effort to pass on the correct information to you.

Marcus, the flamboyant and assertive one in the group, called the meeting of several brothers and sisters, who were trying to get some much needed and well-deserved rest. Marcus is the kind of brother who never seems to be able to rest; he is a veritable *whirlwind.* He always wants to talk, to write plans on organizational strategies, and he keeps everyone on their toes despite their weariness from long days of laboring for their people.

"What is it this time, Marcus?" asked Harriet, "I walked hundreds of miles during my lifetime, bringing slaves to freedom, and quite frankly I am exhausted." She proudly looked at Marcus with loving admiration, which reassured him, as always, that Harriet respected him for his initiative.

"Yeah, Marcus," Frederick chimed in. "Why do you keep marching around in that army uniform? Don't you ever get tired? Don't you know how old you are? You should be getting some rest, my brother." Marcus replied, "I can't rest no matter how much I want to and how much I try. I can't and won't rest until our people are free."

"What do you think, Booker?" Douglass asked. "You fought hard for our freedom, and your life ended quite abruptly and prematurely, during the height of your movement. How do you deal with the plight of our people?" Booker lamented, "Yes, it is difficult to rest while our people are still fighting the same battles we fought more than 100 years ago. I was only 58 years old when I had to stop, so I am with Marcus; we have to continue, and even though our bodies are weary, we must keep our spirits strong."

"I told our people what to do way back in 1829!" interjected an angry David Walker. "I only made it to age 34, but in my short lifetime I appealed to our people to run for freedom, but many of them refused. It's not that I'm tired, my brother, I'm too young for that; I'm just frustrated at our people's lack of resolve to take their freedom."

"Let me say something," said Mother Mary McLeod Bethune. "In my Last Will and Testament I left instructions for our people, among which were directions on how to save and how to build institutions. I told them to save their pennies and nickels, and work cooperatively for our collective wellbeing. From the looks of things, they didn't listen to me, Marcus. So what do you have in mind now to get our people to change?"

"That's right," retorted Maria Stewart. I also told them to unite and open stores; their response was, 'Where will we get the money to do that?' I told them we have all the money we need, but we spend it on nonsense. Nothing has changed."

Then Richard Allen came strolling up to the crowd, imploring them, "Brothers and sisters, I know our people have made several strategic errors by failing to do as we did. Instead of maintaining the institutions we established, they abandoned them and now find themselves in dire straits. If we were able to do what we did back then, surely they can do better today, so let's not get too frustrated; let's see if we can help them"

The conversation started to get a bit heightened and energized; that was just what Marcus wanted. Others who heard it stopped by and sat down to add their wisdom to the mix. One was a fellow named Martin Delany. "Do you remember when I told our people to be producers, to build houses and rent them, to manufacture clothes instead of buying everyone else's? I warned that unless we were committed to make those changes we would walk around with our heads hung in sorrow and our faces hidden in shame. I knew, even then, that our progress resided in the work of own hands. What's wrong with our people? All they have to do is listen to us," Delany said

"I know, I know," Marcus responded, "but we must continue; we cannot stop. Even though our people have refused to hear us and even though they have allowed themselves to be misled, we love them and we must help them. Can you imagine how I felt and what I thought when some of our brothers and sisters were turned against me? I helped start many Black owned businesses and raised millions of dollars toward an economic movement that has not been duplicated since."

Marcus continued to lament, "I can remember when we had our own publishing company in Harlem, during the Renaissance, when many of our Black writers protested about white owned publishing companies discriminating against them by not reviewing or publishing their works. How sad I was to hear our people complain about white folks' publishing houses when our own UNIA publishing house, located in the heart of Harlem on 135th Street, was there for them. We had six million UNIA members who stood ready to purchase all the books Black authors could write, without depending on the largess of white companies. How ridiculous was that? But still, we cannot give up on our people."

"Hey Brother DuBois, you and I have had our disagreements and you have acknowledged that even you, one of our most learned men, fell prey to the divide-and-conquer tactics that caused disunity between us. What are your thoughts on this issue?" Marcus inquired.

W.E.B. answered, "I hear you, and I hear all of the others. I lived on the earth for 93 years, and it took a long time for me to see what was really going on in America. When I left for Africa, I was disheartened and frustrated even at my beloved Talented Tenth. I witnessed the squandering of tremendous intellectual and financial resources among our people, and now as I assess the situation facing our children I am convinced they need our messages even more, and we must aid them in any way we can. We must teach them sacrifice over selfishness"

Brothers and sisters throughout the crowd began to get engaged in the conversation as well, supporting what

Garvey and the others were saying. Martin, Medgar, and Malcolm added, "We agree that our children's most important need is economic. Our messages are there for them to read and heed. Our lives were taken from us as we worked for their freedom. We can no longer be divided and disjointed in our response to this pressing need."

"I wholeheartedly agree with these brothers," responded Elijah Muhammad. "That's what my economic program was all about in the 1960's: self-sufficiency, ownership, and wealth-building."

Looking as though they could no longer remain silent, three brothers leaped to their feet and shouted out in unison, "Amen! Freedom, every aspect of freedom for our people must be the ultimate goal. What is life without freedom?" I wondered who those bold, brash, outspoken brothers were. I soon found out when Marcus acknowledged them as Nat, Denmark, and Gabriel, former slaves who died trying to set their people free.

Kwame Ture and Fred Hampton spoke up too. "Our brothers are absolutely right. What is our legacy if it is not our willingness – and even our eagerness – to make the ultimate sacrifice for the freedom of our people?"

Then Sister Ida B. Wells stood up, and with her usual aplomb and commanding presence, said, "My dear brothers and sisters, we lived during a time when our people were lynched, and those who perpetrated those cowardly acts went unpunished. Their unnamed souls call out to our children who still walk that land called America; they seek relief just as the souls of those in the Book of Revelation called for their rescue. I pray our children will respond and do the things they need to do to help themselves? If they don't change they are lost"

As the crowd grew larger, over my right shoulder I saw a much younger brother standing there, listening intently, with a pensive smile on his face. He obviously had not been there as long as the others. His name was Ken Bridges. Marcus saw him and motioned for him to come closer. "Brother Ken, we know you are a relative newcomer to our midst, but we were watching as you tirelessly worked for freedom for Black people and, like the UNIA, the Matah

Network was a stroke of genius. What do you think now, as you see our people continue to struggle despite all of the wisdom we passed down to them?"

Ken humbly stepped to the front of the crowd and simply said, "Our people have been tampered with, Marcus, and they are suffering from the vestiges of psychological programming that still cause them to dislike everything African about themselves. But I believe if they would just love themselves and their brothers and sisters more, and redirect more of their spending toward one another, they will achieve the goals you promoted and set for them. The messages all of you left are still there with our people but they need to be reinforced continuously. When I left, there were new Kwame's, new Martin's, new Frederick's, new Ida's, and new Harriet's on the way. I am proud of them, for their courage and for their commitment, and I am confident they will make you proud too."

Marcus was relieved, and so were many of the others who heard Ken's words. Jackie Robinson and Paul Robeson were giving high-fives to everyone; Mahalia Jackson was singing, "Glory! Halleluiah!"; Satchmo was blowing his horn; James Baldwin, Bob Maynard, and Amos Wilson were busy writing down everything they witnessed; Queen Mother Moore was hugging everyone near her.

Harold Washington stood up and, with that familiar engaging smile, starting "pressing the flesh," remembering his days as Mayor of Chicago; Ron Brown and Reginald Lewis now felt much better about the future of those they left behind; and Fannie Lou Hamer sat back down in her rocking chair, able to rest once again.

Brother Chancellor Williams was so excited that he actually picked up Sister C.J. Walker and spun her around in his arms. Dr. Carter G. Woodson, Dr. John Henrik Clarke, J.A. Rogers, Langston Hughes, Elders A. G. Gaston, and A. Philip Randolph joined hands in a small circle and silently offered thanks to The Creator. Maggie Walker, Zora Neale Hurston, Sojourner Truth, Mary Church Terrell, Annie Turnbo-Malone, Betty Shabazz, and Gwendolyn Brooks jumped for joy at the thought of their children's awakening.

Tupac, Biggie, Aaliyah, and Lisa "Left Eye" Lopes quietly sat at the feet of these elders, full of regret and remorse for their untimely departure from their loved ones but comforted, nevertheless, by their understanding of what love and sacrifice truly meant. They wept. Mother Hattie McDaniel embraced them.

Garvey was all smiles by now, buoyed by what he had heard and seen. Although he knew his people still had a long way to go, and although Marcus regretted our not having followed the lessons of all the great elders gathered before him, his big smile was a dead giveaway that down deep inside he was confident we would one day soon follow through and fulfill our quest for true freedom.

Marcus was even more reassured when Maynard Jackson, who had just arrived, boldly walked up to him, gave him a huge bear hug, and thanked him for the sacrifices Marcus had made for our people. Maynard, in that beautiful baritone voice of his, thanked everyone in attendance for the lessons and examples they passed on to him.

Garvey was visibly moved by the gesture, as he took his beloved Amy's hand once again, embraced her, and slowly walked away from the crowd. This time he was determined to get some rest, and this time Amy would see to it that he did just that.

My initial feeling of eavesdropping on a private conversation subsided; I was supposed to listen in. After all, those were my brothers and sisters, my family members, and my elders; I have an obligation to listen to them and, more importantly, I have an obligation to acknowledge them and to follow their lead. I was not eavesdropping; I was learning. I thanked them for their words of wisdom, which are echoed throughout this book.

With deep respect and boundless gratitude to those who sacrificed for our freedom; they continue to teach us the "stuff we need to know."

Jim Clingman

Introduction
Knowledge is power ... but only if you use it.

There are some things we absolutely need to know, that is, if we are really serious about obtaining and retaining the "power" we so often discuss. Although many of my readers suggested I write this "sequel" to my previous book, Blackonomics, I wondered, as I still do, if I had written too much on this subject, if I had become the proverbial *broken record* of economic empowerment. Knowing that we can never have too much knowledge, and that we must use such knowledge to empower ourselves, I chose to write and title this book, Black-o-Knowledge.

As I have said many times before, my words are not new or original; they are merely the repetitive yearnings of our ancestors, those who said the same things to us and those who practiced what they preached, leaving their lessons for all to see. I am just one in a long line of *griots,* passing down information from generation to generation.

With that in mind, I decided to work on Black-o-Knowledge, and delay another book I am currently working on, mainly because of the many requests for copies of the essays I had written subsequent to the publication of Blackonomics. Having received so many positive letters, e-mails, and phone calls from across the U.S. and from other countries as well, and even a personal visit from Mustapha Ahmed Sanah, a brother from Ghana (Tamale Region) who read a Blackonomics article on the Internet, I felt compelled, almost obligated, to write this book, which encapsulates all of the information cited in nearly 200 articles written between 2001 and 2003. Black-o-Knowledge is about knowledge. It is also about the execution of that knowledge to the benefit and advantage of Black people.

Once again, the book is divided into sections, and some of the articles have been updated to increase their relevancy and relationship to the economic position of Black people in the United States of America in 2004; they also tell us where we must go and how to get there, as we move forward in this *new millennium.*

Black-o-Knowledge is easy reading; it is written to express, not to impress. Many who read my first two books said they started and finished them in one day. This book is a bit longer, however, and reading it in one sitting may not be practical. So relax, and take your time; read and heed.

The urgency of our need to ascend to new economic heights is stressed throughout this book, as it was in my two previous renderings on economic empowerment. Each day we choose to do nothing to change our situation we lose yet another battle and fall further behind in our quest for economic freedom. This is a call for action. This is not just a book you read and put back on the shelf; it is a book that is crying out for you to take the necessary action steps that will create and maintain an economic base from which Black people in America can collectively build and control wealth.

My contention is that Black people in America have no choice but to work together to build an economic foundation for our children from the resources with which we have been blessed. The establishment is not going to do that for us, and probably not even with us; but what do we expect? They have been in charge of this country since its inception and want things to stay as they are. I suppose, if we are content with the way things are, we will sit back and accommodate the desires of the power structure. If we are not content, we will take the proper action to change our economic demise into what can truly be our economic success.

Black-o-Knowledge is a compendium of views, facts, statistics, and insights that, if taken seriously, can help us in a "mighty way" to fight and win this war. Black-o-Knowledge comprises many of the lessons passed down by our elders, lessons that admonish and direct us along the path of economic freedom.

Black-o-Knowledge, as I stated in my two previous books, is not new in its content. Much of what is said here has been said in some form or another by men and women much wiser, more forceful, and more influential than I will ever be. More importantly, we must realize that the message of economic empowerment is greater than its messenger, and it must continue to be spoken, written, and implemented. It's not about who gets the credit for passing it on; it's about the execution of the strategies and tactics proposed therein.

The economic message is not proprietary; no one owns it and no one holds a patent on it. The economic message of freedom is for everyone – all of us. That fact is exhibited in what other groups are doing collectively to economically empower themselves. They control entire cities, much less economic enclaves within large cities across this country, and they make no apologies for working in support of one another. Sadly, Black folks have been conditioned to hang our heads and shy away from Black issues and from brothers and sisters who are deemed to be "too Black." We have been programmed to do the exact opposite of what it takes for any group in this country not only to survive but to thrive.

Generally, African Americans are suffering from and struggling within a warped world of self-denial. Some of our people seem to delight and revel in self-flagellation and self-deprecation, as though we have done something wrong and we have to spend the rest of our lives apologizing for our transgressions. We deny our children the wealth we gladly provide to others – and some of us even offer reasons for why we should! In his book, **Black on Black Violence**, Dr. Amos Wilson said, "When the Black community squanders the economic inheritance of its own children while it fills to overflowing the coffers of the children of other communities, when it does not regulate is consummatory behavior in terms of its long-term interests – it gets the crime it deserves."

As a result of our "inappropriate behavior," as Dr. Claud Anderson often discusses, we submit and succumb to the whims of others, even against our own people; we often laugh when things are not funny and scratch when we don't itch; and we seldom do things on a collective basis, unless of course they are things "purely social," when it comes to economics. Black-o-Knowledge is another call for an end to the madness of economic enslavement, especially of a people who have $700 billion in annual income and trillions of dollars in intellectual capital, as noted by Brother George Fraser.

There can be none other than psychological reasons for Black Americans to be at the bottom of every economic category in this country. In light of our resources, there can be nothing other than some deeply implanted psychological barrier that has impeded us and caused us to be the 20th century "Reluctant Entrepreneurs" as discussed in Joel Kotkin's article in **INC. Magazine** (1986). My term for it is psychological enslavement. Don King says, "Many of our people are mentally incarcerated, and they don't want parole." Well said, Don.

There can be no other reason for our being so distant from one another, often refusing to form alliances and mergers to grow and strengthen our businesses. There can be no other reason behind our stand-offish attitudes when it comes to doing business with one another and supporting one another, to a greater degree, with our dollars. No other reason. Black-o-Knowledge deals with all of those issues and many more, and offers solutions to ameliorate them.

Beginning with a section based upon the fact that freedom is not free and what the cost of economic freedom will be, Black-o-Knowledge re-teaches the lessons of the past and puts us on the right path.

The next section deals with one of the most important possessions necessary for Black people, or any people, to make economic progress: **Consciousness**. The things we do and the things we refuse to do, in the uplift or compromise of our brothers and sisters, are indicative of our individual levels of consciousness, which then transpose into our overall collective consciousness. Our work must be to increase our consciousness and learn who we are and what our individual obligation is to our people.

Just as Black people readily and proudly acknowledge our obligations as citizens of this country, having fought in all of its wars, even to the point of having won the freedom of this country by fighting in the Revolutionary War, according to Henry Wiensek, in his book, **An Imperfect God**: *George Washington, His Slaves, and the Creation of America*, we must be just as willing to fight for our own freedom as well.

Politricks and **Larceny in High Places** are the next two sections, and it is fairly obvious what they discuss. They point out the fact that we must be vigilant and wary of politicians and corporate *hucksters*, especially when we consider what took place right before our eyes in Florida's 2000 presidential election and on Wall Street, where billions of dollars were stolen by evil, greedy, and selfish men and women.

An Internet buddy of mine, Brother Khalfani, said, "The ultimate responsibility for votes belongs to the people who would, should, and could cast them. If black people don't deal seriously with their own votes, why [do we have] the expectation that anyone else will? Black folks must get out of the skin game and into real politics because we are getting burned by "minstrel" politics (black faces representing white interests). The real politics begins simply with people taking responsibility for their own vote." Therefore, as Maggie Lena Walker admonished us, "You can stand up and be counted, or you can lie down and be counted out." As you read the two-part article about Maynard Jackson, please remember, Black political activism, for the benefit of Black constituents, should be "important" rather than "impotent."

Regarding the corporate and government looting we saw in 2002, the Halliburton contracts and gasoline rip-off to the tune of $61 million, the WorldCom scandal, the Tyco debacle, the Kozlowski $2 million party in Sardinia, and all of the other excesses, I can only pose the following question and response: Politics and larceny? What a redundancy!

We then discuss the games people play on us and the games we play on ourselves. In both cases we lose. The "Minority" game and the "We Won a Victory" game are most dangerous if we are not making the rules and if we are settling for empty platitudes and never-to-be-fulfilled concessions from those who economically transgress against us. Watch out for these games of "No-Chance."

Black-o-Knowledge moves then to the "Doing" stage of our economic freedom quest, giving some examples of groups that are actively involved and walking their talk everyday. Then, understanding that money talks, we pose the question: **What is your money saying?** Listen in, and you may be surprised to hear what Black dollars say.

After that, we take a real close look at education and business. Very few schools are teaching Black children how to start, manage, and grow their own businesses, a vital wealth-building and wealth-retention component. So what should we do about it? Should we simply decry our local education system's lack of concern for our children, or should we take matters into our own hands and assure that our youth too will have access to the skills they need to become entrepreneurs?

Additionally, the art of doing business must first be accepted as the very basis of all that happens in this country. Owning a business (and doing what it takes to stay in business) is one of three ways to create wealth. The other two are real estate investment and investment in stocks, bonds, and other financial instruments. We must increase our ownership and control of income-producing assets and businesses, and not just mom and pop establishments and sole proprietorships, although they are necessary as well. We must establish businesses in manufacturing and distribution. We must merge with other firms and create more jobs for our people, as Thomas Boston tells us in his book, **Affirmative Action and Black Entrepreneurship**, with his *20 by 10 Plan*. He says we should develop enough Black owned businesses to employ 20% of the Black workforce by the year 2010. Ambitious? Yes. Necessary? Absolutely!

We then take a few stabs (Or should I say "jabs?") at figuring out what in the world happened to my hometown, Cincinnati, Ohio. It has been in the national spotlight since the 2001 civil unrest that took place when a 19 year-old Black man was shot and killed by a white police officer, who was subsequently acquitted of his crime. Cincinnati has lessons for all to learn in virtually every area of life. Of course our concentration is on economic empowerment, but it was very difficult to omit some of the other aspects of life in the city I sometimes call *Cincinn-apathy*. You will be "shocked and amazed" as Ali would say, at what happens in this river city on a daily basis. In 1993 we were the "Nation's Most Livable City;" eight years later we were saddled with monikers such as "one of the most racist," "most segregated," and "most dangerous" cities in America. Learn from our mistakes and learn from our apathy.

Finally, we discuss two very important topics, **Solutions** and the **Source of Our Resources**. Whenever I am asked to speak at various events around the country, I always tell the crowd that I did not come just to make them simply "feel" good; I speak to make our people "do" good. I think it's a shame that so many speeches are made, so many panel discussions are conducted, and so many forums are held, only to disperse without an action step, a step that can be taken immediately, to resolve the problems we spend hours talking about. If we are not willing to deal with and act upon solutions to our economic demise, then we have no right to complain about it. So, as we talk, let's "take some action," as Atlanta's Brother Ashiki Taylor says all the time.

The Source of our resources, of course, is God. In all things we should acknowledge Him and give Him the honor for all we have and are able to do. We must also be good stewards of what He has given us, multiplying those resources and using them to help others, because He did not give us what we have just for us; He blesses us so we can be a blessing to others.

Additionally, we must always stand up for what is right and what is just, stand for the rights of the "least" of our brothers and sisters, and stand up for truth, using the resources of strength, commitment, and faith given to us by the Almighty. We are instructed to work, to stand, and to take action when necessary, to resist and put down unrighteousness, and to support the less fortunate. If we understand and believe that our strength and our salvation come from our Creator, we will not be afraid or reluctant to speak truth to power and to stand against injustice.

Use your Black-o-Knowledge. Follow its instructions; combine it with the understanding and practice of good stewardship; be led by spiritual guidance; and help us win our quest for true freedom.

As Harriet Tubman must have asked some of her reluctant, psychologically enslaved travelers, I ask the same question: "Are you ready to go?"

Section I

What Price Freedom?

The future of America depends not on our wealth, our resources, our military power, but on the willingness of a goodly number of citizens to stand up, and – if necessary – risk their well-being, their jobs, their community positions and even their lives to speak out about the injustices and the corruption all around us and then take actions in support of those stands.
Derrick Bell, *Ethical Ambition*

For over three hundred years the white man has been our oppressor, and he naturally is not going to liberate us to the higher freedom—the truer liberty—the truer Democracy. We have to liberate ourselves.
Marcus Garvey

I believe to have interfered as I have done, in behalf of His despised poor, was not wrong, but right. Now, if it be deemed necessary that I should forfeit my life for the furtherance of the ends of justice, and mingle my blood further with the blood of my children, and with the blood of millions in this slave country whose rights are disregarded by wicked, cruel, and unjust enactments, I submit: so let it be done.
John Brown, *Abolitionist*

Still Running For Freedom at Aspen Grove

In June 2001 I had the profound honor and distinct pleasure of spending the weekend at a place called Aspen Grove. Nestled in the woods of Eastern Virginia, one mile off a secondary road in King William County, the 500 plus acres comprising Aspen Grove hold memories of things most of us talk about today. You see Aspen Grove is a former plantation that bares the scars of enslavement but also the triumph of transition, transformation, and true freedom.

The land was purchased by the great-grandson of one of the slaves who worked that hallowed ground. Dr. Walter P. Lomax, a prominent Philadelphia physician, entrepreneur, and all-around excellent example for others to follow, bought Aspen Grove and renovated the "Big House," which was built in 1732; Dr. Lomax also built a guest house on the property. He and his family now lay claim not only to a piece of American history but also a very important piece of their family's past.

As we looked at the pictures of the Lomax family and read the historical information on Aspen Grove, I could not help but imagine what it was like for the slaves on that land 150-200 years ago. When I spoke of it to the group I was meeting with, I felt my emotions rise to the point of tears and asked that we pray and acknowledge our ancestors who, many years ago, were probably doing what we had come there to do: Planning a run for freedom.

Seven Black men met at Aspen Grove in June 2001 to shape a plan for economic freedom for our people. How ironic, I thought, that slaves who once lived there probably held the same kind of meeting. How appropriate, I mused, that we were back on that same sacred ground, with the means to follow through and finally do what the slaves were discussing in the 1700's and 1800's.

I was touched beyond description to be at Aspen Grove. It was an experience that I will always treasure. More importantly, my experience there was a "booster shot" for me and strengthened my resolve to keep fighting for freedom, to keep running for freedom, and to keep spreading the message of economic empowerment among my brothers and sisters.

The shackles on the slaves of Aspen Grove, while they may not have been physical, prevented them from leaving those grounds; some of the slaves are buried just a few yards from the newly renovated home. As I drove away from Aspen Grove, along the one-mile pathway, after our meeting, I thought of the privilege of being able to go where I want to go and my being able to leave that plantation on my own without having to ask anyone.

I also thought about the fact that our ancestors who resided and worked there could not leave unless they ran away and took the risk of being caught and whipped, maimed, or even killed for doing so. I imagined those relatives of Dr. Lomax standing by the side of the road waving goodbye to me and saying "Comeback soon," "Come back and get us," "Come back and finally set us free."

Well, our retreat at Aspen Grove was called for that exact reason, albeit, 150-200 years later, but we came nonetheless. We came to put the finishing touches on a plan for getting our true freedom via what some are calling the final hurdle, the fourth movement, the last moral imperative: Economic Empowerment.

It is our obligation to complete the task of the slaves at Aspen Grove. It is our obligation as Black descendants of those and millions of other slaves who worked the thousands of other Aspen Groves to claim our freedom – to claim their freedom – by doing what they could not do. Can you imagine their desire for true freedom? Can you picture the situation in which they found themselves? Can you feel the pain and suffering they endured? Can you envision their monotonous existence, not being able to go anywhere or see anything or do anything else except work for the slave master?

If you can relate to the struggles and sufferings of our ancestors at Aspen Grove and everywhere else, then you too are obligated, and you should be honored, to do your part in our run for freedom. Visualize it as an economic relay race. The baton has just been passed to us, and we are behind because we dropped it in the 1960's. Our best team member, (a composite of Black entrepreneurs, Black intellectuals, and

Black philanthropists) is running the anchor leg. Coming into the final turn, our anchor is picking up the pace. The brothers and sisters of long ago are in the stands cheering to the top of their lungs for our victory – for their final victory. As the end of the race draws near, the scene *fades to Black.*

Do we win or lose? The ending is up to us. The slaves at Aspen Grove did their part. They survived. They survived to produce a brother such as Dr. Walter Lomax, who does more than his share in our freedom struggle. They passed the baton not only to him but to the rest of us as well. In deference to them, in remembrance of them, in gratitude to them, and in their honor, we must not drop that baton this time. We must win, and allow them to rest in peace.

Note: I made the 500 mile trip to Aspen Grove by automobile; Ken Bridges, after meeting with a group of brothers and sisters in Cincinnati, rode with me. On the journey we learned even more about each other, and we shared our hopes and dreams for the future of our people. After a great weekend of planning and fellowship, early Sunday morning we departed Aspen Grove, excited about what was to come. Ken headed back to Philadelphia, and I came back to Cincinnati.

Fifteen months later, Ken prepared for another road trip back to his family in Philadelphia. He rose early on the morning of October 11, 2002, excited that the first stage of what we had discussed in our initial meeting at Aspen Grove had finally come to fruition. Ken never got to enjoy the fruits of his labor; as he made his way back to his family to give them the good news, he was killed by the DC sniper. Ken was on his way back home that day and, quite ironically, he was on his way home, once again, from Aspen Grove.

Freedom Ain't Free!

We must cooperate or we are lost. Ten million people who join in intelligent self-help can never be long ignored or mistreated. The mass of the Negroes must learn to patronize business enterprises conducted by their own race, even at some disadvantage. W.E.B. DuBois, 1898.

The key word in that statement is "disadvantage." What DuBois was referring to is the fact that Black people must be willing to make a sacrifice for their own economic uplift. He understood the reality of Black owned businesses having to charge higher prices and not being able to compete equally with white owned businesses, and he beseeched Black consumers, in an effort to achieve true economic freedom, to respond to that reality by patronizing our brothers and sisters nevertheless.

Black owned businesses must take care of their business and do the things that will engender support from their consumers as well. The main reason given for non-support of Black businesses is poor service.

The same principles and tenets are just as true today as they were when DuBois and others like him walked this earth. They understood one thing very clearly: If they were going to be truly free, it would cost them something.

DuBois, in 1903, during his Talented Tenth speech, laid out a plan for the uplift of Black people. He called for the top ten percent of our people, after obtaining higher education, to go back and help the other ninety percent of our brothers and sisters. Then, in 1948, DuBois said in his address to the Boulé that he underestimated the selfish aspects of those who made it to the Talented Tenth. He lamented, "Willingness to work and make personal sacrifice for solving these problems was of course the first prerequisite... I did not stress this, I assumed it."

He went on to say, "I assumed that with knowledge, sacrifice would automatically follow. In my youth and idealism, I did not realize that selfishness is even more natural than sacrifice. I made the assumption of its wide availability because of the spirit of sacrifice learned in my mission school training."

Throughout DuBois' speech he noted the importance of individual progress; he also noted and placed more emphasis on the collective economic progress of our people. He was sad to see that his "ten percent" were more concerned with themselves, even after they had attained a certain level of success, than they were with sacrificing just a little to help others.

DuBois, Booker T. Washington, Madame C.J. Walker, and many other brothers and sisters knew our freedom would not be free. Have we learned that lesson? Are we practicing the principles of sacrifice, mutual support, and those "reaching back" and "leave no one behind" strategies we always talk about? According to the position in which we find ourselves today, I would say we are not.

It seems we are so wrapped up in our own individual worlds and have forgotten, either by commission or omission, about the welfare of our less fortunate brothers and sisters. The sacrifices that DuBois discussed are meager when it comes to Black economic empowerment today. Nonetheless, some Black consumers will walk or drive past a Black owned store to patronize one owned by someone else. Some brothers and sisters will drive 15 or 20 miles to the mall to buy a book at one of the larger stores because they can get it for a dollar less than they can at the Black book store. They are willing to spend probably a dollar's worth of gas to obtain a $1.00 "bargain."

This kind of action speaks to a lack of consciousness. Those talented tenth that were more selfish than sacrificial did not have the level of Black consciousness that would move them toward the ideal DuBois sought for his people. Today, our people must first break free of our psychological chains, raise our consciousness about who we are and what our obligations are to one another, and redirect a greater portion of our spending toward one another.

Another thing we have to do is establish more Black businesses, carve out niches in various industries for ourselves, and work together in support of those business ventures for the benefit of our people. We live in the richest country in the world and yet we have the least, in spite of the fact that we have been here since the country was founded – and even before that. We must begin - once again - to build a Black economy.

Martin Luther King, Jr. wrote, "America's industrial production is half of the world's total, and within it the production of Negro business is so small that it can scarcely be measured on any definite scale." Thirty years later, T. M. Pryor, in his book, *The Wealth-building Lessons of Booker T. Washington,* wrote, "If the Black business establishment disappeared from the American scene this moment, the American stock market would not react one smidgen." He continued, rather tongue-in-cheek, "Smoke and fumes from Black-owned businesses do not make measurable contributions to the smog conditions in American towns and cities."

In order for us to have this renaissance of thought, this revived sense of business ownership, Black people must be willing to make individual sacrifices for the collective benefit. We must understand that our freedom is definitely not free. What are you willing to pay for true freedom?

Economic Lessons of the Past

It is always interesting to reflect on certain events that took place in days gone by, especially when it comes to economic issues. In my entrepreneurship classes I often use the example of the Montgomery Bus Boycott to illustrate a very important lesson we could (and should) take from those strong, dedicated, and committed brothers and sisters who walked until their demands were met and bus accommodations were changed. I refer to one of the headlines in Henry Hampton's Black Chronicle (Published by Maloyd Ben Wilson, Jr.) that says, "42,000 Walk to Work." Not only was their action exemplary and admirable, it also offers a very important lesson in economic empowerment.

Here's what I mean. Let's assume the bus fare in Montgomery at that time was 20 cents roundtrip. We know the bus boycott lasted for 381 days, right? And, the headline in the paper tells us that 42,000 people walked. Multiply 20 cents times 381 times 42,000. The answer: $3,200,400! How many buses do you think could have been purchased with that amount of money in 1956 when the boycott ended? Do you think the people could have bought a factory and produced seats, or tires, or signs for those buses? How about opening a maintenance facility to service the buses? Get the picture? Do you see the lesson?

Suppose those who walked to work also put their bus fare into a common fund. If they had done that, in addition to withholding their money from the bus company, they would have had $3,200,400. In 1956 that was a great deal of money and could have effected great economic change.

While there are many other lessons we can learn from and take advantage of today, the Montgomery issue stands out at this time because of a story I read in the Toledo Journal. The headline says, "Restored Rosa Parks Bus heads for new home." As I read the story I could not help but think about the abovementioned multiplication problem, because the article discussed the purchase of the very bus in which Rosa made history.   The Henry Ford Museum in Greenfield, Michigan purchased it.

The bus was found in a field, rusted and riddled with bullet holes.   The museum paid $492,000 for it, and spent $300,000 more for its restoration.   That's nearly one-third of what the brothers and sisters would have accumulated from their bus fares in 1955-56.   With $3.2 million not only could they have bought a fleet of Black owned buses, they could have also bought the Rosa Parks Bus.   Do you see the irony here? Do you see the lesson?   By the way, if you want to see the bus, you'll have to pay between $8.50 and $13.00 for admission to the museum.

Even though our "leaders" have waited nearly forty years to tell us that economic empowerment is what we must seek and fight for, it is vital that we take our lessons whenever and wherever we can find them.   We must remember that it always boils down to economics in some form or fashion.

I don't know about you, but I think we would be much better off today if we owned a few bus companies rather than having to pay to ride on someone else's.   I think Rosa Parks, and those who refused to give up their seats even before she did, would be happier, and they would rest easier if Black people manufactured and owned the school buses our children have been riding for decades.

I know I would much rather go to Detroit and ride a Black owned bus than to go to a museum and pay to see the bus that Rosa Parks and others rode in 1955.   It may be a piece of history, but it's still just a bus, y'all, an inanimate object that played nothing more than a passive role in what we now call our struggle for equality.   Someone has already made a few hundred thousand dollars from the sale of the bus.   Someone else will make another $300,000 to restore it.   And the museum will make who knows how much because people want to see it, to board it, to touch it.   As Don King says, "Only in America!"

I truly appreciate the willing spirit of those who sacrificed, walked, fought, and subjected themselves to the horrendous treatment of the Bull Connors of this world.   It would be a tribute to them if we would use the lessons they left for us and build on what they did by economically empowering ourselves and our children.   Celebration and nostalgia are fine, but what we need these days are ownership and control of income-producing assets, like buses and museums.

Speaking of museums, I trust you will visit the Voting Rights Museum in Selma, Alabama during the annual commemoration of that famous march that began at the Edmond Pettus Bridge. I also hope you will take your children there, not only to be educated by Ms. Joann Bland and others, but because it belongs to Black folks and we should support it all year long. It represents one more lesson from our past – a lesson in strength, determination, and will.

What Price Would You Pay For a Profit?

One of the most sobering questions ever posed is: "For what shall it profit a man if he shall gain the whole world and lose his own soul?" Many who hear or see this question, found in the Bible in Mark 8:36, merely accept it as a rhetorical question. On the contrary, it is not rhetorical; rather it is a question that those of us who believe in life after death should answer on a very personal level. To bring it even closer to home, each of us should ask ourselves this question when it comes to our business practices and our individual dealings in the collective struggle for Black economic empowerment.

What price are you willing to pay to make a profit? In business we hear people complain about being ripped-off, overcharged, and cheated. We hear complaints pertaining to poor business practices and folks not doing what they say they will do for their customers. In social circles we hear the term "sell-out," which indicates that some of us have decided that we are willing to pay the price of another brother or sister, or our people in general, to make a profit (payoff). I have seen and been sickened by both profit-making scenarios, and you probably have as well.

Why are some of us willing to do just about anything to make a profit? Why are we eager, in some cases, to sell our people and ourselves for those proverbial thirty pieces of silver? Far be it from me to pretend I have the answers to those questions, but allow me to elaborate further on the subject.

Profit seems to motivate people to do some awful things to one another. Just look at the savings and loan scandals, the junk bond calamity, and the Enron debacle. Ill-gotten gains are never worth what we have to do to acquire them, but yet we remain willing to risk losing our most precious possession for a mere profit. That profit could be in monetary form, it could be status, it could be power, and it could be influence, but whatever it is, it pales in comparison to what we stand to lose in return. Sooner or later we will have to pay for the illicit profits we make.

The same principle applies in business. Both on the consumer side and the entrepreneur side there are games being played, scams being perpetrated, dishonesty, cheating, and rip-offs. We hear about those kinds of things among our people, especially those who say they will "never do business with another Black person" again. How can we be so concerned about making a "profit," either as a consumer or a business owner that we forget about what is really important – what is important for the long term?

We must treat one another with respect and never do things that will create animosity and distrust between Black businesses and consumers. We should be about the business of moving closer together rather than further apart.

Now, what about the profit made by our brothers and sisters who "sell-out" their people? Why are there still those among us who continue to seek their acclaim, their fortune, and their status by stabbing the rest of us in the back? Is their profit worth what they pay to gain it? Furthermore, is it worth their integrity? In some cases it must be, because we hear about it and many of us see it everyday. Personally, I don't know how folks who do those things sleep at night, but that's for them to deal with and not for me to judge. I will ask, however, that if you are doing things in opposition to the collective advancement of your people, please stop. It's not just about you; it's about us.

So think again when you are tempted to rip someone off via your business or as a consumer of a business. Black businesses must grow, they must expand, and they cannot do that if their owners are dishonest, lazy, or complacent. They cannot grow if we as consumers mistreat them by always asking them for "a hook-up," trying to get them to lower their prices, and on and on. Our businesses cannot thrive if those of us who are employees of those businesses do not care enough to treat assure that every customer is treated with respect, promptness, and consideration. Finally, we cannot grow as a people if we continue to allow a few sell-outs to dominate the scene and control our economic destiny.

Capitalism is great! We should all play. But, please don't sell your soul, or your brothers and sisters, for a profit. Think about it.

Using Our Resources to Help Others. A TALL Order.

" Judge not the poor for their poverty, but judge the community for its indifference."

In **Blackonomics** there was an article titled, "Props to Dikembe." The piece was centered on the charitable work of National Basketball Association standout, Dikembe Mutombo, in his effort to build a hospital in his native country, the Democratic Republic of the Congo. It also cited the assistance he received from a few of his NBA friends. The article showcased a super-rich Black man who was (and still is) willing to share his wealth with those less fortunate. It talked about a Black man who has not forgotten from whence he came and one who is willing to return to do what he can to help his people. Certainly that's a tall order for some of our affluent brothers and sisters.

Those who saw Dikembe's story on the television show, 60 Minutes, surely could not have watched that segment and not have been moved to tears at the sight of children dying from measles and ravaged by polio, two diseases that have all but disappeared and can be prevented with a simple vaccine. If you saw the show, you had to feel tremendous sympathy for Brother Dikembe, who lost his mother to an illness she could have overcome, but for the lack of her ability to get to a facility just ten minutes away. Your soul had to be touched at the thought of this man not being able to help his mother and prevent her demise, despite his great wealth and resources.

I know I felt all of those emotions, and I realized once again that life is short and we should do all we can do everyday with whatever we have to help someone else, just as Dikembe is doing. I repeat, this brother has not forgotten from whence he came, and he is also willing to go back to help those he left behind. I am very proud of him for that.

Were there more of us who felt and acted like our brother, this world would be a much better place. I think about those who have been blessed with material resources; I think about our brothers and sisters who have accumulated tremendous intellectual capital; and I think of all of our mothers, fathers, brothers, sisters, and children who need assistance of some kind or another. It's good to see what Mutombo is doing, and it is definitely another wake-up call for those of us who are sitting on the sidelines underutilizing and refusing to share our talents and resources.

Mutombo also epitomizes what we discuss in this column each week. He understands that through his personal economic empowerment he can help empower others. He says, "When you take the elevator up to reach the top, please don't forget to send the elevator back down, so that someone else can take it to the top. This is my way of sending the elevator down."

In addition, those who have pooled their resources with Dikembe's, namely, Patrick Ewing, Alonzo Mourning, and others, are demonstrating how a collective and cooperative economic effort can do wonders for our people. It's not how much or little you have; it's how much or how little you do with how much or how little you have.

Let's not stop with building a hospital in the Congo. Hospitals are needed in the United States as well, and so are supermarkets, banks, hotels, and many other businesses, especially in Black neighborhoods. Just as Dikembe has charted a course for his contribution to the lives of others, we can do the same, no matter how big or how small we are.

As we said in the title of this article, it is a tall order for us to actually step up and do what many of us only talk about. But Mutombo, along with other brothers and sisters, is at the head of the pack and making sure the elevator is sent back down. He cites a Talmudic proverb to drive home his message, "Judge not the poor for their poverty, but judge the community for its indifference." Well stated, my brother. But well-done beats well said every time. So I also say, "Well done, Dikembe Mutombo."

Reparation Preparation

The demand for reparations for African people is just and simple. It is simply an attempt to "repair," to "make whole" the descendants of the victims of the Trans Atlantic Slave Trade, which was a CRIME AGAINST HUMANITY! Crimes against humanity have no statute of limitations. And our people still suffer from the vestiges of their enslavement and colonization.
Viola Plummer and Dr. Conrad Worrill, National Black United Front

Let's set the stage first. African Americans earn more than one-half trillion dollars annually. According to market research indices we spend highly disproportionate amounts of money on things like clothing, cars, certain foods, travel, and other goods and services.

Black people in the U.S., although we are 12%-13% of the population, comprise less than 1% of business ownership. We own and control less than 1% of the resources of this country. We have relatively few banks, supermarkets, hotels, and other very basic entities that provide many of life's necessities. Finally, each year we hear of Black people who have won hundreds of millions of dollars in lawsuits from major corporations.

The above information alone suggests very strongly that we need to do a whole lot more than we have in the past when it comes to economic empowerment. It also suggests, at least on its surface, that if we had more money we could put ourselves in a much better financial position in this country. But the real kicker in the above information is that Black people in this country continue the trend of conspicuous consumption of many items for which we have no need. Question: In light of these realities, what would happen if we received reparations today?

Some say that if the government and the private sector especially were really smart, they would grant about a trillion dollars in reparations -- like yesterday. Why? You know the answer to that. Because it is likely they would get nearly all of that money back in less than a month.

It follows that if we cannot get together and do something positive with the millions we win in racial discrimination lawsuits, if we had our reparations today, we would not get together and do anything collectively if we received them. Out of instant gratification, some of us would run immediately to the nearest Mercedes, BMW, or Lexus dealer and buy "a few" cars. Out of necessity, some of us would run immediately to the outlets we now patronize and buy truckloads of items because our people do not produce to any great degree the life-sustaining things we must have – like food and clothing.

Who owns the vast majority of the outlets we patronize? Surely not Black people. But wait a minute. Didn't I just say that we have more than one-half trillion dollars already flowing through our hands every year? Seems to me we should be buying a few of those businesses for ourselves now, you know, just in case we get our reparations. It seems to me that we should be busy at work developing strategies for that day when our people will have so much money we literally won't know what to do with it. It seems to me we should be in full preparation to receive our reparations.

Are we prepared now? Of course not, and we can ill-afford to wait around until we get our windfall before we get prepared. We must act now, with what we have, to prepare ourselves, both in terms of our dollars as well as our minds (our behaviors), for that day when we will be paid for the labor and mistreatment of our ancestors. It would make them proud if we receive *their* compensation, our inheritance, and use it to build our own economy the way they did. It would make them smile if we pool our resources to assure a bright future for our children, the way they did. It would make them rest much easier if we would save a greater portion of our wealth, in our own financial organizations, and work together in support of one another, the way they did.

Yes, it would be something to behold if we would use what we have now to prepare for what we are seeking, by refusing to continue to give our money to others without reciprocity. Reparations suggest a repairing of the damage done in the past. It would be great if we would start now to "prepare for our repair" by using the revenue we currently receive to build an infrastructure through which we can channel our reparations.

As I said, if the establishment were smart, they would give us our reparations right now. But they aren't smart, and we must take advantage of that. While they posture, make speeches, and try to get the most political return from this issue, let's take care of our business and make preparations for our reparations.

What Did You Do On The 4th of U-Lie?

Okay, first I will tell you what I did. I thought about Frederick Douglass' remarks regarding the 4th, as many of us did, especially after Uncle Clarence Thomas' feeble attempt at justifying his stance <u>against</u> affirmative action by using Douglass' words. But I also thought of the words of another brother who, for some reason, is not mentioned very often: David Walker.

In his infamous "Appeal," Walker turned the words of the Declaration of Independence back on those who celebrated the victory of throwing off the tyranny of King George (hmmm). In reference to the Declaration, Walker stated, "Do you understand your own language? Compare your own language ... extracted from your Declaration of Independence, with your cruelties and murders inflicted by your cruel and unmerciful fathers and yourselves on our fathers and on us -- men who have never given your fathers or you the least provocation!"

Walker continued to cite the words of the Declaration, particularly those referring to the abuses of the King and the right and obligation of the colonies to throw off such government. "Hear your language further ... I ask you candidly, was (sic) your sufferings under Great Britain one hundredth part as cruel and tyrannical as you have rendered ours under you?" Walker was saying, in today's terms, "U-Lie."

While many of us are familiar with Douglass' famous speech, Brother David Walker's words are a bit more esoteric, but revealing nonetheless. It is no wonder Walker's Appeal, characterized by a Boston editor as, "one of the most wicked and inflammatory productions ever issued from the press," was considered dangerous. Even the great liberal William Lloyd Garrison suggested it was too provocative. But, as I often ask those who read my *Letter to Black Americans*, "Is it true?"

Found dead in his home on August 30, 1830, only in his early 30's and approximately one year after he published the Appeal, Walker was believed by many to have been murdered for his audacious impertinence – or, maybe it was because of the erudite genius he displayed in his writing.

Frederick Douglass had similar things to say in his famous speech in 1852 in Rochester, New York, before the Ladies' Anti-Slavery Society. (Susan B. Anthony, who resided in Rochester, was probably at that meeting. Although she was known as a staunch abolitionist, she had a few striking words of her own when it came to white versus Black voting rights. According to Dr. Anyim Palmer's outstanding book, The Failure of Public Education in the Black Community, Anthony stated, *"The old antislavery school says that women should stay back, that we must wait until male Negroes are voters. But we say, if you will not give the whole loaf of justice to an entire people, give it to the most intelligent first. If justice, intelligence and morality are to be placed in the government, then let the question of White women be brought up first and that of the Negro last."* Like the "liberal" Garrison's response to David Walker's Appeal, some things regarding Black freedom were a little too much to take, even for those white folks who fought for it. Does it remind you of our so-called "liberals" today?)

Frederick Douglass, in reference to July 4th, stated, "I am not included within the pale of this glorious anniversary! Your high independence only reveals the immeasurable distance between us. The blessings in which you, this day, rejoice, are not enjoyed in common. The rich inheritance of justice, liberty, prosperity and independence, bequeathed by your fathers, is shared by you, not by me. The sunlight that brought life and healing to you has brought stripes and death to me. This Fourth of July is yours, not mine." In other words, Douglass was saying, "U-Lie."

He went on to add, "You may rejoice, I must mourn. To drag a man in fetters into the grand illuminated temple of liberty, and call upon him to join you in joyous anthems, were inhuman mockery and sacrilegious irony. Do you mean, citizens, to mock me, by asking me to speak today?"

I wonder if Uncle Clarence Thomas is familiar with those eloquent words from Douglass and, if he is familiar with them, why he did not choose to use them in <u>support</u> of the court's ruling on affirmative action.

Whatever you did on the 4th of U-Lie, I hope you at least thought about our forefathers and mothers; I hope you thought about their struggle for freedom in a country that was busy flaunting its freedom to the world. I hope you considered the state of your freedom today, in our country that is now ruled by another "King George." I hope you took a little time to share some of our history with your children.

I also hope you know that in their latest efforts to bring Black folks into their "big tent," the Republican leadership signed a $2 million commitment to refurbish the former home of Frederick Douglass. Top-ranking Republicans said the Cedar Hill event was to "promote and perpetuate the legacy" of Mr. Douglass and toward "launching initiatives geared at empowering Black Americans."

Two million dollars to "empower" Black folks? I have one question: Who's getting the refurbishing contract? And, I have one statement: U-Lie.

Juneteenth – Are we really free in 2003?

Back in 1865, General Gordon Granger brought the news of freedom to the brothers and sisters in Texas. He told them they were free by reading the following: *The people of Texas are informed that in accordance with a Proclamation from the Executive of the United States, all slaves are free. This involves an absolute equality of rights and rights of property between former masters and slaves, and the connection heretofore existing between them becomes that between employer and free laborer. The Freedmen are advised to remain at their present homes and work for wages. They are informed that they will not be allowed to collect at military posts; and they will not be supported in idleness either there or elsewhere.*

Now in 2003, we still have "generals" telling us we are free, with qualifications of course, similar to those in General Order #3 which Granger read to the people in 1865. The slaves were encouraged to stay with their "former masters" and "work for wages;" they were also advised they would not be allowed to "collect at military posts" or be supported in "idleness." (I wonder if white folks were ever idle during that time) In other words, slaves were told they were free, but they were given no means with which to be free, no back pay for all their years of labor, and no land, the very basis of wealth in this country, especially in 1865, on which they could start a new life. They were advised, however, to stay with their former masters and work for them, thus continuing to create wealth for those who enslaved them.

That reminds me of the 13th Amendment that also supposedly freed the slaves, but says, "Neither slavery nor involuntary servitude, 'except' as a punishment for crime whereof the party shall have been duly convicted, shall exist within the United States, or any place subject to their jurisdiction." Did you notice that little word, "except"? Another qualifier. There's always a qualifier, folks, <u>always</u> a qualifier.

The problem can be appropriately couched in the words of Marcus Garvey. He said, "No one ever frees a slave; a slave must free himself." It's too bad that in 2003 we still have not fully absorbed nor acted upon that message of freedom from our Elder. Yes, there is a qualifier in that message as well, but it's a qualifier based on Black people gaining our psychological freedom, which will then lead us to economic freedom.

Now, let's get back to Juneteenth. It is a freedom celebration, right? Well, the local newspaper in my hometown had an article titled, "Locals pitch in to save festival." It dealt with the 16 year-old Juneteenth Celebration, and described a desperate event organizer scrambling to raise money to save the festival. "I was petrified," said Lydia Morgan, event organizer, obviously at the thought of Juneteenth not being held due to a lack of funding. How much funding? $12,000.

That's right; $12,000 is all that was needed to celebrate Black Freedom Day – Juneteenth in Cincinnati, Ohio. The article went on to describe how WCIN, a Black owned radio station, Kroger, and UPS stepped in to save the day for Juneteenth. (By the way, lest you think I'm just talking and not doing, in 1999 during my tenure as President of the Black Chamber of Commerce, that same radio station and our Chamber funded the event.) While we thank Kroger and UPS for their altruism, I find it weirdly reminiscent of 1865 when Granger read the order that suggested the slaves stay on and work for their former masters or, put another way, remain dependent upon their masters.

I will be blunt. How can we celebrate freedom, which in this case cost a mere $12,000, if we are not willing or able to pay for it ourselves? Does it make sense for Black folks to even celebrate Juneteenth if we don't use our own money to pay for it? It's great that white owned corporations want to give us their money to help fund our events; after all, we certainly give them a tremendous amount of our money every year. But, to have our events <u>dependent</u> upon the largess of corporations, especially events that celebrate our "freedom" in this country, is totally contradictory to the notion of true freedom itself.

It makes no sense for Black folks to pretend we are free, by eating, drinking, and making merry for a couple of days, only because white folks made it possible. They didn't free us in 1865 and they can't free us now, especially with prepaid celebrations. The culmination of the freedom struggle is grounded in economic freedom. And before we obtain our true economic freedom, we must first free ourselves psychologically. If we cannot use our nearly $700 billion annual income to fund our events, especially heralded events such as Juneteenth, then what is the real significance of those events? What are we really saying about ourselves and to our Elders, and what are we saying to paternalistic corporations? Even more important: What are <u>they</u> saying to us? Are we truly free in 2003?

The Economic Legacy of Ken Bridges

All can give some; but some will give all.

I have written many articles about brothers and sisters of the past who have left their marks on our society when it comes to our economic empowerment. Men and women such as Marcus Garvey, Booker T. Washington, Madam C.J. Walker, and Amos Wilson, all of whom, incidentally, died in their 50's. (It's tough fighting for our people) These giants, as well as others, hold a special place in my heart, and I will always revere their accomplishments, their dedication, their concern and love for their people, and their commitment to our economic advancement. But, Kenneth H. Bridges, my brother, my contemporary, who also died in his 50's, will occupy an even higher place, not because he did more than they did, but because I knew him.

It's one thing to read, write, and talk about those great brothers and sisters who did so much for us in years past; it's an entirely different thing when it comes to someone with whom you actually had a personal relationship. Ken Bridges was that and more to me. In addition to working together on the attainment of economic freedom for our people, Ken and I seemed to have a spiritual connection that surpassed the work about which we were both so passionate. We hit it off the first day we met, each having driven hundreds of miles to meet.

During our all-too-short five-year acquaintance, Ken and I spent much quality time together, either in person or on the telephone. I spoke to him the day before he was killed. I was speaking at Tuskegee University and he was closing the "deal of the century" in Virginia at Aspen Grove. We said we would follow up the next day, after we returned home, but that never happened. He was shot by a sniper the next morning as he made his way home.

Ken died working for his people, working for his family, and working for his brothers and sisters in the MATAH Network. And you know what? That's just the way he wanted it. We had conversations about death, and Ken would always say, "Death is something that happens in the middle of your life." He was never afraid because he believed his transition would simply carry him to another plane and allow him to be with our ancestors – the ones I mentioned above, along with many others.

This brother, this proud Black man, was so in love with his people that he literally dedicated his life to the principles upon which MATAH was built, and to achieving a level of business development in MATAH that would propel us to new economic heights. He worked everyday, tirelessly, sometimes losing valuable time with his children. But, he used to tell me that what he was doing, he was doing for his children and for our children. He worked so hard for economic freedom because he wanted our children to have a strong economic foundation on which they could continue to build for future generations. He worked hard because he loved us; he loved YOU.

Now it is up to us to continue what Ken started. Who knows? Maybe one of us will be the next to fall, but whoever is left must keep moving forward. Ken knew, as his friend, elder, and mentor, Dr. Edward Robinson, author of *The Journey of the Songhai People*, always told him, that with any movement it takes a "precipitating event" to push it over the top. Little did any of us know, least of all, Ken Bridges, that the precipitating event that would thrust the MATAH economic solidarity movement forward would be his death, which if you know the entire story on how he came to be in that gas station at the time he was killed, could be called destiny.

This paragraph is for those who are MATAH. What are we going to do to celebrate the life of Ken Bridges? What will be your commitment, your level of dedication, your resolve to continue the legacy of Ken Bridges? If we want to pay tribute to him and do justice to his memory and what he stood for while he was with us, we must not waver or waffle in our struggle for economic empowerment. We must win!

Ken will not receive the accolades of a Martin Luther King, Jr., nor be held up with a Malcolm or Marcus. He will not receive the acclaim of a Medgar Evers, a Huey P. Newton, or a Kwame Ture. Not yet. I submit, as Ken's long-time partner, Al Wellington so eloquently stated in his remembrance of Ken, I submit that one day the world will come to know the real Ken Bridges, and one day it will come to know what this man meant to our struggle for psychological and economic freedom. I submit that Kenneth H. Bridges was one of the greatest leaders of today. And, I submit that one day all of us will realize it.

Ken Bridges was indeed someone we can all be thankful for and proud of as well. Hold his family up in prayer and do your part to continue his legacy. And always remember that Ken Bridges died on his way to freedom; but at least he was on his way. Rest in peace, my brother.

If I Should Die On My Way To Freedom

(The original version of this tribute was dedicated to Ken Bridges and presented to his family, October 11, 2002)

If I should die on my way to freedom, at least I'll be on my way. At least I'll be on the road, pushing against the winds of change, pushing against the grain, making my way toward freedom.

At least, each morning that God blesses me to awaken and put my feet on the floor, I will stand up and stand tall, put one foot in front of the other and begin that day once again, making my way to freedom.

At least I'll be on my way, each day with my family around me – and each moment – pressing toward a future in which they will finally be able to rest from our long and harrowing journey. I know there will be no rest for me, 'cause I'm on my way to freedom, and freedom is always an uphill climb.

But, if I should die on my way to freedom, at least I'll be on my way. Unlike some of the Children of Israel, unlike some on Harriet Tubman's freedom train, and unlike some of our brothers and sisters today, I will always be determined to go forward. I'll be making my way to freedom, and nothing will turn me around.

At least I'll be standing, but **NEVER** standing still.
At least I'll be walking, and **NEVER** looking back.
At least I'll be running, but **NEVER** running in place.
At least I'll be striving, but **NEVER** striving in vain.

If I should die on my way to freedom, at least on my journey the view improves everyday.
At least I'll meet new brothers and sisters along the way.
At least I'll persevere, press on, and keep going, despite the daily roadblocks.

At least I'll trust God to make a way for me out of no way, and He always does, because He never fails.

If I should die on my way to freedom, there's just one thing that I ask. Put your arms of love around my family and keep on going! Fill my space with someone strong and unafraid, someone who can chart new courses, someone who loves and trusts his people enough to continue on to freedom.

If I should die on my way to freedom, whether I am leading or following, pass the word down the line, spread portions of my essence among my dear brothers and sisters, and tell them to keep going. Tell them I'm watching them, and tell them I love them.

Tell them the chain is not broken; it just got stuck for a little while as we were going through a tight space. Tell them what I told them when we had our family talks: "Let's go get our freedom, brothers and sisters!"

So, if I should die on my way to freedom, don't linger too long at my grave. Don't stay too long in your grief. Just hug one another and give them some love; shed your tears, and dry your eyes. Then get back on the road to freedom; and if you should die on your way to freedom, others will be able to say, "At least he was on his way."

Section II

Consciousness – Or the Lack Thereof

Man's consciousness is a creative act and the kind of consciousness one has will determine the kind of world one creates. Consequently, when we look at the world we live in, Afrikan people, we must realize that to a great extent it is a world of our own creation! It is a world generated by the kind of consciousness that we have permitted to be instilled in us as a people.

Dr. Amos Wilson, *Afrikan-Centered Consciousness Versus the New World Order*

It is a peculiar sensation, this double-consciousness, this sense of always looking at one's self through the eyes of others, of measuring one's soul by the tape of a world that looks on in amused contempt and pity. One ever feels his twoness,--an American, a Negro; two warring souls, two thoughts, two unreconciled strivings; two warring ideals in one dark body, whose dogged strength alone keeps it from being torn asunder. The history of the American Negro is the history of this strife,--this longing to attain self-conscious manhood, to merge his double self into a better and truer self.

W.E.B. DuBois

Consciousness is the internal manifestation of knowledge. Consciousness is a valued human asset and every people seek ways to enhance their knowledge – particularly their self-knowledge.

Na'im Akbar, *Know Thy Self*

Being Black When No One is Looking

Have you ever wondered what those Black folks who seem to be afraid of being perceived as "too Black" think about when they look into the mirror? Do you think during that moment in time, a moment when they are alone with themselves that they acknowledge who they really are? Do you think, when they stare at themselves, they appreciate the reflection looking back at them? And, do you think, despite some of our brothers' and sisters' reluctance and resistance in some cases to being Black, do you think they admit who they are and understand their place in history?

I have often said, "You cannot run away or move away from being Black; you cannot graduate from being Black; and you cannot gain enough wealth to remove your Blackness." Unfortunately, some of us think we can, and we are sadly disappointed when we discover the futility of our efforts. Nevertheless, some of us continue to try to assimilate and feel so graciously endowed and "extra special" when allowed in the inner-sanctums of white-owned corporations, country clubs, corporate boards, and all of the other positions that make some of us feel privileged.

Some of our people, to this day, desperately continue to seek that special title of being the "first Black," and use it to rank ourselves one over the other. What do those folks think when they stand absolutely alone and look at themselves? What do they do when faced with a decision that will impact, either positively or negatively, on another Black brother or sister? What do they do when no one is looking?

Someone said good character is "doing the right thing when no one is looking." Being Black has the same application for me. Some of us are so enamored by the trappings of society that when placed in a situation where someone is watching, especially whites, we tend to do and say what we think they want to hear. You know how it is. We want to be accepted as equals, as peers. This is especially true in the workplace. It's the "mask" we wear. But, even if you are one of those Black folks, there will still be times when you will face the reality of your Blackness. There will come a time when you will have to make a decision, when no one is looking, for instance, to make a purchase from a Black owned business as opposed to another business. You may encounter an opportunity to help your brother or sister in a way that may not sit too well with white folks if they found out. What will you do?

Black people make those kinds of decisions everyday. Our level of consciousness more times than not determines what our final decision will be. We can either run and (try to) hide from our Blackness by walking past a Black owned store to get to one owned by someone else, or we can patronize the Black storeowner. We can get lost in the world of status and position and forget about our people, or we can use our intellectual capacity (and financial resources) to help more of our people get to our level – and beyond. We can hold the door open for another brother or sister, or we can slam the door and nail it shut, preventing others to follow in our footsteps.

We can make those decisions and many more, all while no one is looking. No one will ever know, unless you tell him or her, that you decided to go against your people rather than help your people. No one will ever see your reluctance and resistance to being what God made you, and demonstrating your Blackness by doing what you can to help your people. No one will see, but will you be able to sleep at night? Will you be able to face your children when they grow up, more enlightened than you, and ask why Black people don't own more resources than we do, why our businesses fail at such a high rate, why we are no further along economically than we were a generation ago, why our people lead the nation in all the negative categories, why there are so many Black men in prison, why there is such an inordinate amount of Black folks who are functionally illiterate. What will you tell them?

Some of us will not be able to say we did anything to help make the situation better. But, I'm sure we'll come up with something. We can always lie. After all, no one was looking.

Use Me 'Til You Use Me Up

"The greatest weapon in the hands of the oppressor is the mind of the oppressed." **Steven Biko**

Why are some of our brothers and sisters so eager to allow themselves to be used by the establishment to make the rest of us believe everything is just fine for Black folks? And, why do the rest of us keep falling for it? In my hometown, especially when it comes to economic issues such as so-called economic development projects, the scenario is always the same. Black people complain about a certain project being built, because we never get an equitable share of the return on investment for our tax dollars. We complain, and rightly so, because the last time millions of public dollars were spent on a project, we were left out in the cold with little or no economic benefit.

We get so mad, and we march, picket, demonstrate – and go away, never to be heard from again, that is, until the next project comes along. Why do we do this? We do it because we fall for the same old song and dance, performed by the same bunch of Black minstrels sent out on their public relations missions by the establishment to lull us to sleep. And it's always the same ones, which is why I am so perplexed at the ease with which they succeed with their evil mission.

In Cincinnati, Ohio, from 1993 through 2003, several major construction projects were planned, begun, or completed, amounting to more than a billion dollars. We built two sports stadiums, a major highway, and now we are building a National Underground Railroad Freedom Center and expanding our convention center. In each of these instances there has been a call for so-called "economic inclusion." (What's that? Reverse economic exclusion?)

As a result, Black faces have been out front assuring Black people that everything will be all right – this time. Black faces telling their people to chill-out, that everything will be all right. They tell us they are working real hard to "encourage" the powers-that-be to include "Small, Minority, and Women-owned businesses" in these public projects to the tune of 25-30%. It's strange they never say anything about "Black inclusion." It's always, "we are encouraging them" or "we hope to get" or "we are working hard to assure."

Did I say these are always Black folks? Not Hispanic folks, not Chinese folks, not Indian folks, but Black folks are always carrying the "minority" banner. They cut their deals in the back rooms, secure their contracts, and then run to the streets and shout to other Blacks that "Happy Days Are Here Again! This time we are REALLY going to get it right!"

In response to the $180 million expansion of the convention center, the headline in our Black newspaper, the Cincinnati Herald, read, "New Day, New Way," the latest in a long line of tired tricks perpetrated by Blacks against Blacks. And you know what? They even smile when they do it.

This is the same scenario used in 1993 and many years prior to that. Pass a tax bill, with Black folks leading the charge because a few of them have been promised something. Cut the deals behind closed doors, and then inform the public. Tell us things have changed – this time – and make every attempt to convince us to back off, to shut up, to stay calm, and not to demonstrate or do anything else that embarrass them. After it's all said and done, the percentage that Blacks get out of the deal is too small to acknowledge. Oh, I almost forgot, we were talking about "minorities and women" weren't we?

Do you have these kinds of brothers and sisters in your town? If not, let me know. We have an abundance of them here in Cincinnati, and I'd love to ship some to you. As a matter of fact, I think they grow them here on a tree; it's called the Negro Tree. Every time someone wants to get a multi-million dollar project going, and do the okey-doke on Blacks by setting a percentage goal for "minorities and women," they just go to that tree and pick the ripest Negroes. They send them out to do the bidding of the puppet masters, and they use them and use them until the Negroes have no more usefulness. Bill Withers would be proud.

Why would anyone allow himself to be used against his own people? Is it due to a lack of consciousness? Psychological enslavement? Low moral character? Lack of love? Low race-esteem? Low self-esteem? Fear? Or, just plain greed?

Where is DuBois' Guiding Hundredth?

Above all, the better classes of Negroes should recognize their duty toward the masses. They should not forget that the spirit of the 20th century is to be the turning of the high toward the lowly, the bending of humanity to all that is human, the recognition that in the slums of modern society lie the answers to most of our puzzling problems of organization and life, and that only as we solve those problems is our culture assured and our progress certain.
W.E.B. DuBois

Are you aware of the speech W.E.B. DuBois gave to the Boulé in 1948, 45 years after he brought forth his famed Talented Tenth proposal, which he published in *The Negro Problem*? The gist of his words can be summed up with this quote from his speech. "I assumed that with knowledge, sacrifice would automatically follow." DuBois continued, "In my youth and idealism, I did not realize that selfishness is even more natural than sacrifice." Doubtlessly, W.E.B. DuBois was lamenting his famed Talented Tenth proposal because those who he assumed would save the "Negro Race," those "exceptional men," did not perform in the manner he assumed they would.

Thus, in 1948, DuBois proposed another group or at least a doctrine, as he called it, termed the Guiding Hundredth. It seems DuBois, although stymied and frustrated with his Boulé brothers who failed to live up to his high ideals about "exceptional men" saving the race, still had faith that some would come to the forefront and do what had to be done to advance Black people. He knew ten percent was too much to hope for, so he settled for one-hundredth. We ask today, 54 years later: where is that Guiding Hundredth?

Where are the educated, the affluent, the influential, the politicians, the corporate moguls, the doctors, the lawyers, the educators, and all of the other exceptional Black brothers and sisters who will save the race? A more appropriate question is: Where is their money, even if they are unwilling to actually get into the fight? DuBois said to his fellow fraternity brothers that, "They must first of all recognize the fact that their own place in life is primarily a matter of opportunity, rather than simply desire or ability." He continued, "That if such an opportunity were extended and broadened, a thousand times as many Negroes could join the ranks of the educated and able."

He went on to tell those "exceptional men" that in order for the Race to have the things it needed to prosper it would, in DuBois' words, "...need large funds at its disposal," and he asked them to consider the *tithe,* a "tenth of our income" to such a cause.

DuBois died 15 years later and once again obviously failed to see the realization of his second proposal for saving the race. Where was his Guiding Hundredth? Today we ask the same question. Maybe most of them are too busy making money to take the time to give any toward the cause of "saving the race." Maybe they are too involved in "acting as the servants of the political machines supported by the propertied classes in the white community," as E. Franklin Frazier noted in his book, Black Bourgeoisie.

Maybe our Guiding Hundredth is safely tucked away in a comfortable cocoon, waiting for the winter to pass or too afraid of the raging storm of oppression to come out and be seen even standing beside a Black freedom fighter, not to mention offering to help finance the war against injustice. Or, maybe our Guiding Hundredth simply subscribes to the Nancy Reagan mantra of the 1980's of "Just say no." No, I will not help my people. No, I am not a part of "that" group. No, I don't think like "they" think. No, I will not share my money with "them." No, I really don't want to be Black.

There are those brothers and sisters who would be classified by DuBois as members of the Guiding Hundredth who are doing a great deal of positive work for Black people. Thank you! But, there are far too many with the riches, the clout, the influence, and the intellect who are doing far too little to help "their" people. My term for these folks is "Fruit Gatherers."

The brothers and sisters in the streets and in the courts, fighting for Black rights and shaking the trees, are the ones who hardly ever get the benefit of the fruit that falls because of their agitation. Why is that? It's simply because the Fruit Gatherers won't share it with them. Most Fruit Gatherers refuse to share or make a small sacrifice for those who lay it on the line everyday to help them get what they have. Fruit Gatherers get the good jobs as Diversity Managers and other public relations, high-visibility positions – no budget, no power, but a good job. They get the sub-contracts and are held up as the examples of how fair the system is to Black people. They get the appointments to the boards, commissions, and panels, mainly because they are "safe" and will not make too many waves.

What Brother DuBois was trying to tell his audience and those of us who will take the time to listen today, is that we all need one another and we should find our role in this struggle and fulfill that role, whether it is by giving your money, your time, your expertise, or even your life, as was the case of several who have died for "our" people.

W.E.B. ended his speech by saying, "...I do not dream, that a word of mine will transform, to any essential degree, the form and trends of this fraternity; but I am certain the idea called for expression and that the seed must be dropped, whether in this or other soil, today or tomorrow."

Little known is the fact that when DuBois left the United States, angry and disappointed, he uttered these words: "I just can't take anymore of this country's treatment. We leave for Ghana October 5th and I set no date for return... Chin up, and fight on, but realize that American Negroes can't win."

Tree Shakers and Fruit Gatherers

I remember being in a meeting with a group of "high-level" Black folks who were concerned about the economic disparity that exists in our town. We met regularly to develop strategies and resources with which to respond to that disparity and to create real change. I sat and listened to the threats of what they would do, what they would say, and how they would finally get this situation straightened out. They were mad as hell, and they were not going to take it anymore.

The specific situation we discussed centered on the building of two sports stadiums, with taxpayer dollars, but with no real plan of action to include a proportionate number of Black people in the contractual and employment opportunities. I remember them saying they would use their clout to get the rich and powerful white folks to capitulate to their demands for reciprocity and fairness. (Some clout they had; Blacks got less than 5% of the deal.)

After all of the talk, I asked the simple question: "What if they say, 'No'?" They looked around at one another and had no answer. All of their business acumen, their influence, and their contacts, all of a sudden, seemed impotent. I followed up with the suggestion that until we understand we must all work together, allowing each of us to work in our own special area of expertise, we will continue to find ourselves divided and weak in our responses to unfairness and disparity.

My follow-up point to the group was that no matter how many threats and saber-rattling we used to get the attention of those in charge of building those stadiums, while they would listen, they would have no incentive or desire to change until we were willing to stop the project. So, I asked them, "Who will sit on the bulldozers?" And, as I said before, there was no answer.

Those Black folks who are willing to do the dirty work in our fight for justice are the ones who will sit on the bulldozers, and go to jail if need be, are indeed the Tree Shakers. They will not get contracts; they may get a few jobs; but their reward will not be reflective of their work. In other words, they will get very little of the fruit that falls because of their labor.

Those Black folks who sit on the boards with the white movers and shakers, have the high-paying jobs, and own the larger businesses are the ones who gather the fruit that falls from the work of the Tree Shakers. They will get the contracts; they will get the appointments to commissions; and they will go back to their strategy meetings to discuss the victory – oh yes, and to count their money.

The good news is that a few Black businesses will make money from these actions. But the bad news is that the Tree Shakers will go home to the same conditions they had before they shook the tree.

We should all understand that in order to make the kind of economic progress that benefits all of our people, the victories must be equitably shared with everyone involved. The group to which I referred, with all of their clout, could not accomplish their objective (and did not) alone. They needed brothers and sisters who were willing to sit on those bulldozers. The same reasoning applies to most of our strivings for economic justice.

Unfortunately, the Tree Shakers get short-changed, and they are often ostracized and vilified by those who are helped by their actions. You know what I mean. Some of the Fruit Gatherers would never be seen beside a Tree Shaker; they would never come to a meeting of Tree Shakers; they are, in many cases, ashamed of the Tree Shakers and do not want to be identified with them.

By the way, the Fruit Gatherers are at it again in my hometown. Another sports stadium is under construction, and the same scenario is repeating itself. During the initial fiasco the hue and cry for economic justice went out from the Fruit Gatherers, without the assistance of the Tree Shakers, resulting in Black people receiving a pittance of the stadium business. Of course, the vast majority of that pittance went to the Fruit Gatherers.

Now, again without working with and for the Tree Shakers, the wails of injustice and unfairness rise. To make matters even worse, the Fruit Gatherers are pleading for fairness by asking that 15% of the deal be given to "minorities,

women, and small business owners." Not once did the Fruit
Gatherer I saw on television, standing before the three white
county commissioners, mention what he wanted for Black
people; he was speaking up for minorities and women. Is it any
wonder that we are in such a sad predicament? Black people
who are afraid to seek fairness for Black people are shameful.
Why do some of us fight for reciprocity for everyone else –
including women, most of who are white and of other
ethnicities – before we will fight for ourselves? We cannot help
anyone else from our position on the bottom of the heap.

Fruit Gatherers, eating very well because of work being
done by Tree Shakers, should do some reflecting and realize
they are doing more harm than good by not advocating for,
looking out for, and working with those who make it possible
for them to eat – the Tree Shakers.

Throw-away People

There are two categories of leaders in our communities, especially when it comes to issues and activities related to economic empowerment. According to Dr. Carter G. Woodson, *"Negroes ... sometimes choose their own leaders but unfortunately they are too often the wrong kind. Negroes do not readily follow persons with constructive programs. Almost any sort of exciting appeal or trivial matter presented to them may receive immediate attention ... and liberal support."* That dilemma cited by our Elder has never been more pronounced than it is today.

There are so-called Black leaders who, despite their unseemly tactics, their portrayals of themselves as "honest" brokers, and their shadowy deal-making and sellout prowess, seem to be exempt from exposure by our people. While Black folks have always had to deal with these scoundrels, we have been reluctant to call them out – to expose them for what they really are.

On the other hand, we have leaders among us who are totally dedicated to the collective economic advancement of African Americans. These are the leaders who are usually sacrificed by Black people -- thrown out because they are a threat to the establishment or because they are "too Black." That frightens some people and, sadly, we play into that fear by participating in the demise of the very people who would help pull us out of our economic enslavement.

I have witnessed the "death" of brothers and sisters who go all out for their people, who don't take sell-out bribes, who don't back off when it comes to speaking up for Black people, and who are unafraid to be Black. These conscious brothers and sisters are virtually thrown-out, in many cases simply because someone from the establishment thought they were crossing the line and getting out of their place. They are let down by the very brothers and sisters they have helped. Through our acquiescence and apathy many of us turn our heads, afraid to speak up for the ones who speak out for us.

I have, on the other hand, seen certain folks stroll through our communities and be held up as paragons of Black liberation, all the while filling their pockets with the *filthy lucre* from their sell-out deals with the powers that be. They lurk in the shadows, afraid to come out in the open, using lackeys to promote their causes. They have their hands in every deal, every program, every transaction, and every scenario that involves Black people, making certain that they will be the first in line to be paid. They rob the community and blame that same community for not moving forward. How can we move forward with crooks like these in our midst?

These are the ones we should throw away. These are the ones from whom we must run. These are the very ones who will continue to hold us back because they will sell us out for their individual benefit and acclaim. The saddest aspect of this reality is that we accept it. For years we have seen the same persons in our neighborhoods and our communities selfishly plot and scheme to fill their pockets and then make some shallow overture to their brothers and sisters who ignorantly hold them in high esteem.

We have seen these people move up, economically, while those they are suppose to be helping are pushed further away from the actualization of their economic dreams. We have also seen the brothers and sisters in the opposite category fade into oblivion, never to be heard from again. And then, more times than not, we sit around and reminisce about not having listened to them and not having followed their prescriptions for collective economic success.

We must learn, as a people, to identify, respect, and follow our true leaders. Heed the words of Carter G. Woodson and do not be swayed and mesmerized by charisma and rhetorical ranting. Fake leaders are very good at the things that will not take Black people where we need to go, especially economically. They will not and cannot put the collective first because they are too wrapped up in themselves. It makes me wonder if they ever think about death, responsibility, legacy, and accountability. They may not have to account for their actions to us, but one day that accountability will come. Most of us would be fearful of that day. But these fake leaders not only have no consciousness, they have no conscience.

So what do we do about these people? The first thing to do is look at what they have done for our people – not what they have said, but what they have done. Look behind the deals they bring you; see who else is in support of them. Check them out completely before you place your confidence and trust in them. If they are using you to do their dirty work, afraid themselves to come out into the open and speak, be wary of them. They mean you no good.

If you see their fingerprints on everything that has money attached to it, none or very little of which is being used to truly empower our people, watch out. It's very likely they are getting theirs off the top (and probably off the bottom as well) leaving very little for you. Look for the common thread that always leads back to this person. After a while you will be able to discern the nuances and *modus operandi* of this person because he will do the same things, say the same things, plan the same things, and always have his hand out for his cut.

Let's *throw the scoundrels out*, as they say in political circles, and support those who are dedicated to serving rather than merely appointing themselves as leaders (or being appointed by white folks); they are the "keepers." Follow the ones who do not seek the spotlights, the cameras, and the headlines. Follow them; protect them; revere them.

Frederick Douglass' Tribute to Harriet Tubman, 1868

"I am glad to know the story of your eventful life has been written. You ask for what you do not need when you ask me for a word of commendation. I need such words from you far more than you need them from me, especially where your superior labors and devotion to the cause of the lately enslaved of our land are known as I know them. The difference between us is very marked. Most of what I have done and suffered in the service of our cause has been in public, and I have received much encouragement at every step of the way.

You on the other hand have labored in a private way. I have wrought in the day – you in the night. I have had the applause of the crowd and the satisfaction that comes of being approved by the multitude, while the most that you have done has been witnessed by the few trembling, scarred, foot-sore bondmen and women, whom you have led out of the house of bondage... The midnight sky and silent stars have been the witness of your devotion to freedom and of your heroism..."

Condo for Sale – Bushes Included

The lie can be maintained only for such time as the State can shield the people from the political, economic and/or military consequences of the lie. It thus becomes vitally important for the State to use all of its powers to repress dissent, for the truth is the mortal enemy of the lie, and thus by extension, the truth is the greatest enemy of the State.
Joseph Goebbels, *German Minister of Propaganda, 1933-1945*

Sometimes I am at a loss for words when it comes to some of the things Black people say and do, especially when it comes to politics. I have seen some of them grovel before politicians and walk in lock-step with political parties, even to the detriment of other Black people. I have witnessed our so-called Black leaders compromise (a softer word for sellout); I have seen them collaborate against their own people; I have seen them stand idly by and do and say nothing when they see with their own eyes gross injustice all around them. It's as though some of us just want to be accepted or need to be validated by the white power structure, so much so that we are willing to lie, distort and skirt the truth, and run interference for our former slave masters even today. Gabriel Prosser would be outraged.

As I sat and watched National Security Advisor, Condoleezza Rice on television explaining the debacle in Iraq, I was outraged, I was ashamed, I was insulted, and I was hurt. Here is a woman, a highly intelligent woman, a respected woman, an affluent woman, answering questions about the escapades of George W. Bush and what he and his comrades have done since his rise to power. Tim Russert would ask her a question and you could hear her voice quivering, something I have not heard before, shaking at the prospect of having to say some of the most ridiculous things ever to come out of the mouth of a person. She had to know that some of her answers were not quite true, not quite to the point, and not quite convincing. She was just there to cover for Bush.

Rice, also having worked for George H.W. Bush, George W's father, is always there, always close to the village idiot's side to take the slings and arrows that come his way. She jumped to his rescue to defend those infamous 16 words in his State of the Union Address. She fell on her sword, after George Tenet did the same thing, and some underling before him, to protect George Bush.

By that time I was asking myself how much more Rice and Powell could take before they would speak out, before they would resign from this corrupt and horrid administration. Apparently, either they think they are doing a great job or they are in so deep they cannot find a way out now.

Whatever the situation, it is shameful that Ms. Rice, recipient of the N.A.A.C.P.'s President's Award for advancing the ideals of the N.A.A.C.P. through image, personal achievement and service to all people of color. N.A.A.C.P. President even said those attributes accurately describe Rice. Yes, Ms. Rice has a nice image and she has certainly achieved a great deal on a personal level. As to the part about "service to all people of color (whatever that means), I don't know.

Looks to me like she's doing more for people of non-color, and if you count the people of Iraq, Korea, Iran, and Syria as "people of color," then it is questionable if she is living up to all of the award's credits. Of course we certainly could not be talking about people of color in this country, except for the warm feeling some of us might get when we see a Black woman walking just behind the President, staying at his ranch, going to Camp David with him, and sometimes whispering sweet nothings in his ear for dramatic effect.

So what is it? What makes Condo tick? What keeps her going? Is it money? Probably not, at least not to the highest bidder. If this Condo is for sale, it's only to the Bushes – or, as the title of this article slyly implies, this Condo comes *with* the Bushes. Besides, surely she has a little somethin' somethin' tucked away from her days with Chevron Oil. Is it power? Probably so; power is such an aphrodisiac to those who already have all the material things they ever wanted.

But what about ethics? What about responsibility? What about principle? What about truth? In the midst of a storm such as the one we are in now, it sure would be great to see someone of Condo's stature stand up and proclaim that what we are doing in this country and in this world is wrong.

What an image that would make. What a role model for our children to see.

On Meet the Press, when asked about the additional $87 billion requested by Bush, Condo said, "We did not have perfect foresight into what we were going to find in Iraq." What in the world is "perfect foresight"? How much of the future is foreseeable? On another occasion she justified the Iraq debacle by saying the terrorists are there now because Iraq is the center of the war on terror. Well, who made it that way, Condo?

Yes, this Condo is for sale, but, *caveat emptor*: Bushes are included.

"I don't think anybody could have predicted that they would try to use an airplane as a missile, a hijacked airplane as a missile," said national security adviser Condoleezza Rice on May 16, 2002.

"How is it possible we have a national security advisor coming out and saying we had no idea they could use planes as weapons when we had FBI records from 1991 stating that this is a possibility," said Kristen Breitweiser, one of four New Jersey widows who lobbied Congress and the president to appoint the commission [investigating the Sept. 11 attacks].

All Money Ain't Good Money

There is an excellent book titled, Betrayal by Any Other Name, written by Dr. Khalid Al-Mansour, in which he notes that the original charter of the N.A.A.C.P. prohibited the ownership of land by that organization. Of course, we know it was white people who started and initially funded the N.A.A.C.P. at its inception, thus, in light of that historical reality, let's look at one example of what Dr. Mansour says about the differences between the solutions offered to solve Black problems versus those offered to solve similar problems faced by white people.

One example Mansour uses centers on the problem of the establishment and maintenance of a viable economic infrastructure for white and Black organizations. He cites the solutions that white organizations implemented included *investment of private capital, government incentives, establishment of banks, trade and exports, development of infrastructure, and great emphasis on business, education, vocational training, and strong leadership.*

Solutions offered by the N.A.A.C.P. included the *elimination of segregation, desegregate, vote, and own no land.* According to Dr. Mansour's book, the N.A.A.C.P. Charter prohibited that organization from owning land. Now, you figure this one out. If the majority of those who established the N.A.A.C.P. were white, and we know they were, why did they insist that the organization not own land, the very basis of economic empowerment? Too often we allow our organizations to fall into the role of puppet because we take money and assistance from those who would "keep us in our place."

There is a similar situation occurring in Comedy Central USA, Cincinnati, Ohio, that will culminate in a confrontation between pro boycott groups and the Black organization known as the Cincinnati Arts Consortium. For over ten years, the Consortium has held a Martin Luther King, Jr. Breakfast in downtown Cincinnati, at the Hyatt Hotel. This year's event will be held on January 20th and will find itself embroiled in national controversy and massive local protest.

The organization will hold its celebration in the boycott zone despite, of all things, a personal request from Martin Luther King III asking them not to do so. As of the date of this writing (January 6, 2003), the organization's "Board," made up of different people, white and Black, but funded primarily by white-owned corporations, the Consortium has refused to comply with King's request.

The main reasons given for its refusal to comply is (wouldn't you guess it?) money. First of all, those sponsoring the breakfast are surely behind the scenes calling the shots. Just as we experienced with our local N.A.A.C.P. and Community Action Agency, there are those, Black and white, who hold these organizations hostage by threatening them with withdrawal of their precious sponsorship funds if they do not conform corporate desires and motives.

The national office of the N.A.A.C.P. called our local office and told them not to hold their annual dinner in the boycott zone; they ended up moving it. The Community Action Agency, did not comply with the wishes of the boycotters because its corporate funding was threatened by corporate lackeys, one of which is former Federal Judge, Nathaniel Jones, who is on the Toyota "Diversity" advisory board that was formed after Jesse Jackson threatened, of all things, a boycott of Toyota.

My point is this. We just celebrated a series of days called Kwanzaa, one day of which was dedicated to self-determination. How self-determined are we when we allow organizations that are suppose to benefit Black people to be co-opted by corporations that do not have the best interests of Black folks in mind? Where is our self-determination when we submit to the demands and commands of puppet masters? All money is not good money, especially money that is attached to a rope with which to hang our people.

My contention is that we must create revenue streams that give our organizations long sustainability and viability. Sure it's all right if some corporation wants to assist, but if they also seek to control our organizations it's time to give them their money back or just say "No" to it. Additionally, if our organizations are doing what their mission statements describe, and they are providing a necessary service to Black folks, it follows that Black folks have the primary obligation to support them. If, as our local Arts Consortium has stated, they will lose corporate funding if they go against the grain, so to speak, then it follows that Black folks should step in and fill that corporate gap. We should also punish the corporate culprit for its attempt at compromising our organization.

And finally, if a particular Black organization is doing such a good job for Black people, and it loses some corporate funds, Black people will surely take care of it, won't we? If not, maybe that means we don't really want or need that particular organization. After all, as Brother Walter Fauntroy once said, "We buy what we want and beg for what we need."

The Correct Psychological Moment

Professor John Sibley Butler notes in his excellent book, Entrepreneurship and Self-Help Among Black Americans, W.E.B. DuBois' comments about Booker T. Washington's economic program. DuBois said Washington's "[economic] program emerged at the correct psychological moment; the nation was ashamed of giving so much sentiment to Afro-Americans and was turning to the task of making money." Of course, we know Booker T. was making valiant attempts to get Black people to take the economic path to freedom. We can see several "then and now" similarities as we take a look at what is happening in this country vis-à-vis the all-out assaults on affirmative action and the very real prospect of a war with Iraq.

Just as the country was turning its attention to money (Or should I say, "back" to money?) during the latter part of the 19th century, so it was and continues to be the case in the waning years of the 20th century and now into the 21st. The country has gone stark-raving mad over making money – and stealing quite a bit of it as well – and we stand on the brink of a war that brings back memories of other wars that started under false pretenses and ended up being all about the almighty dollar.

While I will not go into the specific history of those wars nor the one we are about to enter. Suffice to say that this one is also about money. This is not so much about "owning" the second largest oil reserves on the planet, as much as it is about "controlling" those reserves. Do some research on the oil industry and the dollar, the standard of purchase for oil, and you will see the real deal.

But let's get back to the correct psychological moment. Marcus Garvey said we should know when to strike our enemy. He said the best time to strike is when he is busy doing some evil to someone else; that's when he is at his weakest against us. Malcolm X said, "...We have made advancement in this country only when this country was under pressure from forces above and beyond its control."

Do those statements sound germane to you today? They sure do to me, especially since I saw Jerry Falwell on television saying that now we are facing a war, this country must show all of its citizens, especially Black Americans, that they are important to this country. Do you see a pattern here? Good. It's been the same for hundreds of years, folks.

I have no idea where this latest fiasco, this geopolitical comedy of errors, this web of falsehoods, this Woodrow Wilson-like grab for world power, this buffoonish, laughable, but tragic scenario will end. But I am very quick to learn from the past, especially when it comes to what Black folks should be doing to strengthen our economic position, you know, like Garvey and Malcolm admonished us.

I can see that this, as W.E.B. said, is the correct psychological moment for us to act and take advantage of Falwell's plea that we come together and sing Kumbaya – now that we are facing war. This is the correct psychological moment for Black folks to assess our situation and make a determination on how to fix it or at least improve it.

History proves that we are only valued and valuable when the country is being threatened. What have we gotten from the deal for being some of the first in line to get shot by the enemy? Well, old Crispus Attucks got a few schools named after him. Runaway slaves who fought for the Union got Jim Crow, second-class citizenship and the Klan to keep them in check. Black soldiers, who fought in World War One, even though they breathed the same toxic gas as some of the white soldiers, were not allowed the same medical treatment.

Black soldiers who fought in World War II got to ride in the back of the train, while the German prisoners they captured were given much more comfortable seats. Korean and Viet Nam Black warriors got duped into believing they were fighting a just war, one they could and would eventually win, and came home brainwashed or drugged-out. Gulf War Blacks were doused with Agent Orange and returned to a cadre of white police officers who were hell-bent on killing Black men.

Now, while the country's attention is focused on another outside enemy and while it is doing all it can to make and control even more of the world's resources, another correct psychological moment has come for a Black program that will, once and for all, move our people forward economically. Black leadership should not waste its time discussing the war. After all, we already have our "HNIC's," Condoleezza Rice and Colin Powell, leading the war chants. Real Black leadership will use this time to pull our people together around an economic agenda and, whether we have a war or not, we may be able to catch them while they are looking the other way and take full advantage of this correct psychological moment.

Plan for what is difficult while it is easy, do what is great while it is small. The most difficult things in the world must be done while they are still easy; the greatest things in the world must be done while they are still small. For this reason sages never do what is great, and this is why they can achieve that greatness.
The Art of War, Sun Tzu

Internal Reparations –
Repairing Ourselves from the Inside Out

On August 17, 2002, the anniversary of the birth of the Honorable Marcus Garvey, many brothers and sisters traveled to Washington, D.C. at the request of Dr. Conrad Worrill and the National Black United Front. The Millions for Reparations March and demonstration will be the collective demand for the United States Government to pay Black folks what *"They Owe Us,"* and to let them know *"It's Time To Pay Up!"* Those are the words of Dr. Worrill, and certainly we agree with him and others who are calling for this country to pay what we call, "External Reparations."

You may not know it but there is another form of reparations that we must seek, and these reparations are easy – almost elementary – to obtain. Internal Reparations. That's right, Internal Reparations. By taking (not asking for, not seeking, not petitioning) our Internal Reparations, Black folks will not only be preparing ourselves for our external reparations, we will simultaneously strengthen ourselves and future generations of Black children. Please notice that I am saying we must simply "take" our Internal Reparations. It is that simple, brothers and sisters.

From the inside out, we can start to repair ourselves simply, and I emphasize simply, by redirecting a greater portion of our $700 billion in annual income to ourselves. Considering our own internal economic and psychological infirmities, we should understand that it's going to take a dose of strong medicine to cure us. We should know that unless we take that medicine we will not get well. And, guess what, folks, the medicine does not taste bad at all.

Here is the main difference between external and internal reparations. The external reparations we seek are essentially outside of our control and must be given by people who really do not love Black folks. Internal reparations are well within our control, and most of us love our people and ourselves. You do control what's in your pocket, don't you?

Can you imagine what would happen if we used that control to internally repair our people? We have the internal assets to change our economic condition in this country. All we need to do is USE them to benefit US.

The external reparations movement must continue, and it surely will because of the strong and committed leadership heading up this effort. So this is not an *either or* situation. Both movements must proceed simultaneously. The beauty of pursuing internal reparations is that people of African descent get a positive return everyday. We don't have to wait for the largess of recalcitrant legislators. We don't have to listen to the excuses, the filibustering, and the negative rhetoric from those who would keep us "in our economic place." Internal reparations allow us to pay ourselves everyday of our lives and to build a system that will be here when our external reparations come – and they will come.

This is vitally important because, as many of us know, if we have no channel through which our money can flow, in a circular direction, touching as many Black folks as possible, we will simply end up giving our external reparations right back to the ones about whom we complain so much. Any rational thinking man or woman knows this is pure insanity. We could never maximize the benefits of external reparations without first being internally repaired.

The ultimate goal of internal reparations is for people of African descent to love ourselves and our people enough to continuously *Give and Buy Black* and unapologetically support Black efforts. The benefits of internal reparations are obvious: Greater income; increased employment; increased political strength; increased hope and less crime; improved housing; and a stronger negotiating position for external reparations.

How do we gain internal reparations? The first thing we must do is educate ourselves economically and historically. Then we must make individual commitments to regularly spend more of our money at Black owned businesses. Look inward as well as outward for economic justice and freedom. As Jesse Brown's book says, "Pay yourself first."

No Deposit, No Return

Not only do I want you to be conscious, I want you to be "consciously disturbed." I want your consciousness to be disturbed enough to cause you to act – to use your economic resources to empower yourselves.
Jackie Mayfield, *Founder and President, Compro Tax, Beaumont, Texas*

Why do some of our people continue to believe that we can achieve our collective economic freedom without doing the things necessary to obtain that freedom? We seem to think it will come to us simply because we want it, or simply because we march and demonstrate, or simply because we hold a conference and come away from that gathering feeling good about what we heard. Why don't we realize and accept the fact that if we do not follow through and act upon the information we receive, and the threats we make during our marches and demonstrations, we will never achieve economic freedom? These are not rhetorical questions. Please answer them for yourself.

I have answered them for myself, and I act upon the information I have by following through on the solutions to our problems rather than merely going home and waiting for the next crisis, or refusing to contribute to the solution. What is the solution? The solution is grounded in actions we can take – right now – to relieve our people of the horrendous economic conditions in which we have been, especially for the past 39 years. The solution can be found in what we are willing to do after the marches, after the speeches, after the rallies, and after the forums.

Aren't you tired of just talking? Aren't you exhausted after all of the marching? Don't you want to see some real change, some real return for your actions and your outrage? What is the solution? The solution is right in our pockets, right now. We may not be able to control very much in this land we call home, but we can certainly control what is in our pockets and purses. We can certainly control our money.

So what do we do with our money? Well, we all know that if we go to the bank expecting to make a withdrawal we had better have made a deposit first. As often as we complain about not being treated fairly by the banks that hold our money, we should be searching for alternatives for our dollars. We should be looking for repositories that will give us something in return for our dollars – and I am not talking about the stock market.

We should also understand that we cannot move forward economically without individual sacrifices in favor of the collective. That is, we must make deposits into our own economic accounts, so to speak, if we expect to get something out of them. Our Black institutions, organizations, banks, clubs, businesses, and of course, the MATAH Network, the only Black owned and operated consumer packaged goods distribution channel in this country, can do much more for our people and would be much better off if we would support them more.

I cannot tell you how great I felt when I attended a MATAH Conference a couple of years ago and noticed the sponsoring banners on the walls. They were all Black; the conference was paid for with money from Black folks. Black deposits – Black returns. With as much money as we have in our control, albeit for a short while because it leaves our neighborhoods so fast, we could fund our own conferences and organizations, you know, just like we fund our churches. Have you ever seen a Black church with a banner behind the pulpit saying "This week's service sponsored by Toyota"? Uh oh, I had better quit this line of reasoning before some preacher gets a bad idea.

John Brown, investment/merchant banker and associate of the Bedford Group, Culver City, California, asks the question, "Why can't we invest in ourselves? We invest in others everyday without question, always giving other businesses the opportunity to fail, with our money at stake. Why don't we invest in our own businesses and give our own brothers and sisters that same opportunity to fail as well. Who knows? They just might succeed."

Brown, in addition to his tremendous workload, is also working as a board member of the MATAH Network and on his personal dream of building a $1 billion Real Estate Investment Trust – endowed and controlled by Black folks. He understands that if we don't put anything in, we can't take anything out.

Let's make some deposits into Black children's accounts for their economic future. Let's understand that we cannot have anything of substance without making some kind of sacrifice. Let's invest more in one another, not just from the consumer side of things but from the Black business side as well. What I mean by that is, let's not put the entire burden on consumers to support Black owned businesses. Black businesses not only have an obligation to do what they say they will do, they must also spend as much as they can with other Black businesses, and they should give as much as they can to Black organizations.

When we do that, and do it consistently, we will be able to make withdrawals from the tremendous returns we will have accumulated from our deposits in one another. Always remember: If we don't put anything in, we can't take anything out.

Section III

Politricks and Other Games of *No-Chance*

"There are two ways of making politics one's vocation: either one lives 'for' politics or one lives 'off' politics.... He who strives to make politics a permanent source of income lives 'off' politics as a vocation, whereas he who does not do this lives 'for' politics."
Max Weber, German Sociologist
From the book,
Coleman Young and Detroit Politics,
Wilbur C. Rich, Author

"Real politics...is deeply rooted in the economic foundation of the social order."
Dr. Carter G. Woodson

Every student of Political Science, every student of Economics knows, that the race can only be saved through a solid industrial foundation; that the race can only be saved through political independence. Take away industry from a race; take away political freedom from a race, and you have a group of slaves.
Marcus Garvey

Two Wings on the Same Bird

Any time you throw your weight behind a political party that controls two thirds of the government, and that party can't keep the promise that it made to you during election time, and you are dumb enough to walk around continuing to identify yourself with that party, you're not only a chump, but you're a traitor to your race.
Malcolm X

Prior to the 2000 Presidential Election (or should I say, "Selection"?) I wrote an article titled, "Will we be Gored or Bushwhacked?" Two years later, we all knew the answer to that question. The article was written to point out the similarities between the two candidates and the ridiculous nature of our so-called two-party political system. Even more important, I wanted to point out that no matter who was "selected" as our next President we would generally get more of the same. Right wing, left wing, who cares? They are both wings on the same bird.

If you look closely you can easily see the similarities of the left and the right. Sure their rhetoric is different, but they are more alike than different. A bird must have both wings to fly, a right wing and a left wing, and it's the bird that makes the decision where to fly, how high to fly, whether to fly north or south, to take off or to land, and whether it will turn right or left. Just who or what is this political bird, the one that controls both the left and the right wing? Corporate America, that's who.

We sometimes pretend that politics is so pristine and so untouched by corporate shenanigans, especially when election time rolls around. We pull out the banners of righteousness and character, we start beating the drum for honesty, and we dust off the old political clichés that conjure up the days of "Vote for me and I'll set you free." Yes, we would love to think, even during a brief period of utopian thought, that our politicians, the ones we personally elect and send to various offices, are as pure as the driven snow and would never be swayed by the corporate temptations that lie in wait for them. We should awaken from that dream.

This is not to say that all politicians are bad people, and this is really not so much about politicians as it is about politics. As I have said before, if we could just take the politics out of our politicians, we would be much better for having done so. But for us to think that corporations are not in control of politics is Alice in Wonderland thinking. Both of the political wings attached to the corporate bird must be controlled by the corporations, and control them they will.

If you look back at how this country started and how it has been maintained, it will be quite clear to you that everything is based on economics. Of course we need a political system to keep things cool, but the bottom line is who controls the money. Procedures and organizations were set up in this country and in England, despite the political constraints and the outrage of some politicians, mainly to gain and maintain control of the world's monetary system. The prime examples of that are the Federal Reserve System and the Internal Revenue Service.

Right wing, left wing, it does not matter who is in charge, and that's just the way the rich and powerful wanted it to be. They couldn't care less who wins office, and that means even the Office of the President of the United States. To paraphrase Baron Rothschild, he said as long as he could control the world's finances it mattered not who was in political office. In case you have not checked lately, the Rothschild family is still *large and in charge* globally, hundreds of years after the master plan was developed.

As we approach yet another election, don't be duped by all of the left wing versus right wing talk. Don't get hung-up on the labels, i.e., Republican, Democrat, Conservative, and Liberal. And don't fall yet again for the ridiculous practice of always voting for a person simply because he or she is in a certain party, or simply because he or she is Black. Haven't we learned our lesson yet? A few decades ago most Blacks voted Republican; now most of us vote Democrat. What has that gotten us? Just take a look around and you can answer that for your self very easily.

We must always remember that politics is about self-interest, so we should always vote for the candidates who will see to our interests, whether those candidates are white or

Black, Democrat or Republican. Corporate moguls understand that and take full advantage of it by giving money to both parties. They obviously agree with old Baron Rothschild and continue to spread their money around, expecting and getting their needs met by whoever happens to be in office.

Left wing, right wing, it does not matter to the bird, for he knows he is always in total control of those wings and he can make them do whatever he wants – and needs – anytime he chooses. There may be two wings, but there is only one bird: The Big Business Bird.

Wanted: Maynard Jackson Politics – Part One

My election was the result of the greatest grassroots effort in the history of Chicago. My election was made possible by thousands and thousands of people who demanded that the burdens of mismanagement, unfairness, and inequity be lifted so that the city might be saved...Most of our problems can be solved. Some of them will take brains, and some of them will take patience, but all of them will have to be wrestled with like an alligator in the swamp."
Mayor Harold Washington, Inaugural Address, April 29, 1983

I don't claim to know a great deal about political strategy, campaigning, and elections, but there are two periods in our political history of which I am aware and quite proud: The election and incumbency of Harold Washington in Chicago, and the election and reign of Maynard Jackson as Mayor of Atlanta, Georgia. Despite being a political numbskull during those times in my life (some might say things haven't changed in that regard), I knew something special had taken place in those two great cities. This article speaks specifically about the Jackson victory.

Blacks from the north were going back home to Atlanta during the early 1970's; I made my first trip there in 1970, albeit with a "heightened level of security" if you know what I mean. I soon found that Atlanta was on the move, trying to get it together. Then Maynard Jackson came along.

Initially I was proud simply because I knew Mayor Jackson. He and I sang in the famous North Carolina College choir under the direction of Dr. Samuel Hill, way back in 1964. Maynard had this deep bellowing voice and he was so articulate. I used to marvel at his impeccable enunciation as he narrated one of our Christmas renderings. Another memory I have of the Mayor is the night in Washington, DC, during an east coast singing tour, when he and I missed the bus because we were eating together in a Hot Shoppe.

Since I was a lowly freshman and Maynard was a first year law student we did not have a personal relationship, but I greatly admired him, and I claimed him for my own some ten years later when he won that election in Atlanta. I bragged about the new Mayor and my brief association with him. I was proud to tell my friends about my days at "NCC" with Maynard Jackson, and Leon Pendarvis, who has played piano for Saturday Night Live for probably 20 years now, and the beautiful Brenda Randolph, the former wife of Randall Robinson, and all the other choir members who had such an impact on my college life.

Then along came the Atlanta Hartsfield Airport. My first lesson in political savvy, strength, and resolve was about to begin and, I might add, so was this nation's. The powers-that-be wanted to build a new airport and were quite reluctant at the prospect of Black folks being involved in any meaningful way. You know what I mean. Black businesses were relegated to second-class, hand-me-down, crumbs-falling-off-the-table status. The plans for building the airport were being made without significant inclusion of Black contractors and others who paid their fair share of taxes and held a stake in the city "too busy to hate."

Bad move. Apparently the good old boys had no respect for the Mayor (Mr. Jackson, if you're nasty), or they had not heard of him, or they simply believed they could walk right over this Brother. They were most assuredly mistaken. The Maynard Jackson brand of politics was about to be unveiled. He very plainly said, and I am paraphrasing, "If we don't get ours, you don't get yours." In other words, if there is not a significant percentage of Black business involvement in the building of Hartsfield, there will be no Hartsfield. I loved it. I began to brag even more about knowing this giant of a politician.

The rest is history, as they say. We are all familiar with the ensuing years in Atlanta vis-à-vis development and contracting, and we can look back at that watershed moment in history and appreciate it even more. It was truly a "Rosa Parks moment" as Pastor Damon Lynch III so aptly noted during the April unrest in Cincinnati, when he valiantly took his stand against injustice. Maynard Jackson, by standing up for what was right and fair for his people, had changed the landscape in Atlanta. He had redefined Black political empowerment simply by doing what Marcus Garvey and others said we could all do: Stand up!

Now, here in Cincinnati, we have a similar situation, a similar defining moment in the history of a city still trying to maintain status quo and continue business as usual. There is no Maynard Jackson here – there never has been a Maynard Jackson here, so it is up to the 43% of the city's population that calls itself Black to take a stand.

They are building a National Underground Railroad Freedom Center on the riverfront, which just happens to be between the two new stadiums that were built without significant economic benefit to Blacks. In addition, plans are underway to build what will be known as The Banks, a riverfront development of housing, retail, entertainment, lodging, and office space. What is estimated to be an $800 million project, as of this writing, will not – I said, "will not" include an African American development team. The only majority Black development team of the 12 teams that submitted qualifications was not allowed to submit a bid for even one of the 12 blocks on the riverfront!

The team, comprising top-notch, best-of-breed, second-to-none businesses from across the country and in Cincinnati was eliminated from the opportunity to have development rights on this mega-project. Sure, there will be a few Blacks who will get subcontracts, but that's the way the game is always played here in river city. Our fight for economic justice will continue in part two of this column. In the meantime, I'm putting a call out for Maynard Jackson.

Wanted: Maynard Jackson Politics – Part Two

Part one of this article described my respect for Maynard Jackson and what he did as Mayor of Atlanta during the construction of the Hartsfield Airport. I also introduced a new "Rosa Parks Moment" that is taking place in my hometown, Cincinnati, Ohio. Like Hartsfield back in the 1970's, the $800 million Cincinnati riverfront development project known as The Banks will either be an opportunity for economic justice or it will turn out to be a permanent monument of economic injustice and exclusion of Black people in this city. So far, status quo has been the order of the day, despite the shallow and shadowy efforts of a few "black" folks and their white counterparts on the Greater Cincinnati Port Authority, which excluded the only majority Black development team from the bid process.

A brief history is in order here. The Paul Brown Stadium in Cincinnati, Ohio, was built at a cost of approximately one-half billion taxpayer dollars. Of course, a deal was cut by just one County Commissioner who, by the way, now works for Mike Brown's Cincinnati Bengals, that literally gave away the entire store to his current boss, i.e., concessions, parking, guaranteed sellouts, and a long term lease made for a Sultan. Black folks received their token share of subcontracts – and some were elated about that – but the final number for "economic inclusion," a term that by definition suggests previous "economic exclusion," was less than the stated goal of 15% -- and that was for all "minorities," including white females! No need to discuss what percentage Black folks received.

Then we had the expressway project (approximately $200 million) and another stadium, a baseball park for the Cincinnati Reds (approximately $300 million). Same song and dance. Business as usual. A lot of clamoring about "this time we will do it right," subsequent complaining, and finally bricks and mortar start to fly with minimal participation by Black folks. (Does anyone know Maynard's number?) Now we have a National Underground Railroad "Freedom" Center ($100 million plus) being built on the riverfront, the board members of which are determined to change the landscape of economic inclusion with this project, and to their credit have made significant progress. After all, how could a "Freedom" Center be built without considerable participation by sons and daughters of ex-slaves? That wouldn't go over too well with the country, now would it?

That takes us to the current project, The Banks. It looks like the same game is about to be played once again. The sad part about it is that some of our recognized Black "leaders" in this town are standing on the sidelines cheering for the visiting team, having already given them our playbook; they are now secretly giving them the signals for our plays. Nevertheless, the fight continues.

A reconsideration of the Maynard Jackson era in Atlanta and his brand of politics that said, "If we don't get ours, you don't get yours," suggests that Black Cincinnati should begin to chant, "Remember Maynard!" "Remember Hartsfield!" Or, will we slither back into our dark caves of apathy, only to go down in history as a group of Black people who were satisfied with *crumbs,* in the form of minor subcontracts from white developers, over *loaves,* in the form of development and ownership rights of income-producing assets on Cincinnati's riverfront? Instead of this being our "Rosa Parks Moment," it could be described as our Ida B. Wells moment. If you are familiar with the stand that strong sister took seventy years before Sister Rosa made her statement, you know that she refused to give up her seat on a train and was subsequently put off the train. She did not give up; she filed a lawsuit and won, but her victory was denied by a higher court. Wouldn't you know it?

What will our statement be? A better question is, "What would Maynard Jackson do?" Well, that strong Black leader would say, "If we don't get ours, you don't get yours." If there is no real economic opportunity for Black people on the Cincinnati Riverfront, which is now ironically being touted as *The Freedom Banks,* even though when slaves reached this side of the river they still were not free, (that's why there was an underground railroad in the first place), should we support this project? If we are not in a position to benefit from the billions of tourism dollars generated from the *Freedom Banks*, shall we even allow it to be built? What would Maynard Jackson do?

This situation very clearly suggests that even though Black people were qualified to build the mansions in the antebellum south, the buildings of state in Washington, DC, and the homes of former slave holding Presidents in Monticello and Mount Vernon, Virginia, they are not qualified, at least in *Cincinn-apathy*, to build stadiums, hotels, office buildings, expressways, and retail complexes. Of course, we know that's nothing but hogwash, but if we settle for it, if we accept it, we deserve nothing more than the usual crumbs they always give to Black people. Maynard Jackson would not accept the crumbs. What about you? These situations take place in cities all across this country. What are you willing to accept?

Had Enough Yet?

"Any people who would vote the same way for three generations without thereby obtaining results ought to be ignored and disenfranchised."
Carter G. Woodson, *The Mis-Education of the Negro*

Well, they did it to us again. Bill Rehnquist and the *Supremes* saw to it that "We the people" would have no say in determining who would be our President. They selected the President for us. And that's not the worst part of the travesty we witnessed during the national "selection." We saw the Supremes use their ultimate authority to decide who would be king by dragging out the 14th Amendment and using it against rather than for Black people – the people for which the amendment was written in the first place.

Yes, we saw the politicians jockeying for position on this, the most important election of our time, as some put it. We heard all of the speeches and saw hopes dashed when the decision was announced. And then Uncle Clarence Thomas was sent out to quell the masses by suggesting that politics had nothing to do with the Supremes' decision. Thomas, after saying virtually nothing during the "deliberations" we are told, was the one who came out to explain, or should I say, "mitigate," the process. I nominate him for an Oscar; he's good.

It reminded me of the Rodney King incident. We all saw what happened, but they told us we did not see it. Oh well, that's water under the bridge. There's certainly nothing we can do about it now. Protest? Yes, but it won't change the result. They are certainly not going to reverse their decision and they are not going to re-call Dubya from the Presidency. So what's the lesson here?

Let's go back to the 14th Amendment. In order for the rights of Black people to be protected, this amendment was adopted, although some called it illegal because it was never fully ratified. Little by little, we have seen an erosion of the power of this amendment, vis-à-vis the rights of Black people. We have seen, and in some cases Blacks have participated in, the transferring and co-opting of this amendment from Black people to all people. The Supremes used it against Blacks in deciding the Presidential Selection.

Some of our so-called Black leaders have found it convenient to promote the protection of the 14th Amendment for everyone, including white females. That's what this term "minority" is all about, and what we see today is the result of allowing ourselves to be called minorities along with every other group that wants to piggy-back on the struggles and victories of Black people. To think that we are so downright naïve to suggest we can help everyone else, before first helping ourselves, is ludicrous. We are on the bottom of the heap and some of our leaders say we must help everyone. I wish they would tell us how to accomplish such a daunting task.

So, have you had enough yet? Have you had enough political charades and love fests? Have you had enough promises? Have you had enough lies, enough posturing, and enough pandering? Have you had enough of losing every time there is an election? Black people always lose in the political game because we do not have an economic base from which to operate and wield power. We do not have a collective national strategy that addresses non-crisis situations. We always seem to be behind the curve – or in front of the train; and we get run over every time. Have you had enough yet?

Quite honestly, I don't know what it will take for us to change our ways and do what other groups do in this country. Bob Law, former host of the popular radio talk show, Night Talk, says, "Black people must protect our interests by creating and maintaining an economic infrastructure rather than seeing how many Black people we can get elected." I agree wholeheartedly. If we continue to seek parity by putting most of our eggs in the political basket, we will never win. We must have a national strategy that addresses our overwhelming need for economic empowerment. We should all be able to see that now. Economics controls politics – and we seem too enamored with elections to figure that out. Think about it. Who was the first person Dubya went to see in Washington? It wasn't Clinton; it wasn't the security advisors. It was Allen Greenspan. Hello!

If you have had enough of the political game, get involved in the economic game. That's what this is all about anyway. Why do you think Jesse Jackson made that call to Dubya after he told <u>us</u> to "stay out of the bushes"? Do you think the Supremes selected Dubya because they think he's a nice guy? Why do you think Uncle Clarence went on the offensive to justify what happened? Why do you think Gore slithered away with hardly a mention of Black voter disenfranchisement? What we saw is the result of what Jesse and his son told us in their book, "It's all about the money," folks.

We had better take heed of that fact real soon, or we will find ourselves in this same situation four years from now. If you have had enough, check out Dr. Claud Anderson's plan for economic empowerment via Powernomics, and act on it. Get involved with Recycling Black Dollars or the MATAH Network or the Visions 2000 economic power movement. Just DO something, rather than continue to merely talk about the problems. For our children's sake, get involved in some kind of economic empowerment program. Our future is at stake!

Can You Hear Me Now?

You knew someone would use this line sooner or later, and considering what happened in the latest, "most crucial election" in our history, I could not pass up the opportunity to ask the question, "Can you hear me now?" Why? Because I have been writing this column since 1993, telling our people to wake up from our political deep sleep, and move toward collective economic empowerment, and it seems most of us still fail to heed the message. After seeing the latest "selection" of those who will rule the political roosts for the next two to six years, I ask, "Can you hear me now?"

In my neck of the woods the local Black politicians, as well as a few national ones, told us once again that this election was crucial (aren't they all?) and it was imperative for Black folks to get out and vote to change the political landscape of our city and the country. I have not seen the final results, but I would venture to guess our turnout among Black folks was once again quite dismal. They know us so well, they predict low turnout when it rains. That's ridiculous! On Election Tuesday, I drove 500 miles, every mile of which was in driving rain, to get back to Cincinnati in time to cast my votes. I am not buying that rain excuse, but I do understand why some of our people don't vote. The more we do it, the less power we have.

We woke up on Wednesday after the election and found no Black person with any significant control in this country's entire political system. No Black Governors and no Black Senators, in 2002, despite our being here since the country started. Does that mean anything to you? Does it say that we have been doing something wrong? And, already some of our Black leaders are telling us to get ready to vote in 2004. Is that the best they can offer us?

We get so hyped for elections that we lose sight of what happens between elections. Just in case you haven't heard, economics happens, folks. Business happens. Economic empowerment happens. The question is: What do we do between elections? Do we wait until the next "crucial" election, or do we build our businesses and lay the foundation for an economic future for our children? From what I have seen, the answer is obvious.

But, can you hear me now? Can you hear me when I say we must change our attitudes and our actions when it comes to economics? Can you hear me when I say, "Wake up, my people?" Stop placing all your eggs in the political basket, please. If a Katherine Harris and a Jeb Bush can get elected and re-elected in Florida, of all places, doesn't that tell you something? Can you hear me now?

If what was anticipated to be a new day for the Democrats to control the Senate by an even greater margin and maybe even take over the House of Representatives, as predicted by some, if that turned out to be the biggest debacle since the Contract on [Black] America, can you see a need for change? If you thought Black folks had political power before this election, what must you think now? Black folks don't control jack in the political system. You know it and I know it. And, as Martin Delany, Booker T., Marcus Garvey, Amos Wilson, and many others have told us, if we want to control anything politically we had better get our economic act together. Can you hear me now?

I am not saying I told you so; I would never do that. I am only trying to get us to change directions. I love our people too much to sit idly by and not continue to share these messages of empowerment in my Blackonomics column. But the next step is yours. What are you going to do?

There is the MATAH Network, the work of which carried our brother, Ken Bridges, to his death after he and other forward thinking brothers and sisters culminated one the biggest deals in Black business history with Grenada Nutmeg Oil (GNO). MATAH has also formed a partnership with Mariandina Nutritional Products, developed by Dr. Charles Ssali, from Uganda, now residing in London. What are you waiting for? What more do you want? This is the opportunity we have awaited for years, brothers and sisters.

Black people now control the entire vertical business process of Grenada Nutmeg. Blacks control the growing, the processing, the wholesaling, and the retailing of this product, a multi-billion dollar industry, which has many significant uses, including medicinal uses. It's yours, Black people. It's under your control, unlike the political system you so greatly admire. If we do not support this historic partnership by purchasing the products on the MATAH Network, especially the GNO, then we have no one to blame but ourselves. And if we fail to take advantage of what we have and keep complaining about what we do not have, we will soon look around and find ourselves relegated to permanent underclass status in this country.

I say it once again, for what is probably the 10,000th time. Start and support Black businesses. Form partnerships among Black businesses. Create more capacity to do business. Create more jobs for Black people within Black businesses. Love one another more. Trust one another more. Get on the economic empowerment track and stop concentrating most of your efforts on politics. **Can you hear me NOW?**

You Asked For It

You have heard the saying, "Be careful of what you ask for, you just might get it;" and it's really true. When the Trent Lott debacle was upon us I was shouting, "Let him stay; don't ask for his resignation." Obviously those who wanted him to step down won that battle, but I wonder what will happen now that he is no longer the leader of the U.S. Senate. There were those who asked the Senate to censure Lott instead of defrocking him, namely, the Congressional Black Caucus (CBC), and I commend them for that. Time will tell if their suggestion was the best, and I think we will find out very quickly.

In my opinion, it would have been better for Lott to remain in his position because during his numerous apologies he also made some very interesting statements. He said some things for which he could have been held accountable to Black folks, thus opening the door for possible concessions on our behalf. But nooooo, we wanted him out because he said what he'd been feeling and thinking for years, and this time we not only heard him (I assume we also heard him in 1982 when he said the same thing), we paid attention to it.

If we had not gone along with his Republican cohorts, Armstrong Williams leading the charge, we would be able to say to old Trent, "Hey, didn't you say you support affirmative action? Aren't you the guy who said you didn't really appreciate the contributions of MLK, but now after a recent epiphany you are a changed man?" We could have asked Trent Lott several questions in reference to his apologetic statements, but now African Americans can hold him accountable for nothing.

It was really funny how things played out. The CBC asking for Lott to be censured, John Lewis accepting his apology and saying, "Let's move on," Armstrong Williams decrying Lott's remarks as unacceptable in the party with the "big tent," and finally, after he was granted permission by his boss, Colin Powell came out and spoke against Lott's remarks as well. The whole thing smacked of ridiculous theater if you ask me.

The Republicans saw this Lott thing as a way to engender Black folks and to take greater advantage of the Democrats' laxity when it comes to their primary "minority" voting block. George Dubya has an agenda he is desperately trying to ram through, and scapegoat Trent Lott proved to be an unwilling assistant. Bush could not afford to be derailed and Lott was not such a big deal that he could not be sacrificed. To top it all off, Black folks, at least those who just had to have Lott out of there, played a major role and actually helped Bush in the process. I bet it was congrats and *attaboys* all around the big tent when Lott stepped down.

I don't know what the new majority leader will do for Black folks, if anything, but already Black folks are stepping to the front of the line endorsing him, praising him, lauding him, and holding Bill Frist up as though he were the Messiah himself. I guess we'll have to wait to see. But with Lott, we knew what we had, and we finally had something on him. What do they say about the bird in the hand?

I hope you can see this is all charades and more of the same when it comes to politics. Bush sacrificed Lott, but he re-nominates Charles Pickering for Federal Judge (A payback to Lott?). So much for the "big tent." Bush says he's concerned about the poor and downtrodden, but he puts forth an economic program that will give the richest among us a windfall, while the poorest get little or nothing. Our President has also issued a brief that speaks against the affirmative action program at the University of Michigan. Lott said he was in support of it; I wonder what *Uncle Clarence and the Supremes* will say.

Bush is determined to go to war in Iraq and sacrifice more young lives, and he needs the support of the people. Trent Lott was an obstacle to that support, and he had to go. As for the role of Black folks in this whole thing, Jerry Falwell said it best in an interview about Trent Lott. I paraphrase: *We are about to go to war and now is a time when we have to let everyone know, especially Blacks, that they are important to this country.* I guess so, Jerry, especially when we will be the primary victims of the war. It's a shame Blacks can't be as highly regarded any other time.

Yes, we should be careful, very careful about what we ask for, because we may get something worse than what we have. Just remember, politically speaking, Bill Frist owes Black folks nothing. He made no commitments, no promises, and no deals, except those deals he may have already made with a few Black people. But that's cool; it's not personal; it's just politics. Right?

Standing in the Door of No Return

How did you like the photo op of George Bush on Goree Island, walking through the slave dungeons, looking solemn and interested in the plight of our ancestors, and making a speech that strongly suggested he was genuinely concerned about Black people? As he stood in the sacred "Door of No Return," mugging for the cameras, I have since heard and read the accounts of the brothers and sisters who were there and actually experienced the impact of Bush's trip to "The Bush."

Personal accounts of Goree Islanders being herded into a football field at six o'clock in the morning began to surface after Bush left The Bush. People said the town was deserted, except for secret service agents everywhere – even in the ocean. They told how they were mistreated and disrespected by Bush's protectors without regard for their rights as citizens of Goree Island, not to mention their relationship to those about whom Bush was speaking.

Bush probably didn't even make the connection. There he was talking about how bad slavery was, all the while the relatives of the slaves to which he was referring were being held captive in a football field, only this time they were waiting not for their departure but for Bush's departure. One sister said, "We never want to see him come here again."

So, what we witnessed on American television was our President standing in The Door of No Return, making a speech to no one but his secret service agents. Of course, Condi and Colin were there. (Too bad the two of them were not at the World Conference on Racism in Durban, South Africa a couple of years ago. Oh yeah, Bush told them they couldn't go.)

I don't know about you, but I think our President needs a lot more help. The information he gets, and then passes on to us, is wrong; the words he uses are inappropriate; he must have failed World Geography with flying colors; and he needs a new walk. (I can't stand that arrogant cowboy strut of his) To top it all off, he goes to Africa and demonstrates a total lack of decorum and respect for the African people.

This is the same man who, according to a recent statement by Strong-arm Williams, the black (small "b") apologist for Strom Thurmond, who said, "President Bush has done more for Black people than any other leader in modern history." (Did I say Strong-arm Williams? I'm sorry, I meant Armstrong Williams.) I wonder how Williams defines "modern history." Must be two years or less, and if Georgie Boy has done more for Black folks than anyone else, in such a short period of time, we should elect this guy to the lifetime office of "King of the World."

The Door of No Return was obviously the highlight of Bush's trip. It was the crowning glory of our President's commitment to and concern for Black people – in Africa. He has yet to show the same thing in this country. However, the trip continued from Senegal to South Africa, where he did not meet with Mandela or Mugabe of Zimbabwe. He thought he would let Mbeki take care of Mugabe, but once again made a fool of himself when the cameras and his microphone were turned on. And then, on to Botswana. Botswana? What was that all about? Scouting for a new military base, no doubt.

He left there and went to Uganda; I guess they figured with Idi Amin near death it was safe enough to go there. Finally, the *coup de grace*, Nigeria, the country that has the 5th or 6th largest oil reserves in the world, the last stop on the tour. Hmmm. Now we're getting somewhere, George. We went all over Africa pretending to care about human beings and some how we ended up in Nigeria, the most corrupt country on the continent.

Nigeria, a place where people are protesting high gas prices, despite having tremendous oil reserves, it is a country where the annual per capita income is only $290.00. Did I say Nigeria has the 5th or 6th largest oil reserves in the world? Why would people protest high gas prices with so much oil under their feet? Because they have no control of their own resources. I guess that's why I get so many e-mails from the relatives of Mr. Abacha, offering me millions of dollars if I would just....

Big oil conglomerates such as Chevron-Texaco and Shell make tremendous profits exporting millions of barrels of oil from Nigeria to other parts of the world, while the Nigerian citizens remain extremely poor. Can you say, Bush, Cheney, and Rice? Among those three, there is an oil connection somewhere. I am sure more oil deals were cut during Bush's visit to Nigeria. After all, why make the trip if there is no money in it for his corporate buddies?

Finally, since Bush was so concerned about Africans, I wonder why he didn't visit Kenya to offer his personal condolences to the families of those killed when our embassy was bombed? Then again, what must have I been thinking? There's no oil in Kenya, at least not a lot, right?

It was quite significant that Bush began his trip in Senegal, visited Goree Island, and stood in The Door of No Return. I can hear the people in that football stadium saying, "Please make it come true once again, Mr. President; don't you ever return."

Eureka, Eureka! – I've found it!

It is said that when Archimedes discovered how to determine whether the King's crown was made of pure gold, he jumped out his bathtub and ran naked through the streets of Syracuse shouting *"Eureka, eureka!"* – I've found it! Well, I am not about to run through the streets naked, but I will shout, "I've found it! Or, in this case I should say, "I've found them!" What have I found? I have found the elusive Weapons of Mass Destruction, sometimes called Weapons of Mass Deception. I wonder if there is a reward for finding these weapons, after all, the entire contingent of U.S., British, Australian, and let's not forget about those other fearsome countries like Latvia and Eritrea, could not find them.

Before I tell you where they are, let's do a brief review of recent history. Our President and his cohorts, during the weeks leading up to the war in Iraq, told us they knew there were WMD's in Iraq. They were unequivocal in their assessments of the situation. They looked us in the eyes, just like they said Clinton did when he said, "I did not have sex with that woman," and said they knew Iraq had WMD's and they even knew how much and how many they had. Our man Colin Powell laid it all out for us, and our girl Condi Rice backed him up, not to mention old Rumsfield, Wolfowitz, and the boys. They knew Hussein had those weapons and they were determined to go over there and disarm him, and kick some Iraqi butt in the process. After all, like George W. Bush said, "He [Saddam] tried to kill my daddy!"

So, as the story goes, the Bushites knew so much about the WMD's that I was all but convinced they were there, that is, until I asked myself the following question: If they know these weapons are in Iraq, why don't they just tell old Hans Blix where they are? That way Blix and his crew, instead of looking every where but the right place, wasting millions of dollars in the process, could just waltz right up to the place where those 100 to 500 tons of weapons are being stored and they could say, Eureka! Made sense to me.

If you are that certain the weapons exist, it logically follows that you would know where they are. After all, you had satellite photos of them, you had intelligence on the ground in Iraq, and you had your best and brightest CIA and FBI infiltrators already snooping around in Iraq. What's more, you had Iraqi spies and turncoats who were sending information to you as well. Surely you had to know where the WMD's were being stored. There is a great deal more in background information, but if you have kept up at all with the war in Iraq, you know most of it.

Now, as in Bill Clinton's case, there are cries for impeachment. Even though Clinton confessed on national television, he was still vilified and taken through the impeachment process. Bush has not yet confessed; as a matter of fact he still says the WMD's are there and eventually they will find them. Oh yes, pardon the fact that on average one U.S. Soldier per day is being killed in the process, about 50 at latest count – all since Bush's "top gun" appearance as the conquering hero on the deck of that aircraft carrier. Pardon the fact that the very soldiers who were used to fight this war were "left out" of the administration's initial tax-cut proposal. Pardon the fact that the very soldiers who fought would come home to a massive cut in military veterans' benefits.

Pardon the fact that both Wolfowitz and Rumsfield have all but admitted the whole thing was just a ruse, that WMD's were the one thing they felt everyone in the country could "get behind," that they only used the WMD story "for emphasis," and the real deal, because Iraq "is swimming in oil." Told ya! (See article: "It's Iraq's Economy Stupid!")

("Pardon." Now there's a word from the past. Remember Gerald Ford's pardon of Richard Nixon? As Gil Scott-Heron once said about that pardon, "He (Nixon) had phlebitis. Rats bite us; no pardon in the ghetto.")

Well, Bush and his guys and *Gal Friday* have not yet found the WMD's; they have taken over the oil wells and gotten the Black Gold flowing again, but they have not found the WMD's. So I figured I would help them out by looking into this matter myself to see if I could find them. And, Eureka! Eureka! I found them! I found them in the most unlikely place. Little did I know, those dreaded weapons were right under our noses. Much to my chagrin, they were located in a place we should have searched a long time ago.

The Weapons of Mass Destruction, weapons that have killed masses and destroyed massive infrastructure in Iraq, are in Washington, DC. They are in the White House, in Congress, and in the Pentagon. Now that we know where the WMD's are and who they are, let's disarm them in November 2004.

The Arrogance of Power

What we witnessed during one of George Bush's rare Presidential News Conferences on July 30, 2003, was simply embarrassing. Frankly, I don't know why the members of the Press Corps even bother asking this guy questions. He insults them and hardly ever answers their inquiries. His command of language, geography, and history are abhorrent, and his arrogance knows no limits. But, that's what we get from a person who was "selected" to be the leader of the United States by the one Supreme who was appointed by his father, our own Uncle Clarence Thomas, who could have dissented, thus, reversing the decision under which we now suffer.

I have come to the conclusion that George Bush, the King of Malapropism, is not a mean-spirited, devilish, ogre, who hates certain people. I am convinced that our President is not a conscious racist, a hate-monger, or the antichrist, as some would suggest. I do not think Bush is an evil, blood- thirsty, maniac, who has a plan to take over the world. (The only plans he has are the ones given to him by his handlers.)

Here's what I do think about this man. He is a simpleton, the village idiot, placed in an office by those who knew he was such. I think Bush is an arrogant, swash-buckling, cowboy, stuck in a John Wayne past, who doesn't even realize his situation. Although he is not trying to be King of the World, his "handlers" are desperately pursuing that end. I think he is but a puppet in the scheme of things, and he does not even know it because he is too ignorant and, quite frankly, too stupid to understand.

Unfortunately, the only characteristic emanating from this so-called leader of the free world is arrogance – the arrogance of power. Watch how he walks; listen to how he answers questions and how he describes the war in Iraq. I think he is lost on a giant war game board somewhere, the kind we used to play with as children. I can hear him now, "Boom!" "Gotcha!" "Pow!" "Bang," making all the sounds of a little child lost in his imaginary world, oblivious of the consequences of his actions.

While U.S. soldiers die everyday in Iraq, Bush arrogantly says, "Bring 'em on. He plops down on the flight deck of an aircraft carrier to declare victory in Iraq, and then proceeds to say and do things that anger the vanquished to the point of a guerilla war.

These are not the acts of an intelligent person. These are the acts of an ignorant, pitiful, idiotic, lost in fantasyland, spoiled brat, who is used to getting everything he wants. It is sad that we must continue to suffer under this kind of arrogant, shallow, misguided, vacant, clueless leadership.

As one brother in Africa said when Bush made his five-country trip, "The United States has sent their Village Idiot to our village."

Let's Take the Politics Out of Politicians

"The new Negro in politics, moreover, must not be a politician. He must be a man." Those are the words of our Elder, Carter G. Woodson, and far be it from me to change the meaning of his words but, since Brother Woodson wrote these words in 1930's, I would add, "She must be a woman." Since voting is appropriate in politics, I vote we take the politics out of politicians. Politics gets in the way, especially as relates to Black politicians getting things done for "the race," as Woodson says in his timeless work, **The Mis-Education of the Negro.**

I have seen Black politicians, at home and on the national scene, come around prior to every election seeking votes and saying exactly what their Black constituents want to hear. They go to the churches hoping to get an opportunity to speak after and even during the service, and they show up at the oddest places making every attempt to garner those precious votes. Win or lose, in many cases we never see or hear from them again, that is, unless they decide to run for office again. Isn't that what white politicians do also?

I have seen politicians trying to get elected for the second or third time around, reciting everything they did during their previous term, which most of the time amounts to little or nothing, promising even more this time. All the while knowing they cannot deliver half of what they promise, some politicians continue to mislead the people into thinking "this time it will be different," and the sad part about it is that we fall for it every time. Yes, let's take the politics out of politicians, Black folks, because it is obvious that our love for this *game of chance* will not change in the near term.

Let's take the politics out of politicians because we need to get positive things done for the broad base of Black people in our local districts and on the national front, and if Black people are mere politicians that will never happen. If we get the politics out of politicians maybe then we will elect brothers and sisters who have backbone enough to stand up and say, "I am not going to allow this position to contaminate and destroy me, thereby, destroying my relationships with my people and minimizing my effectiveness. I will always do what is right, and if they vote me out of office for that, so be it."

Ron Daniels, convener of the recent State of the Black World, in Atlanta, Georgia, and an active participant in the 1972 Black Political Convention held in Gary, Indiana, wrote an editorial, titled Tracking Black Elected Officials, in which he decried the "marginal" difference new Black officials will make. Brother Daniels relates, "The political bodies in which they will operate have not favored liberal public policies in the past two decades. In fact, we know that institutional politics is marked by gradual change -- if there's any change at all – which is another reason for the younger generation to continue to consider more dynamic methods of achieving their goals."

Daniels is certainly politically astute, and I respect him tremendously. I also agree with him wholeheartedly. If he can make this kind of assessment regarding politics, I know I am on the right track. But our Elders such as Woodson, Booker T. Washington, Marcus Garvey, and a host of others understood that Black people must first gain an economic foothold in this country, and then the political gains would be much easier to attain.

As Daniels cited, "The newest roster of Black elected officials released by the Joint Center for Political Studies shows that their number has grown to 9,040...a long way from the 1,500 Black officials counted in 1970... but it raises the question of the nature of the gains that have been made because of such growth." Those who have followed my writings are aware that I have asked that same question for some time now. Thus, with no disrespect intended, and with much love and appreciation for those Black men and women politicians who have done as Carter G. Woodson suggested, I say it's time to take the politics out of politicians.

The economic salvation of Black people is not and has never been in politics. On the contrary, political salvation lies in economics. After forty years or so of chasing the illusive butterfly called political power, only to attain political influence, Black folks must now (as we should have done a long ago) make some drastic changes, as Ron Daniels has told us.

A good start would be with the Hip Hop political movement as recently noted in Savoy Magazine. Instead of, or at least in addition to that, we must have a Hip Hop economic movement. While there certainly are thousands of new votes to be had from the Hip Hop crowd, would anyone like to count the dollars controlled by this group, starting with the likes of Russell Simmons, P Diddy, Jermaine Dupri, and Master P? Then let's take a look at the brothers and sisters on the street and count all the money they spend on this music genre, not to mention the clothing, the concerts, and the videos.

The same level of effort we put into registering and pooling our votes at Hip Hop Summits should be put into registering and pooling our dollars at an economic Hip Hop Summit. The term "politics as usual" is insulting to Black people, especially considering all the political shenanigans and scandals we see these days. It must change; we must change.

At a minimum, if we refuse to take the politics out of politicians, please, let's add a little *economic flava* to the mix.

Section IV

Larceny in High Places

"I have no financial ties with Halliburton."
Dick Cheney, Vice President, United States

"I have never felt better about the prospects for the company... Our performance has never been stronger; our business model has never been more robust; our growth has never been more certain."
E-mail to employees from Ken Lay, Enron, August 14, 2001

"What I did was not against the rules."
Martha Stewart, ABC's "20/20"

[Dennis] Kozlowski vows Tyco's earnings will once again grow by more than 20% a year.
Business Week, January 2002.
(In September 2002, Kozlowski was charged with enterprise corruption and grand larceny.)

Congressmen Henry Waxman and John Dingell reveal the prices that Halliburton has charged to import gasoline into Iraq. Oil industry experts say Halliburton's prices are 'outrageously high,' a 'huge rip-off,' and 'highway robbery'.
Truthout Newsletter, October 16, 2003

Update: It's sad to see that what I wrote and spoke about prior to the war in Iraq, vis-à-vis the monetary reasons behind the whole sordid affair, have come to fruition. The first things secured when the troops got to Baghdad were the oil pipelines. The soldiers found as much as $1 billion in cash but those spoils were never fully accounted for by the victors. Then the real reason for the invasion became evident: The lucrative contracts to "rebuild" what we destroyed.

Three months before the invasion and "liberation" of Iraq I started writing articles on the economic impact of the war. At the time of this writing we can plainly see that what many of us believed about Bush's motivation to go to war was not his compassion for the Iraqi people, rather it was his desire to fill the pockets of his friends and, of course, to "break a little piece off" for his family too.

But beyond the financial shenanigans taking place, there is a human side to this charade. The lives lost and the thousands of soldiers injured, the made-for-TV melodrama of Jessica Lynch coming home to a million dollar book deal and nearly full disability benefits juxtaposed against Shoshana Johnson coming home to far less in disability benefits and no "hero" status, even though she was the one who actually suffered gunshot wounds.

And let's never forget Sergeant Vanessa Turner, who lapsed into a coma while in Iraq, came home partially paralyzed, had to wait for months before being treated at the Veterans' hospital, and that only after a U.S. Senator intervened, ended up homeless and, with her 16 year-old daughter, had to sleep wherever they could. All of this after "serving" her country and risking her life doing so.

I chose to preface the following section of articles to highlight what is currently taking place with this war, now that an additional $87 billion has been approved for the "rebuilding" of Iraq and maintenance of the troops who remain there – albeit, dodging bullets and R.P.G.'s.

The following article on the hypocrisy of it all was written in September 2003 as a result of my frustration with George Bush's "bring 'em on" war rhetoric and the almost daily disclosures of corporate thievery and deceit. Three months later, as I work on this book, we hear Bush explaining to the world why only certain companies and countries will share in the $18 billion sweetheart deals to "rebuild" Iraq.

In his typical finger-wagging style, Bush said something to the effect that American soldiers made the sacrifices in Iraq; they risked and in some cases lost their lives in the war. Thus, America would give the lion's share of the contracts to Dick Cheney's former company, Halliburton, and dole out the rest to countries within the "alliance." You remember the alliance, don't you? Bush claimed, "We have ally after ally after ally," during his infamous press conference with England's Tony Blair. Albania, Poland, Eritrea, and all of those other fearsome allies that Bush referred to, will be rewarded because of the sacrifices of American soldiers.

George Bush used the lives and livelihoods of American soldiers to justify giving Halliburton billions in sweetheart deals, after he recommended a funding cut for veterans, after Sergeant Turner's demise, and after soldiers came home to live at Fort Stewart, Georgia, in conditions worse than they had in Iraq.

How hypocritical is that? Halliburton gets a multi-billion dollar raise, and the soldiers get killed, maimed, and a reduction in their current slave wages. Have you had enough yet? I know I have.

Politricksters, Corporate Thieves, and Hypocrites (Please Pardon the Redundancy)

"An hypocrite with his mouth destroyeth his neighbour; but through knowledge shall the just be delivered." **Proverbs 11:9**

As I always say, every issue we find ourselves dealing with in this country, and probably around the world, has some connection to economics, which makes me wonder why we still don't get it.   Is it that we don't want to know certain things because that would actually cause us to have to do some work? Is it because it's just too uncomfortable to face the truth about crooked politicians and corporate thieves? Are we mimicking Nero, as our country and the world are destroyed right before our eyes? I don't know about you, but I refuse to stand idly by, saying and doing nothing to help change our situation.

Admittedly, I am not a celebrity-opinion leader; I am not an affluent corporate leader; I am not a person seeking some high status in life; and I am not some *high and mighty* sage who only pontificates and never gets involved in the work of helping others. But, I am a man, a man who will not and cannot go quietly into the night, fading away as if I were never here on this earth and did nothing to make it better.

In my walk everyday, although I stumble sometimes, I do whatever I can, within my simple sphere of influence, to make a positive difference in the lives of others by sharing information and knowledge through this column and in the classes I teach. Most important to me, as I find myself on the national stage via radio talk shows, speaking engagements, and Black newspapers across this country, most important is that I have a conscience that will not allow me to mistreat my brother or sister, and I have a consciousness that pushes me to contribute to our economic uplift.

It's too bad we do not have more political leaders, from the President on down, who are just as concerned about the welfare of their fellowman as they are about filling their pockets with billions of dollars in ill-gotten wealth. It's too bad we don't have political leaders who will not sacrifice the lives of young men and women for profit, pretending they hold these young people in high esteem but leaving them abandoned and neglected when they come home from war.

It's too bad we don't have more corporate leaders who care enough about the state of our country, its citizens, and our children, to stop stealing money, to stop their utter greed, and their ridiculous lust for "things" at any cost. It's too bad, as we have watched several tycoons be hauled off to prison for bilking their customers and employees, that what we saw was just the proverbial tip of the corporate scandal iceberg. It's too bad we can sit back and watch these things only to think that as long as we "get ours" everything is all right.

A few examples of the hypocrisy and thievery that seem to pervade this country include the recent case of Vanessa Turner, a 41 year-old army sergeant who suffered an allergic reaction during her tour of duty in Iraq. It put her into in coma and caused nerve damage to one of her legs. This mother of a teenage daughter came home to the bureaucracy of our ineffective and inefficient veterans' hospital system, homeless, and having to sleep on her friends' floors and couches. While George Bush says "bring 'em on" Ms. Turner can't find affordable housing nor get the proper help she needs as one who served her country under this cowboy of a President we have. He's safe and sound and well taken care of, having never even served in a military conflict, not to mention a war, while Sergeant Turner and her daughter have no place to live.

How about Dick Cheney and his so-called "no financial ties with Halliburton" mantra? This guy has a job that pays him around $200,000 per year, which he doesn't have to spend because all of his expenses are taken care of by "the people." In addition, he gets a couple of hundred G's from Halliburton every year, the company he used to head but now has no financial ties with, and sits back and watches while Halliburton gets no-bid contracts from our government to reconstruct Iraq, the country he and his evil cabal invaded and destroyed. It was reported that Cheney made $36 million from Halliburton the year he accepted the lowly job of vice president. Why would he leave? Does he love his country that much? Or, does he just love that no-bid money he gets from a company with which he has no financial ties? Cheney does justice to the title of "Vice" President. What crooks we have in charge of this country!

One last example is, Richard Grasso, former chairman of the New York Stock Exchange. He left his position with a $140 million "pay package," more than four times the profit made by the exchange last year. He made $30 million in salary in 2001! No wonder they clap and cheer when the market opens and closes. That's nice work if you can get it. Grasso made so much money that it even embarrassed the insiders on Wall Street, those hardened profiteers who never have enough. They said they just could no longer rationalize giving this guy that kind of money, but they are the ones who allowed Grasso to select his own compensation team. He started out at $2 million in 1995 and increased his salary fifteen-fold to $30 million in 2001. The insiders called his pay a bit too "generous." Well, duh!

These are the kinds of people who are running our country into the abyss of hell. They are the hypocrites, but now you have the knowledge. What are you going to do about it?

Wall Street Implosion

As we look back on the events of September 11, 2001, and remember what the pundits were offering as one of the reasons for the attacks, they said Osama and his men targeted the World Trade Center to make an economic point. They said the WTC was struck and destroyed by two airliners to prove that the heart of this country's financial and economic systems could be gravely wounded. The WTC represented commerce, unimaginable riches, and power, and by showing the world they could destroy those two symbols, or mortally wound them, the 19 men who planned and carried out the heinous attack would also strike fear in the hearts of U.S. citizens and raise doubts about its financial stability.

Obviously, we did receive a terrible wound, one that will take a long time to heal. But, we also know that Osama's two airplane bombs, although they physically took down the two towers of strength known as the World Trade Center, did not take down the system they had targeted. Yes, the stock market went down very fast the Monday after the attack. Lots of people lost lots money, at least on paper, that day and during the days that followed. But it did not destroy the system; it came back, it rebounded; it showed tremendous resilience by returning to levels prior to the attacks.

As we move closer to the anniversary of that tragic day, we wonder if another attack will come. We wonder of we should hunker down and make plans to cocoon our families during that anniversary period. We are afraid once again that we will lose more money if our financial district is attacked again. I say, put all of those worries aside. Put them aside because Osama and his army can never do the harm to our financial system that our very own people can and have done over the years. That's right, what Osama could not accomplish, Enron, WorldCom, Global Crossing, and Arthur Andersen did.

They say organizations and systems are seldom destroyed from the outside; rather they are destroyed from within. We are witnesses to that truth as we speak. We see greed at its highest – or should I say, lowest – point. We see lying, cheating, blaming others, and literally *passing the bucks* from one account to another, all for the love of money. We see the people who run those companies taking all they can get and leaving their employees and stockholders holding the *empty* bag. We see the politicians scrambling to at least act like they are concerned and are going to do something about the pervasive greed and deceit that have been running rampant in corporate America.

We see it all today, nearly one-year after the attack on the heart of our economy. We are witnesses to CEO's, Board Chairmen, and high-ranking executives, who are suppose to be concerned about those of us who pour our hard-earned dollars into their companies, we see them doing the Papa Doc and Baby Doc two-step with billions of dollars entrusted to their stewardship.

These hucksters, these liars, these cheats, these unethical immoral men and women who have perpetrated one of the worst crimes in history against this country have done more damage than Osama could ever do to our financial system. I truly wish Osama had known about the "fuzzy math" accounting practices of Halliburton and Harken, managed by Cheney and Bush respectively. I wish he had known about the strange accounting practices of one of our nation's largest accounting firms, the venerable Arthur Andersen. I really wish Osama had just taken a look inside Enron and WorldCom and seen the deception and greed of their executives.

If Osama had just known that what he was trying to do would be done by the very folks he was trying to financially destroy, maybe, just maybe, he would have called off his attacks. Maybe those 3000 plus innocent lives would not have been lost. Maybe we would still have a WTC. If he had only known. Better still, if we had only known. If those 17,000 WorldCom workers had only known. If the Enron investors had only known.

Well, if you did not know before, you do now. What are you going to do about it? Are you going to continue to believe the Martha Stewart's of the world are really your friends because they can make up a bed nice and pretty? Are you going to continue blindly and naively to believe that top corporate execs don't tell their friends and relatives about deals that are about to occur? Are you going to continue to buy the lies and condescension from the politicians? I hope not. I hope we, especially Black folks, will finally start to look inward, start to invest in ourselves, start to redirect a greater portion of our money toward our own businesses, start to build even more businesses, and start to expand and partner and merge with one another.

If we continue to place our economic salvation in the folks who are running this country, we can forget about advancing economically. They are stealing the country (and the world) blind. When and if Osama comes calling again, the job of destroying this country will have already been accomplished – by our people, from the inside out.

Give And Take

Organizations and individuals have collected more than one billion dollars for the victims of the New York tragedy; I would imagine those funds would also be used to help the victims in Washington, DC and Pennsylvania. Americans certainly moved, with all haste, to dig deep into their pockets and come to the aide of their fellow citizens. Children collected pennies, entertainers held benefit concerts, and the money flowed into New York, or to somewhere, so fast that fund administrators had to pause to figure out how they were going to disburse the much needed contributions. The money also grew so fast that apparently those in charge are still trying to "figure" the whole thing out and get things right.

One billion dollars and counting, and the families of the victims are still waiting for their assistance from these various funds. That's the sad part of it. All of the giving that has taken place over the past month or so, probably the fastest and most successful fundraiser in history, and either the people in charge do not know how to administer the funds, or something else is going on with all of that money. We know that where there is giving there is taking, and experience tells me that wherever there is a huge amount of money there will be someone who will figure out how to take some of it. After all, there were people so money-hungry that they tried to forage in the wreckage at "ground zero" in New York for the victims' money.

The overriding question in this case of the not-yet-distributed billion dollars or so is: Where is the money? Or should we say, "Show me the money." The victims for whom the funds were donated should have something by now. I would submit that some administrator(s) has been paid by now. I also submit that these funds should be flowing, expeditiously, to the families that need assistance. No excuses. Send the money to the families so they can get on with their lives.

This country has a reputation for reacting positively when a crisis occurs. We have certainly responded, even as the call continuously goes out, by sending millions of dollars to

New York, but the people in charge have dropped the ball – or, have been negligent in doing their part.   Even more tragic would be our discovering that much of the money we raised has "disappeared."

I think it's a sad commentary on our country and some of our citizens that we exploit the tragedies and misfortunes of our fellow citizens. Is money so important to us that we will risk our very souls for it? People are suffering from the worst calamity to ever hit this country, and there are those who would deny them their compensatory relief: money donated by well-wishing and concerned fellow citizens.

But, as I always say, "Where there is a large sum of money, there is always some crook lurking nearby to steal as much as he or she can. Whether it's the "Lootery" (Lottery to some people), social programs, the stock market, or any other money-laden business activity, we eventually read the headlines about some dishonest person facing trial and punishment for absconding with the money.

While I hope and pray this is not the case with the donations sent to New York, I kinda' doubt it. It should not have taken this long to move those funds to the grief-stricken families affected by the tragedies. I know we can do better. Why haven't we? Let's not sleep this one, folks. Don't allow this latest venture in fundraising to go unchallenged. Too many people have sent in their hard-earned money. Too many children have worked hard to pool their pennies. Too many other charitable organizations have fallen short of their goals because so many dollars were diverted from traditional contribution channels. More importantly, too many lives were lost in the three tragedies on September 11th for us to tarnish their memories, ignore their children, and disgrace this country by not following through on our promise to assist their families.

We have done a whole lot of giving since the disaster in New York. Who's doing the taking?

Red, White, and Blue Trumped by the Green

The recent call for patriotism by our government leaders, with George W. leading the charge, was received by millions of African Americans the same way it has always been received. Having fought and died in all U.S. wars, Black people are always at the head of the line when it comes to standing up and defending this country. Thus, the call for patriotism and the positive reaction by many African Americans was not surprising, notwithstanding the underlining meaning of patriotism as it relates to those espousing the message and those receiving it.

So what does this latest round of patriotism mean to all of us? There are calls for U.S. flags to be displayed on everything moving or standing; there have been rallies, concerts, and impromptu "acts" of patriotism by baseball and football teams; we have seen millions of dollars donated to charitable organizations to help the victims of the tragedy; and we have even seen the congress stand together under the banner of patriotism and sing *God Bless America*.

In my neck of the woods, the call for patriotism came forth as a call for consumers to buy, buy, buy, and for investors to hold, hold, hold. I expressed my thoughts on my radio show the Sunday following the tragedy by saying "We will see how patriotic we are on Monday morning when the stock exchange opens." My words were not prophetic; it did not take a genius or a prophet to predict what the folks with the "real" money would do following the disaster.

As I watched the market drop each day, I thought about the calls for patriotism issued by Bush and others, asking us to sacrifice, to stay the course, to continue to purchase goods and services, and to refrain from selling our stock shares. Well, somebody was selling and it was not a pretty picture, nor was it the picture of patriotism many were promoting. While the "little people," who have a few shares of stock and our entire futures wrapped up in 401-K investments, watched the depletion of our relatively meager savings, the "big boys" (and girls) were busy unloading and making moves that were completely contradictive to the calls for economic patriotism. But, are you surprised?

We live in a country where people gouged consumers for much needed plywood and nails after Hurricane Andrew hit Florida; we were witnesses to profiteers who raised the price of gasoline to $5 and $6 per gallon immediately after the planes hit the World Trade Centers and the Pentagon; we saw volunteers ask a local Starbucks for water to help victims, only to be charged $130.00 (The CEO of Starbucks later apologized and refunded the money); and we received notice of scam artists selling postcards of the WTC for $30.00, asking for social security numbers of bereaved relatives under the guise of charitable motives, and even combing through the macabre wreckage at the WTC to find a way to take economic advantage of such a tremendous loss of life and property.

We also live in a country where the economic interests of the few individuals who control 80-90% of all the resources always come first, despite tragedies, catastrophes, or terrorist attacks. The money and the control of that money come first. Case closed. End of story! So much for patriotism.

Those who will be hurt the most, irrespective of this new wave of patriotic flag-waving, are the front-line employees who have already been laid off from their jobs. Is there any fund available for them and their families? The corporate patriots of this country who make $10 million, $20 million, and even $100 million and more per year were busy making their lay-off lists instead of decreasing their mega-salaries to help retain some of those lower wage employees on payroll. You know, in the name of patriotism. Maybe they should follow the example of the CEO of American Airlines, who will not take a salary for one year. (Somebody pinch me 'cause I must be dreaming.)

The bottom line (pardon the pun) is this. Patriotism is more than flag-waving and making tear-jerking speeches laden with emotionalism and very little substance. Patriotism is sacrifice – on everyone's part – to keep this country economically sound and to keep the least of us from bearing the brunt of the pain and suffering. Patriotism is a full-time commitment to do the right thing, ALL the time, by ALL the citizens of this country, not just when it's convenient and expedient. Patriotism, as it was solicited by our political and economic leaders after the disasters in New York, Washington, and Pennsylvania, should and could have been practiced by all. Rather it was immediately put into action by young men and women being called to war, many of who will not return to their families. It was applied by those who sent donations to the families of the victims. And, it was the evinced by those of us who refused to sell our stock and continued to make purchases and travel.

Those Americans who scammed and gouged consumers, and exploited the markets, proved once again that the green will always trump the red, white, and blue.

Enron's End-Run

As we have said so often, it's always about the money. We see it so clearly in what the 7th largest company in the country just perpetrated on its employees. We see it so clearly that corporate executives care little or nothing for the proletariat ranks as they sold their stock and drove down the value of the company, while at the same time preventing their subordinates from selling their shares. They hid their evil activities and are now scurrying for excuses, oh yes, after destroying important accounting documents that would have apparently incriminated them and sent them all away to jail for quite some time. Who knows? Maybe that will still happen.

What should be done now? Well, there should be some relief for the employees who lost their retirement funds as a result of Enron's "Let them eat cake" philosophy. How about allowing them to share in some of those billions that were collected after 9/11? How about giving them some of the billions in relief that are going to the corporations affected by the tragedy? How about siphoning off some of that corporate welfare money that is earmarked in the proposed economic stimulus package? Give some of it to those employees. They deserve relief too.

Unfortunately, there are people in this country who want everything, and they will go to any end (as in Enron) and hurt anyone to obtain their filthy lucre. I wonder how they can sleep at night; maybe they don't require sleep. Treating people the way Enron executives and their cohorts did is beneath anyone who has an ounce of compassion for his fellow man. I guess these folks don't even have that much.

A very important lesson in this for Black people is the fact that we must always recognize and understand the value of ownership and control of income-producing assets, business ownership and entrepreneurship, and supporting our brothers and sisters on all levels. Most of us depend upon the largess of white corporations and government bureaucrats for our livelihood. At any moment in time they could do their end-run on us. What would we do if that happened?

Well, if we would work together in support of one another, pool our resources and buy assets, use the only Black channel of distribution available to us, The MATAH Network, follow the teachings of Dr. Claud Anderson of Harvest Institute, John Brown and Ernestine Henning of Visions 2000, and Bishop Frank Stewart of the Black American Family Christian Agenda (BAFCA), we will survive. If we do not follow these very basic principles of economics, we will continue to lose, and our children will continue to lose.

Enron is just a hint of what goes on in this country's boardrooms. Corporate greed has run rampant for years, while the "little people" suffer in silence waiting to see what the moguls will do. We cannot afford to maintain our silence and our current economic position in this country. We must take things into our own hands by lessening the possibility and the probability of anyone doing an "Enron End-Run" on us.

There is no way, after what our ancestors went through in this country that we as modern day, educated, affluent, intellectual Black folks should capitulate to the whims and greed of the establishment. It is an insult to our ancestors for us to rely solely upon the sons and daughters of their "owners" for our sustenance. It is a sin for us to be such poor stewards of what we have accumulated in this country that we will simply turn 95% of it over to those who hold us in disdain.

We should be doing our own end-run with our dollars and our sense. We should work together to develop ways in which we can cooperatively and collectively progress economically. We should put aside the attitudes that keep us apart, shake off the psychological programming that makes us think we are better than our brothers and sisters, deflate the massive egos that cause us to strut like peacocks among one another, and find ways to make life better for our children and their children.

Economically speaking of course, we could make a tremendously positive impact on our future by simply changing the relationships we have with the so-called powers-that-be. If we use more of our dollars and sense to produce, distribute, warehouse, and sell our own products, our end-run would be like no other in the history of this country. If we would adopt the principle of good stewardship of our resources, withholding them from others and giving more to ourselves, those resources would multiply.

Let's not get caught by another Enron End-Run. The next one could affect you and your family. Stay vigilant. Stay informed. Work everyday for economic empowerment and self-sufficiency for our people.

Martha's Stewardship

The charges against Martha Stewart carry a potential prison term of 30 years, although she would get far less if convicted under federal sentencing guidelines. Stewart told ABC News in an interview aired in November 2003 that she is scared of prison. "I don't think I will be going to prison, though," she said. Maybe old Martha is wrong this time.

I write a lot about stewardship and how we should apply it in our daily lives; I have also written a considerable amount on liars, cheats, and thieves, when it comes to the bastions of capitalism such as the stock market, banks, insurance companies, and savings and loans. You just read the article titled Enron's End Run? Well, now we have WorldCom and 17,000 workers thrown into the streets by this company whose leaders lied, cheated, and stole their way to temporal riches. And to top it all off, there is the Miss Martha (Stewart) connection. What did she know, and when did she know it?

You know, it's almost comical to hear the latest "shocking" revelation about the possibility (and some say the probability) that dear Martha may be involved in yet another huge rip-off by the elitists of this country. While I don't know a great deal about Miss Martha and her empire, and really don't care to know, it is intriguing to hear all of the news reports concerning her alleged collusion in the insider trading scandal. I don't understand why so many people virtually worshiped her in the first place and bought all of her "stuff." But, those same folks are now jumping on the Get-Martha bandwagon, saying they hate her and they are showing it by causing her company now to suffer a tremendous loss in the value of its stock. As the old television show said, "People are funny."

This debacle reminds me of stewardship and what it means to be a good steward of the resources God gives you. Miss Martha, if she is guilty of wrongdoing, has lost millions of dollars because she cared so much about saving a measly $200,000. Martha's stewardship leaves a lot to be desired if she is that greedy and short-sighted. How much money does she need anyway? How much does she want?

Despite the mounting evidence against Miss Martha, a top-level executive for Forbes Magazine, in an interview on Fox News recently said we should leave Martha alone. After all, it was only a small amount of money, and it is not important enough for us to spend time discussing. In other words, if Martha broke the law, we should just wink at her and move on. I wonder if he would say the same thing about others who break the law, especially if they don't have as much "jack" as Miss Martha. It's funny how the rich stick together. If those of us who are less fortunate would stick together half as much, we'd be in real good shape.

An interesting aspect of this money madness is the new Black love affair with the stock market and the current hoopla being promulgated regarding how many Black folks own shares of stock. At a time when billions are being stolen from the market, some of us are bragging about how good it is to finally be in the game. Some of our leaders are telling us to invest more of our hard earned money in the stock market and to ride out the rough period we are in right now. And Blacks are doing just that, according to the latest reports. Martha Stewart, a mega-millionaire, is yelling Sell! Sell! while Black folks are saying Buy! Buy! Stay in! Stay in! Black folks comprise the group that can least afford to lose our money on the market or anywhere else. Go figure.

I say Black folks should place a greater emphasis on investing in ourselves and the businesses owned by our people, in addition to the blue chips. Instead of continuing to make everyone else rich, like the Martha Stewart's of the world, we must invest in ourselves and create and retain wealth for our children. How much more do we need to see before we change our tactics? How many Enron's, ImClone's, and WorldCom's do we need to experience before we turn inward and start doing for ourselves?

The bottom line is this. So-called insiders are lying, stealing, cheating, and ripping-off the markets everyday. Do you really believe that an executive who knows his company is about to be sold, or has been cooking the books, does not tell someone in his family or his closest friends? Do you really believe insider trading does not go on everyday in this country and around the world? How do you think the rich stay that way? Why do you think those folks are always clapping and cheering at the closing bell of the New York Stock Exchange, even if it has been a bear of a day? C'mon brothers and sisters. Let's get real.

My guess is that Miss Martha will not do one day in prison if she is convicted of acts of *unjust stewardship,* but I could be wrong. After this blows over, we will return to our state of euphoria and wait for the next crisis to come — so we can have something to talk about. We will either go back to buying Martha's sheets and everything else she makes, or we will find another hero or heroine to worship. I hope we don't miss the lesson on stewardship, however, because Martha's stewardship is one for the books.

It's the Iraqi Economy, Stupid!

While it's not much to speak of now, the economic potential that lies within the borders of Iraq is mind-boggling, and old Georgie-Porgie is determined to take control of it. I know, I know, it's not about the oil, right? Then what is it about, y'all? Let's see, could it be the <u>control</u> of the oil? Could it be the assurance that Iraq's oil standard will be the dollar instead of the Euro? Could it be that George and his friends are just licking their chops at the profits to be made after the "awesome" bombing ceases and reconstruction begins? Oh yes, I completely forgot; it's about the fact that Iraq is a threat to the United States and old *SoDamn Insane* will fire a nuclear weapon he does not have to a place it cannot reach. I'm sorry. What must have I been thinking?

Those of you who know anything about wars of the past are probably falling out of your chairs during the evening news; and it really must have been hilarious when you saw George "Papa Doc" Bush *perform* at only his second press conference. By the way, of those *allowed* to ask questions, there were 13 white males, 2 white females, 1 Black female, and one Asian-looking man. Where were the Brothas? But I digress.

This latest upcoming war in Iraq is yet another in a long line of wars that have been started and fought for economic reasons. It's not about national security, just like the first and second world wars were not about security. Woodrow Wilson and Franklin Roosevelt knew what was coming. There's nothing like a good war, you know, to put billions in the pockets of the moneychangers.

Iraq is second to Saudi Arabia in oil reserves and, according to an article on Alexander's Oil and Gas website, "...controlling Iraqi oil is at the heart of the Bush campaign to replace Hussein with a more compliant regime." Additionally, another related article points out, "...the need to dominate oil from Iraq is also deeply intertwined with the defense of the dollar ... that all OPEC oil sales be denominated in dollars. This requirement is currently threatened by the desire of some OPEC countries to allow OPEC oil sales to be paid in euros."

Colin Powell gave a glimpse of US intentions when he told the Senate Foreign Relations Committee on February 6 that success in the Iraq war "could fundamentally reshape that region in a powerful, positive way that will enhance U.S. interests."

The same report stated, "The Federal Reserve's greatest nightmare is that OPEC will switch its international transactions from a dollar standard to a euro standard. Iraq actually made this switch in Nov. 2000 (when the euro was worth around 82 cents), and has actually made off like a bandit considering the dollar's steady depreciation against the euro. (Note: the dollar declined 17% against the euro in 2002.)

There is much more, if you'd like to do a little research on the subject. And they say the U.S. does not care about the oil in Iraq. They even tell us the U.S. does not purchase Iraqi oil. Well, consider this: America imported about 290 million barrels of crude oil from Iraq in 2001 according to the Department of Energy, about 795,000 barrels per day, making Iraq America's sixth-largest supplier in 2001. The US was "the main market for Iraqi crude" according to the Middle East Economic Survey.

Can't you see it's about the Iraqi economy? Can't you see it's about maintaining the riches of this world under the control of a few families? Can't you see it's about U.S. dollar hegemony over the world's major sources of oil? If you can't see those things, I don't know what you can see.

This entire scenario is nothing more than a centuries-old continued attempt to maintain control over the world's resources and fatten the pockets of a few sinfully wealthy families in Europe and America. It was that way in the 1500's and it's that way in the 2000's. It's about power over resources. That's why our Vice-President refused to turn over the reports from his secret energy policy board meetings, and it's also why he left a multi-million dollar position to take a meaningless and relatively low-paying job as V.P. By the way, wasn't he in Iraq and running the show back in 1991? Wasn't Powell there as well? Why didn't they finish the job when they were there, if things were so ominous?

Yes, brothers and sisters, it's all about the economics of war. Billions are flowing now and billions more will flow for a long time after the shooting starts. Baby Doc Bush has already committed to rebuilding an entire country, using the oil profits for that purpose, and he is saying he will liberate the people of Iraq. Who do you think will get the contracts to rebuild Iraq? Have any of your Black owned contracting companies been called yet? And don't forget about the oil-well fires. Red Adair and his boys can't wait to make those millions.

Bomb 'em and then feed 'em; take their oil profits and pay for reconstruction of their country (Most of which will go to the Halliburton Corporation); install a puppet government that will exchange dollars rather than euros for oil; and then maintain military presence in the region to make sure things don't go back to the way they were. What a plan! And half of the people in the United States believe in it!

Peace Profits

Well, I hate to say, "I told you so," again, but... Several weeks ago I wrote an article titled, "It's the Iraqi Economy Stupid!" I reminded us that if we follow the money we will see history repeat itself when it comes to the profits of war; and now we see the same thing when it comes to the profits of peace. As I watch the dastardly acts of arrogance and avarice by our so-called government leaders, I often wonder if these guys and their girl have any conscience at all. I wonder if they think they are going to live forever and never have to account for what they have done. I guess not.

Now that the war is winding down we are seeing the real reasons for thousands of people losing their lives. We are witnessing the real reasons we forgot about Osama, who merely served as our Marinus van der Lubbe (The Dutch terrorist who, in 1933, firebombed the German Parliament, the Reichstag, jump-started the Hitler regime, and changed the German constitution), and went after Saddam. As the O'Jays once said, "Money, Money, Money."

We see closed bidding for reconstruction contracts, and "bidding" is a mild word for what is really going on behind those closed doors. We see the two leading firms, Halliburton and Bechtel going to the head of the line and getting huge contracts, so large that no one can really say how much they will be in the end. We see the new sheriff of Baghdad, Jay Garner, hand-picked by you know who, riding into town on his white horse determined to mine the black gold of Iraq, under the guise of humanitarian compassion for the people of Iraq.

We see more than a billion dollars in cash, so far, being found by the troops. Who knows where that money will end up? Of course, they tell us they have to determine if it's counterfeit or not. Do you really believe this stuff?

We see the old guard like George Schultz, Henry Kissinger, and James Baker, standing in line to make millions from their war on terrorism. We see the Spiro T. Agnew of the 21st century, "Tricky Dick" (Where have we heard that term before?) Cheney, rubbing his hands together gleefully waiting for another windfall. And where is Condoleezza these days? The last I heard, she was in Russia negotiating some deal for Hussein's safe passage out of Iraq; maybe that's why they can't find him and maybe that's why there was so little resistance when we crossed that mythical "red line" around Baghdad.

And let's not forget about our pal, Colin Powell, the brother (and we have another one on the rise in General Vince Brooks) who let himself be used to the point of now being blamed by Newt Gingrich for his "diplomatic failure" vis-à-vis the Iraqi war. Although, according to a recent CNN report, the White House expressed its confidence in Powell, saying he had done an "excellent job" in promoting the president's views and advancing his agenda. Well, they got that part right. You know what they say about lying down with dogs, Colin. You find yourself scratching even when you don't itch.

What we see in the post-war era is a mad scramble for money – a headlong plunge into an ocean of profit – by some of the most treacherous men of our time. They comprise a cast of characters the likes of whom the world has not seen since J.P. Morgan and his ilk and the Rothchilds before him. We see a veritable cavalcade of stars with names such as Perle, Wolfowitz, Fleischer, Rove, Feith, Libby, Woolsey, and several others. Talk about the in-crowd; Ramsey Lewis would be proud of this group.

Finally, there is the Kingpin, the guy who was there from the beginning, the guy who was shaking Saddam's hand and smiling as people were being gassed, you know, back in 1983. He is the guy who had Reagan's ear; he is the guy who could not wait to go to war with Iraq; he is the guy who for more than 20 years has plotted and schemed and lived for this day. He is Rumsfeld, the glib, arrogant, and flippant, Secretary of Defense, and architect of it all. (Did you know there is an effort to run him for president in 2008? He'll only be 75 years old by then.) And you thought it was Bush who planned this; Bush has to plan how he is going to walk and what facial expressions to use. How could you have thought he planned all of this?

No, it's Rumsfeld, the John Gatti of the new economy, the boss of bosses, who laughs at the news reports of the looting of antiquities in Iraq by suggesting we are seeing the same television reports of a few 5000 year-old vases being stolen by the same persons. He asked the reporters at his news conference, "How many vases could there be in Iraq?" I guess that means he couldn't care less about things that were on this earth during its infancy; he just wants to find the money, to get the contracts signed for his friends, and move on to the next "Axis of Evil" country and take over its resources or change its "Regime."

As for my disagreeing with this underhanded, evil, and despicable war policy, and risking being called "unpatriotic" by some, read the words of former Republican President, Theodore Roosevelt regarding Woodrow Wilson's crackdown on dissenters to the U.S. getting into World War I. He said, "To announce that there must be no criticism of the President, or that we are to stand by the President, right or wrong, is not only unpatriotic and servile, but is morally treasonable to the American public."

How Much Money Do You Need Anyway?

I am reminded of the passage in Luke 12:15-21 that discusses the greed that some men harbor, how they build up huge caches of material things on earth, and overlook their moral and ethical responsibilities. You should read it sometime, and after you do, think about not only your personal situation but also the fact that are some in this country, and throughout the world, doing the exact opposite of what the passage admonishes. Their answer to our question of how much money is needed is obviously, "All I can get." Let's take a look.

The headline in the local newspaper stated, "Worker/CEO pay gap widens" and cited J.P. Morgan Chase & Co. boss, William Harrison, received $22.2 million from salary, bonus, and stock options in just one year. The article went on to report that an average worker could make that same amount – if he were willing to work for 440 years at $50,000 annually!

As you probably have as well, I have heard all of the arguments for such exorbitant compensation packages, not to mention those golden parachutes awarded when a CEO gets fired. They say we should look at the big picture, at what the CEO brings to the table. That's all well and good, but any *Joeblow* could fire thousands of employees and then boast huge cash surpluses. That's what I see happening today and in years past.

An example of this excess is AT&T Chairman and CEO, Michael Armstrong, who earned $4.01 million in salary and bonus in 2001. That was a 70.8% increase over the previous year. Meanwhile, 5100 employees "had left" the company's payroll by the end of 2001, and 5000 more positions would be eliminated by the end of this year. (This information was reported in the Cincinnati Enquirer on December 30, 2002)

But let's get back to the mega-salaries. A survey done by Forbes Magazine points out that in 1970 the average full-time worker earned $32,522, according to the National Institute of Pension Administrators, while the average compensation for the top 100 CEO's was $1.25 million. In 1999, the average worker made $35,864, while the average salary for the top 100 CEO's was $37.5 million – a 2800% increase! How much is enough?

Take a look at the following statistics for company CEO's in my hometown. Between 2000 and 2001 of the top 25 public company executives, the lowest percentage of increase in salary was 34.7%, a lowly $200,041 per year to $269,403, and this executive owned 66,652 shares of company stock. In the number one position a local executive enjoyed an increase in compensation of 514%, from $1.4 million to $8.7 million; he owned no shares of stock. Number 14 on the list was S. Craig Lindner, CEO and President of Great American Financial Group, Inc. His increase was only 42.8%, but he owned 35,169,868 shares of stock!

I don't think there is a threshold upon which these greedy executives will say, "That's it. I have enough." And if there is a threshold, and they finally reach it, then their quest for more salary becomes a quest for more power. Old Ben Franklin is said to have been very afraid of this lethal mix of money and power, when he lamented, "There are two passions which have a powerful influence on the affairs of men. These are ... love of power and love of money ... When united ... they have the most violent effects." And, we all know what Lord Acton said about power corrupting and absolute power corrupting absolutely.

We are living in an era of unprecedented avarice and disregard for those who have not. When we see CEO's stealing billions of dollars from publicly held companies and buying $8,000 shower curtains and the like, we should all realize that we are in deep trouble, especially when those who commit the thievery get nothing more than a wink and a nod. We should realize as a collective that we are living in a corrupt society and we should – no, we MUST concentrate more on our future economic foundation by working together to build a legacy that we can leave here for our children and grandchildren. On an individual level, I hope and pray that we reconsider our economic position and make sure that we are storing up our treasures somewhere other than on this earth, because just like the man in the book of Luke, we will soon be separated from our stuff.

I am not accusing all executives of being greedy and power-hungry. Many of them are doing wonderful things for many people, and they are building up their asset base to pass on to their children. However, there are those who are so greedy and who have such a low regard for their fellow man that they would steal, lie, and cheat to gain material possessions. And then they lavish themselves with the trappings from their ill-gotten gains.

Our country is steadily becoming more and more divided, not only by race but also by class. We are swiftly moving to two levels of participation in this society: Those who have it all and those who have nothing. But you who have it all had better give some serious thought to what you are doing with all the riches you are accumulating. As God told the man who said he would build more barns in which to keep all his stuff, "You fool! This very night your life will be demanded from you. Then who will get what you have prepared for yourself?" How much money do you need anyway?

Blackout Keeping Us in the Dark

Do you believe the recent blackout of New York and other areas of the country was caused by a lightening strike? Do you believe a fire at a power station caused it? How about the one that suggests consumer demand caused the outage? What about mismanagement? Whatever you believe to be the cause of the blackout, the largest in the history of this country – maybe the world – please add this to your thoughts: Economics, namely, the economics of deception and the tremendous wealth that can be obtained from deceiving the people of this country. We have seen it throughout our history, especially when it comes to war, and we saw it during the Enron scandal, and all the other corporate shenanigans. Are we seeing it again with this blackout?

If you have not noticed, the first thing that came out after the blackout, amid all of the blaming and finger-pointing, was the fact that this latest incident was going to cost billions to fix. Say what? Billions? And who is being tapped to pay those billions to upgrade a system that was supposed to have been maintained by greedy, dishonest, deregulation-crazed, rip-off artists like Enron's crooked executives? I'll give you one guess: Consumers, of course.

They don't know what caused the problem, but you'd better believe they know it's going to cost a whole bunch of money to fix it. They know our utility bills are going to rise because of this problem. They know that the same companies that ripped people off during this period of deregulatory madness now stand to make billions because of the blackout. They know that.

This reminds me of the war in Iraq. Prior to Bush ordering the bombing, he asked Saddam not to blow up his oil wells. Immediately after the troops entered and occupied Baghdad, the oil wells and pipelines were secured, and the black gold was flowing once again. Giving food, water, and medicine to the people had to wait. It was all about the oil anyway, so why are we surprised? It's always about the money; it's always about economics. Just take a look at gasoline prices, and now because of the blackout, they will rise even more. In military parlance that would be called "mission creep."

So, let's review this situation. First of all, can you say Dick Cheney? Can you say Halliburton, the company he presided over before taking that fantastic job called Vice President? Anytime I hear anything having to do with energy, I think of Cheney, the guy who refused to release the minutes of his meetings with the energy Czars. And then I think of George Bush, oilman and friend of Ken Lay and some of those other energy crooks. Then there's our girl, Condoleezza Rice, who sat on the board of one of the largest oil companies in the world and has an oil tanker named after her. Energy = Bush Administration.

So now we have the blackout, an energy-related fiasco, and the first thing they really know is that it's going to cost a few billion dollars to fix and consumers will have to pay for it. I'm sorry, but once bitten twice shy. Fool me once, shame on you; fool me twice, shame on me. Until I am convinced this latest taxpayer rip-off started by a company in eastern Ohio, or a fire in a transformer, or a lightening strike, I am leaning toward the conspiracy side of things. I cannot believe that this blackout, one the experts say should not have moved throughout the grid the way it did, was the result of what we are hearing right now. But, I could be wrong.

Here's the bottom line. Ever since the *Bush-Masters* came into office, energy-related incidents have occurred. Cheney, after leaving Halliburton (the company getting those non-competitive contracts in Iraq), conducts meetings on energy policy and refuses to disclose what was discussed. Ken Lay and his posse rip off thousands of Enron (an energy-related company) employees for millions of dollars, and let's not even talk about energy in California.

Bin Laden does his thing in New York, Washington, and Pennsylvania, and all of a sudden we are chasing Saddam and oil in Iraq. (By the way, in December 2000 Saddam changed the currency Iraq accepted for its oil from dollars to euros) Home heating oil skyrockets; gasoline is as expensive as ever; and Nigeria, with its 5th or 6th largest oil reserves in the world, becomes the last stop on Bush's Tour of Africa. There are more peculiarities, but I will stop there.

I don't know about you, but I am a little gun-shy right now, especially when it comes to believing anything I hear on energy-related crises. There is a lot of money to be made from energy, and I have always been told that a leopard cannot change its spots. Once an oilman, always an oilman.

Just because the lights went out for a while doesn't mean we have to stay in the dark. That's where the establishment wants to keep us. Do you know how to grow mushrooms? You keep them in the dark and feed them a lot of *bull manure*. Are you a mushroom? Wake up, America!

Rush "From" Judgment

If there is one point I always try to make in these articles it's the one Booker T. Washington pointed out. He said, "At the bottom of [everything] lies economics." In this country we see it everyday in everything and yet it seems we don't heed the lessons nor do we play the game to our advantage. While there are many examples we could consider, let's look at the criminal justice system. Or, should I say the injustice system? We saw in the O.J. trial that having enough money can get you out of a capital crime. We saw what it did for Michael Jackson, the first time he was accused of pedophilia. And now we see what it is doing for Martha Stewart and some of those crooks who stole billions from their stockholders. What a country we live in, huh?

With all of the examples before us, both past and present, Rush Limbaugh's case is probably the most glaring and blatant. Here is a guy, admittedly quite rich and well thought of by his "Ditto Heads," who broke the law, declared himself guilty to the world, and then sentenced himself to four weeks in drug rehab. He is now back on the air doing his thing, and he came back without a hint of what judges like to see: remorse. But I suppose if you are the judge of your own case you don't have show remorse.

Limbaugh assumed the titles of arresting officer, prosecuting attorney, defense attorney, witness, jury, and judge, and then issued his own sentence, all in one flamboyant, made-for-Hollywood mea culpa on his radio show. This happened shortly after he was asked to leave ESPN for his comments about NFL quarterback, Donovan McNabb. Talk about Teflon; old *Rushbo* must have graduated from the Reagan School of Nothing Sticks, along with his buddy, Dubya, of course. What a piece of work!

Back behind the golden microphone, arrogant and above the law at this point, because neither he nor his drug dealer has been arrested, Rush Limbaugh awaits the legal decision from, of all places, Florida. Isn't that where Jeb Bush is

Governor? I thought so. Isn't that where some 100,000 or so votes were thrown out and thousands of people were intimidated and lied to about their voting rights? This is getting better all the time, folks.

Let's look deeper. Is Manuel Noriega imprisoned in Florida for drug dealing? You remember him I'm sure; he's Daddy Bush's friend. Drugs? Florida? Limbaugh? Bush? Noriega? What a winning combination. How many of you think old Rush will do one day in jail for breaking the same law that keeps hundreds of thousands of poor people in prison? As Jesse Jackson said on Scarborough's show, "Either the law must be changed or Rush must be subjected to that same law." I agree, but my opinion and a dollar might buy you a cup of coffee at the IHOP.

One more thing you may want to consider: The Grand Old Party needs Rush Limbaugh. It needs him to continue and even increase his daily attacks on the political left, and the party will surely need him as the 2004 presidential election draws near. There is no way they are going to allow him to go to jail now. And you had better believe, if Jeb and his posse can fix a statewide election and steal the larger national election for his brother, you best believe they can fix a little drug charge. They can even make it disappear.

How do all of these transgressions go unpunished? How can some offenders choose when to turn themselves in and others are whisked off to jail before they have time to change their clothes? How is it that some privileged folks are allowed to decide what their fate will be for the same offenses that would get you and me considerable time in the slammer? Could it be, as the Church Lady says, "MONEY?"

Maybe through this example you can see what I have been trying get us see for over a decade now in my newspaper column. No, I am not recommending we increase our economic empowerment so that we can commit crimes and get away with them (you never really get away with them anyway). I am simply saying we must first understand that in this country everything revolves around money and power, and then we have to act upon that reality by keeping a great deal more of ours in order to "buy" our way out of this crime of injustice and economic disparity.

Now if you are upset about the Limbaugh case, I mean really upset, why don't you listen to his show for a little while, if you can stomach it, and see who his advertisers are. Then do what Scarborough and O'Reilly do when something happens they don't like: Boycott. They do it all the time, and they get what they want. Can you say CBS and the Ronald Reagan movie? While you're boycotting, take all that money you're withholding and spend as much as you can with your own businesses.

While folks like Rush control the criminal justice system, they do not control what's in your pockets. Use what's in your pocket to fight against injustice of all kind and, like others, you will win.

Section V

The Games People Play – On Us

"The definition of minority continues to expand and to become more amorphous. Today, almost everyone is a minority in some way. Anything that applies to every group has no real meaning for any group. However, the term 'minority' holds major political advantage for those who wish to maintain status quo. Blacks are further undermined when included in a minority category because none of the other so-called minorities were statutorily deprived by the government of their humanity or their right to enjoy the fruits of their own labor.

Dr. Claud Anderson, *Black Labor White Wealth*

They wrote in their Cointelpro papers about how they would keep blacks separated from each other... and most importantly, separated from progressive activist whites. They wrote that they would discredit black activists so they would lose favor within their community and in [America]. They also wrote that they would replace authentic black leaders with what they called "clean Negroes" whom they had groomed to be more loyal to them than to us. Those aren't my words, they're their words.

Cynthia McKinney, U.S. Congress Representative

This Racism Thing

We believe that all men are created equal -- yet many are denied equal treatment. We believe that all men have certain inalienable rights. We believe that all men are entitled to the blessings of liberty -- yet millions are being deprived of those blessings, not because of their own failures, but because of the color of their skins.

The reasons are deeply embedded in history and tradition and the nature of man. We can understand without rancor or hatred how all this happens. But it cannot continue. Our Constitution, the foundation of our Republic, forbids it. The principles of our freedom forbid it. Morality forbids it. And the law I sign tonight forbids it.... **U.S. President, Lyndon Johnson signing the Civil Rights Act of 1964**

In my hometown, fondly called *Cincinn-apathy*, Ohio, the politicians are at it again. They are starting up another campaign against racism. They have called for yet another "dialogue on race" to figure out how we can stop racism. Did I mention this is an election year for city council? The leading councilman who called for the "summit" is white. He also surmised who the "Black leaders" are in this town and summoned them to City Council for this landmark meeting to discuss racism and racial profiling. The Mayor is on board, saying racism is the number one problem in our city. Man, with all of this high-powered authority, assisted by our "Black Leaders," we should finally get this racism thing solved. Right?

Wrong! Dead wrong. This is just another effort that Black people refer to as the *Okey-Doke*. How some white people can be so patronizing when it comes to racism is beyond my understanding. Oh, I know <u>why</u> they do it; I just don't know <u>how</u> they can do it, and sleep at night. They must think we are really stupid.

I always say if people of goodwill, of all stripes, would simply stand up and point out racism wherever it exists, our need for these kinds of meetings would greatly diminish. Politicians who all of a sudden, and very conveniently, find it necessary to call the community together around racism have known all along that racism exists, that it is the scourge of this nation and has been since the country started.

This farce being perpetrated on Black people, some of us being willing accomplices, must not be the guiding force behind what we need to do to secure our future. We must not allow white politicians, or any others for that matter, to decide who we are, what we are, and what our number one problem is. This only takes our valuable attention away from issues like true freedom. They want to keep us actively running after the solution to racism, trying to make us believe, that we can solve the problem. Well, allow me to let you in on a secret: We cannot solve the racism problem.

White people invented racism not Black people. White people commit racism; Black people only react to it. White people only deal with the issue when it is expedient and convenient for them – especially when there is another election on the horizon and they need Black votes.

For white politicians and other white people to call meetings between Blacks and whites to solve racism is nothing more than window-dressing. They should call meetings among themselves, meetings for which the agenda has one item: The Elimination of Racism. All they want, instead, is for us to be sidetracked by the dialogue, mesmerized by a *photo op*, and enamored with the possibility of being more acceptable to white people.

As I said, and I reiterate, Blacks did not start racism and Blacks cannot stop it. Only white people can stop racism. And until they do, what are we going to do? Are we going to continue to fall for the *Okey-Doke*, or are we going to realize and follow up on the fact that we must be about our business, just like they are? Do you think racism is really THEIR number one issue? If you do, I have some nice oceanfront property in Kansas I'd like to sell to you. They simply want racism to be OUR number one issue, and they want us to be diverted from taking care of business.

Let's get this straight. Racism is a condition of the heart, and changing hearts is God's business. Racism is structurally imbedded in the fabric of this country. Focusing all of our attention on this structural inequity by reacting to the calls for summits and dialogues will always keep us on our heels. More importantly, it keeps us from dealing with economic issues, and that's exactly what the profiteers want us to do.

One last note to those "Black Leaders" who are always called to sit on racism boards and panels, don't you fall for the *Okey-Doke* either. You are being used. You are not in some kind of acceptable position, crowned by white people, never again to be treated unfairly, never again to be harassed when a racist cop stops you, never again to be attacked by the establishment. You are still Black and you will be treated the same as any one of us if you get caught in the right or the wrong place at the wrong time. You are not special; you are being propped up as an emperor with no clothes.

Please don't allow yourself to be used that way. It will only help keep your people down. Yes, you may get a few extra perks, a few extra dollars, a contract or two, but are those things worth what we stand to lose collectively?

Racism is here to stay. It is a condition of the heart, a flaw in perception and moral character. Government cannot legislate it away and man cannot protest it away.
Jerroll Sanders, *If you've got my dollar, I don't*

We Have Been Programmed by Programs

Have you noticed every time a problem arises between African Americans and "the establishment" the usual result is another program for Black folks? Have you also noticed that the programs we get usually result in economic progress for the establishment? Have you ever wondered why we accept "programs" as the solutions to our problems, all the while standing on the sidelines and watching "the establishment" get progress in their efforts to "help" us? Well, I have noticed these and other *Black strategies* being implemented over the years, and I have come to the conclusion that we have indeed been programmed by programs.

Let's look at some examples, but first let me clarify what I mean by "the establishment;" it comprises members of our local societies who always seem to "get the call" or come to the rescue when a socially oriented problem needs to be solved. They can be Black, white, or otherwise, but they are considered "safe" by those who really run the show.

They get together and make the plans, which more often than not result in new (and sometimes old) programs for the rabble-rousing, dissatisfied, angry Black folks. But those who make the plans are the ones that get real economic progress. They get the high level positions; they get the consultant contracts; they get access to the funds allocated to set up the programs; they get development rights to build more housing. They get progress; we get programs.

And check this out. Even when we get our programs, you know, like affirmative action, set-asides, and the like, "they" develop ways to get in on that action as well. For instance, affirmative action benefited white females more than any other 'group. Hey, wasn't that "program" developed in response to past injustices against Black people? Some of the set-aside programs, again originally designated for Black folks, were soon compromised by changing the names of those programs to Women Business Enterprise (WBE), Minority

Business Enterprise (MBE), and Small Business Enterprise (SBE) Programs.

The result: Black businesses, for which the programs are written, get lost in massive "certification" paperwork (Can you imagine having to "certify" your Blackness in order to get a portion of the meager percentages set aside for all of these groups?), and end up, if they are lucky, getting the crumbs that fall off the set-aside biscuit. To make it even worse, white males get the lion's share of the resources, without having to certify they are white, and because they are married to and are the fathers of white females, they get in on the WBE action as well.

In my hometown, white males can now also get in on the City's 30% "Small Business" Enterprise Program, due to its "race-neutral" criteria and its increase in the net worth ceiling of an individual small business owner from $325,000 to $750,000! Thus, white males get all of the 70% and even some of the 30%. They get progress; we get programs.

We have been programmed to believe that all we need is another program and things will be just fine. We have fallen for the ruse of corporate greed shrouded in a cloak of largess toward Black people; we have accepted Black politicians who pretend they are working to "level the playing field" all the while advancing themselves and forgetting about those upon whose shoulders they stand; we have been programmed by programs, mesmerized by programs, hypnotized by programs, put to sleep by programs, and we are being killed, literally and figuratively, by programs that put millions into the pockets of others and leave us dangling by a thin string hoping there is a safety net below. That safety net: Another program, of course.

Why do we keep buying the same old song and dance? Why do we keep allowing others to play us that way? How can we look at ourselves in the mirror and not see the sad eyes of our children who long for a better world? How can we not hear the desperate cries of our youth, who are asking us to stand up as Black men and women and stop this madness? How can we sleep at night when what is happening to our people is so blatant and overt that even a child can recognize it? When are we going to stop feeding on the *pablum* placed before us, fighting over the portions originally and entirely meant for

Blacks, only to end up with a small *percentage of the percentage* designated for "minorities," women, and "small" business owners?

Programs would be all right if they were doing what they were originally set up to do. But we have allowed them to deviate so far from their purpose that they have become nothing more than a joke – with Black folks being the punchline. If white females have been discriminated against, then they should have a long talk with their fathers, uncles, and husbands. Blacks didn't have anything to do with that, so why should white females share in our *programs*?

Minorities did not suffer the horrendous treatment that Blacks suffered in country. So where did those minority programs come from? Small businesses, according to various definitions, can employ hundreds of persons, have receipts in the millions and, as I said earlier, comprise owners who have a net worth, not income but net worth, of $750,000. How can Black-owned (or any other for that matter) micro-enterprises and sole proprietorships compete with that, especially within the same Small Business Program?

Yes, programs have programmed us, and we had better start deprogramming ourselves right now.

*If Black people are at all disappointed in our present level of achievement, it may be because our roots are not planted deeply enough in the past – resting upon such a shallow, inadequate and faulty data input of only **400** years of history.*
Dr. Frances Cress-Welsing,
The Isis Papers, The keys to the colors

"Minority" Programs Keep Us Fighting Over 15%

What about the 85% of the contracting, the employment, the development, and the tourism dollars? Who gets that? And, what entitles them to get it? You have probably heard the term "economic inclusion" being bantered about lately, so here are some other questions while we're at it. Who is doing the including? Who are they including? How does a public project, or one funded with public dollars, come under the authority of a white contractor or developer who, in turn, has the right to "include" a certain percentage of "minorities?" Why is it that white men, for the most part, are always the ones doing the "including" and "minorities" are always the ones being included, to the tune of an average of 15% of the pie?

Isn't it amazing that we continue to fall for the games people play on us? Disparity studies (Croson Studies) state very clearly that Black people and other groups have been discriminated against via city contracting opportunities. What solution do they offer? Well, our city council, led by our Black "vice" (there's that term again) Mayor, voted to implement a "race-neutral" program, laced with a few small percentage goals, to make up for past discrimination. Mind you, the problem was based on race, but the solution was not.

We have all sorts of "minority" programs that call for goals, aspirations, goods intentions, hopes, wishes, and have encouraging words attached to them. However, they are not enforceable, and they are centered on a relatively small percentage of a particular project; that 15% (a little more in some cases) is designated for so-called minorities. Now check this out. The minority group, which sometimes comprises as many as five or six individual groups, collectively, often makes up more of the total population than the so-called majority, which is given the right to "include" minorities in public projects.

Does this make sense to you? Does it make sense for Black people to, first, allow ourselves to be called "minorities" and then allow a group of white men to dominate and control our tax dollars to the point that we end up fighting for 15%? Why are we competing with other groups for the "minority" share of our tax dollars and allowing the other 85% to escape into the hands of white men?

Maybe we should look at the percentages of population or the aggregate number of "minorities" in various areas, and base our economic inclusion efforts on that. Once again, I draw your attention to Cincinnati, Ohio. We are building the National Underground Railroad Freedom Center for more than $100 million. The "goal" for "minority" inclusion is 25%. The Black population is nearly 50% and Hispanics and Asians comprise between 5%-7%.

First of all, the last time I read my history, the only characters who participated in the Underground Railroad in Cincinnati, Ohio were Black folks and white folks, not "minorities." No one ever taught me about a Chinese person swimming or wading across the Ohio River, or a Latino person, or a person from India or Pakistan participating, either by running from slave-catchers or by helping slaves get to Canada. That being the case, why then are "minorities" the focus of the Freedom Center's Economic Inclusion Program? And where is the rule that says white men and women must always be the ones who determine how much everyone else will get? The same thing applies when it comes to other minority programs. Black people are the ones who were discriminated against, but everyone else has stepped up to get the benefits of our pain and suffering. We're gettin' played, y'all!

While we are scrambling to get our share of the 15% allotment, others are getting the 85% without the slightest problem. And to make it even worse, Black people have to comply with so-called minority set aside regulations and horrendous "certification" programs to get their share of such a small piece of the pie. How can you call me and treat me "special" and make me jump through five hoops to get a contract while white men don't have to jump through any hoops, yet they get the lion's share of public funds and development opportunities? They keep our attention diverted toward 15% and they get away with 85% in the process.

I can hear the detractors now, saying, "What about the fact that Black people do not have the professional and business capacity to perform even if they were given a greater percentage." While it is true there are far too few Black businesses, whose annual receipts are far too low, that fact makes the case for more "access" to opportunity, information, education, and capital. It makes the case for Black businesses to form partnerships, mergers, and alliances to capture a larger share of the proverbial pie. It makes a case for those in control to spend some of that 85% on the things that will enhance the opportunities for Black business development. (Maybe that's what George Bush means by that nonsensical term "affirmative access," no doubt following in his father's footsteps, or missteps, when he coined the term, "A thousand points of light.")

Brothers and sisters, let's stop fighting over a share of the 15% allocated for "minorities," and start fighting for more of the 85%.

Booker T. and W.E.B. – Two Schools of Thought

Why did we feel we had to make a choice between these two giants of Black history? Why do some of us, to this day, continue to argue about which one was right and which one was wrong? Why do we allow ourselves, then and now, to be pitted against one another and subsequently divided and conquered? We know how the game is played and we certainly know when it's being played on us, but we fall for the game every time. Why?

The classic example, of course, is the Booker T. Washington versus W.E.B. Dubois discussion. These two brothers came from extremely different backgrounds and experienced drastically different childhoods, one of extreme poverty and one of relative affluence. At the turn of the 19th century, they both grew to understand and to act upon their understanding of what Black folks needed to survive in this country. They both worked hard to make the changes they felt were necessary to move our people forward.

Quite simply, Booker T. took the education and economic road, and W.E.B. took the education and political road. History is replete with their disagreements and how brothers and sisters of their day chose which one they would support. Things got pretty nasty between the two camps of supporters too. Sabotage, false accusations, character assassination, and all of the other dirty tricks you can think of, were used one against the other. You know the story, I'm sure. But have you ever given any thought to how and why those things happened? Have you ever wondered who was really behind the scenes orchestrating the chaos among Black people in the early 1900's? There's always a hidden hand in the mix.

Here's my thinking on it. Booker T. started Tuskegee Institute, and set up a program *par excellence* to teach Black youth how to use their talents and how to become economically self-sufficient. Education? Economic empowerment? That combination was (and still is) a big problem for the establishment. W.E.B., although he also understood and supported Black folks going into business and supporting one another, encouraged Blacks to obtain college degrees and seek political offices to participate in the rule-making process of this country. Education? Political empowerment? That was (and still is) far less threatening to those in charge.

When Booker T. started the National Negro Business League in 1900, a few white folks helped by giving money for the effort. There was not, however, a groundswell of white support to get the group organized, which is very important in my comparison. And, maybe Booker T. and the organizers did not want white folks to do anything except give their money.

When W.E.B. and his associates convened the Niagara Movement in 1905, a few white people assisted with his effort. Four years later, white folks called their own meeting and invited some of the members of the Niagara Movement, one of whom was W.E.B. Outraged by a lynching that took place in Springfield, Illinois, this group of whites formed what is now called the N.A.A.C.P. We can be sure they put some money into that organization as well.

Here is where the difference comes to light. The Business League was an economic empowerment entity started by Black folks. The N.A.A.C.P. was a civil and political rights entity started by white folks for Black folks. (Or was it really for Blacks?) We soon began to choose which effort we would support. We began to debate whether Booker T. was right or if W.E.B. was on the right track. Meanwhile, the two organizations were established and growing. Booker T. headed the economic organization and W.E.B. was relegated to the position of Editor of The Crisis Magazine and in charge of publicity and research. Publicity? Now there's something to which we can all relate. Oh yes, a white man named Moorfield Storey headed the N.A.A.C.P.

Why didn't white people get behind the Business League the way they got behind the N.A.A.C.P.? Why didn't they push for economic empowerment for Black people the same way they insisted upon civil rights for Black people? Why didn't white folks see how important it was for Blacks to gain their economic rights? Why was there not an economic movement built into the N.A.A.C.P.? (Maybe we would not be hearing a call for economic empowerment from Brother Mfume in 2002 if there had been one in 1910)

Those are very interesting questions. They also point out very clearly where we went wrong and why we should not allow ourselves to be made to choose between and among our great leaders. We should have taken the best of both Booker T. and W.E.B. and used their thoughts and directions to empower our people completely. Instead, we eventually gravitated to the political side of things. I am sure "outsiders" helped in that choosing process as well as orchestrated the demise of Booker T. because, while political influence and "civil rights' were really no big deal to the establishment, economic power was (and still is) everything to the establishment.

Booker T. died in 1915 from a sudden onset of a mysterious illness, just before Brother Marcus Garvey, who was on his way to meet him, could have a chance to pick Booker's brain (Coincidence or Conspiracy?). In 1961, W.E.B. left America for Ghana, angrily saying, "I just cannot take anymore of this country's treatment." He died on the eve of the March on Washington in 1963 (Conspiracy or Coincidence?).

Two schools of thought from these two giants? What must they be thinking now – about us?

"It seems to me," said Booker T.
"I don't agree," said W.E.B.
From a poem by Dudley Randall

Sibling Rivalry? I hope not.

The snubbing of the N.A.A.C.P. by George Bush, followed by his acceptance of an invitation to speak at the National Urban League (NUL) Convention, could lead to a rivalry between the two groups. And as we look back in history, that's just the way the establishment wants it. Will we fall for it again? Divide and conquer is the name of this game. Remember that commercial where the kids were singing, "My dog's bigger than your dog"? I hope the N.A.A.C.P. and the NUL don't get into comparing the size of their dogs, especially over who gets most of George Bush's attention.

The N.A.A.C.P. should not only be insulted but thoroughly embarrassed as well, not only because of Bush's snub (What else did they expect? At least he's honest about his disdain for them.), but because of the Democrat candidates' snub of them too. Of course the Dems came in and gave their apologies, hugged and kissed, and moved on with their agendas. Bush has not only refused to meet with the N.A.A.C.P. during his tenure in office, he is rubbing salt in their wound by attending the NUL conference, even though all he did was give the League an Economics 101 Primer on goods and services.

Isn't the N.A.A.C.P. the same organization that gave Bush's National Security Chief the Image Award? Well, maybe they should have called Condi Rice to intercede on their behalf. I don't know why they gave her the award in the first place, but they should have leveraged their relationship with Rice to see if she has "the juice" everyone professes she has with Georgie Boy. You know what I mean: *Quid Pro Quo*.

Why would Bush accept the Urban League's invitation and shun the N.A.A.C.P.? Maybe the N.A.A.C.P. is a bit too vocal in its criticism of Bush and his policies. Maybe Bush just does not like Mfume and Bond. Maybe Bush believes that since the NUL focuses more on job training than it does on politics, he's better off dealing with the NUL over the N.A.A.C.P..

Maybe, when faced with the choice of which organization to support, it is a matter of who gets the most money from white corporations, thus, keeping the door open for more control over that organization. And, maybe it's the age-old game of creating an atmosphere in which Black people are made to believe they must choose. Remember W.E.B. and Booker T.?

Maybe Bush is listening to that black (small "b") apologist, Armstrong Williams, who was recently quoted by CNN, saying, "Some of these organizations have been downright hostile to this president, and he realizes that there is more than one avenue to reach black Americans. Early on, he wanted to attend the Urban League's convention, and the president should be praised for this. And Marc Morial has not been willing to buy into the demagoguery that [N.A.A.C.P. President Kweisi] Mfume, Bond, and Jackson have heaped on the president. He, too, should be commended." Uh oh. I smell something. Who's it going to be, Black people, Marc or Mfume?

According to the same CNN report, in 2000, Morial said, "I'm fearful of a George Bush administration. I'm fearful because when I'm reminded of Reagan-Bush, I'm reminded of the most difficult economic times in this state in my lifetime." But Mr. Morial subsequently praised Mr. Bush for meeting with the U.S. Conference of Mayors, which he headed before leaving office in 2002. "We've had a good start with President Bush," Mr. Morial told a crowd at the National Press Club in 2001.

A good start? Why? Because of a meeting? I have always been told it's not how you start; it's how you finish. We will see if the rhetoric turns to progressive action for Black folks, but history tells us it will not. So, let's not get too hyped about a meeting, or a speech, or a hug and a kiss.

Here is the interesting point about the entire matter, also included in the CNN report, which said, "Most recently, the Urban League lost an annual $15 million federal grant that it used to assist low-income seniors, after the U.S. Department of Labor announced an open-bid competition for the grant money. The Urban League this spring lost the funding, which it has received for 25 years, in the bidding process." Hmmm.

What's the lesson here? The N.A.A.C.P. should realize it has absolutely no clout with Bush, Condoleezza's Image Award notwithstanding, but neither does the NUL. They really don't have much clout with the Democrat Party either. So what should they do to gain clout? In my opinion, they should rally their constituents around collective economic strategies, and build a solid economic foundation from which to leverage not only the mere "attention" of Bush, the Democrats, and their corporate puppet masters, but also their genuine support. Seems to me, we just want to be liked, paid attention to, and accepted. Oh yeah, and be apologized to as well. We buy the sizzle while everyone else gets to eats the steak.

The most important lessons are those of the past. The NUL and the N.A.A.C.P. had better look back at those lessons and finally recognize the divide and conquer tactic worked then, and is still being utilized in 2003. Black folks can least afford to be divided. Imagine what we could accomplish if the NUL and the N.A.A.C.P. worked together and stood up for one another, and rallied African Americans around what both organizations have deemed to be the last hurdle in our freedom race: economic empowerment.

The Minority Majority

Some Black people have been so well programmed that we have allowed ourselves to be thrown into this vast category called, "Minorities," and we are the only ones leading the fight to "level the playing field" (what an overused and meaningless term that is) for all so-called minority groups. Some of us also refer to ourselves with that despicable term in spite of the fact that we comprise the majority of the population in some cities. How could you even use the term for yourself, as a Black person, if you live in a city where the majority of the citizens are Black? I was participating in a panel discussion in one of these cities where Blacks outnumber whites, and I heard a brother who lives in that city refer to his people as "minorities."

Our dear Brother Walter Smith, Publisher of the New York Beacon newspaper, in an editorial in the June 27 – July 3, 1996 edition of the Beacon, cited a very important point. He said, "We are the only ethnic group in America who are defined by our deficiencies. The word that most defines us is 'minority.'" Brother Smith went on to give more "deficiency" information by citing the data such as annual household income and our "minority" stake, as Black people, in the total American economy.

We have fallen, hook, line, and sinker, for this minority thing, and we are paying for it every day. The folks on the city council of San Diego, thanks to one of its conscious members, recently called for a ban on the term "minority." Too bad others haven't followed their lead.

Now here's the real kicker. The term "minority" is often used by those in power to keep various "minority groups" in constant competition for that proverbial *piece of the pie*. They set up efforts called *economic inclusion* for minorities and include themselves by adding white females to the "minority" category – and Black folks lead the charge in support of such nonsense. Since when have white females suffered from discrimination and injustice? Since Susan B. Anthony? And if white females have suffered these things, then they need to have a heart-to-heart talk with their white men, many of whom are their husbands.

Check out the "minority" programs in corporate America; look at who is at the helm of "minority" offices in Chambers of Commerce. To make things even worse, many more times than not, these positions are occupied by Black folks, some of whom are afraid, or at least reluctant to even use the word "Black" or the term "African American." They say things like, "We want economic inclusion for minorities, people of color, small businesses, and females." They never get around to standing up for their own people by saying what they want for Black people.

Back when the 13th, 14th and 15th Amendments were written, everyone knew they were enacted for Black people, not minorities. We all know that so-called Affirmative Action was established for Black people because of past unfairness and mistreatment, not for white females and other "minorities." What went wrong, folks? Why do we allow our numbers and ourselves to be dispersed and misused the way they are?

The other very important consideration is this. What Pat Buchanan writes (and fears) in his book, The Death of the West, and what our dear sister Francis Cress-Welsing wrote in The Isis Papers, is fast becoming a reality. In the aggregate, all so-called minority groups in this country will soon comprise a majority in this country. Just as Blacks comprise a majority in some cities and still call themselves minorities, certain ethnic groups collectively allow themselves to be called minorities even though they are moving swiftly toward becoming the majority in this country, and Buchanan is sounding the alarm on all the talk shows.

This farce that has been created and perpetrated against Black people should be stopped. And it will only be stopped when Black people stop it. Why would we allow others to place us in this "minority" category, along with white females in some cases, especially when most of us know it is not for our benefit? It simply helps the establishment to maintain the status quo and to keep doling out small portions of the wealth and resources of this nation to "minority groups."

Resist the "minority" title. You are much better than that. Rebuke anyone who refers to you as a minority. It carries no benefits – it only stigmatizes you. Stop being timid and speak up for your own people. Stop saying "Minority" when you really mean "Black." Check all the statistics, folks. We are on the bottom, even among so-called "minority" groups, when it comes to net worth, median income, unemployment, and other economic indicators. We are on the top among so-called "minority" groups when it comes to annual income ($700 billion). Don't you think there is something drastically wrong with that picture? We must help ourselves before we can help anyone else, so get off this minority kick, brothers and sisters, and get about the business of helping your own people – Black people.

By the way, who will be the minority forty to fifty years from now? Maybe that's the end game for the use of the term minority. Hmmm.

Somebody's Calling You Out of Your Name

Let's do a little test. I live in Cincinnati, Ohio. It has a "minority" city manager, a "minority" vice-mayor, a "minority" fire chief, a minority chairman of the visitors' bureau, a "minority" assistant city manager, a "minority" head of contract compliance, a "minority" city solicitor, a "minority" clerk of council, a "minority" director of human relations, and a "minority" school superintendent.   Can you tell me the ethnicity of each of these persons? C'mon now, surely you can do it. Are they Hispanic-American? Are they Asian-American? Are they African-American? Are they Native American? Are they Indian-American? Are they women? Are they white women?

I'll give you some time to compile your answers while I answer the question: What's in a name? First, a name is an identifier. It let's you know when to turn around when you are called.   A name can also be a disparaging term used to denigrate and demean. So, a name can be positive or it can be negative, depending on who is doing the naming-calling and who is being called the name. Names have connotations and denotations. In other words, names can conjure up anxiety, stereotypical images, fear, and other uncomfortable feelings, despite their true meaning. Names can also lead us to believe we know something about a person simply because of the name they may carry when, in fact, their denotation could be entirely different.

So what's in a name? How about pride? How about heritage? How about culture? How about history? How about cohesiveness? How about continuity? How about structure? What else is in a name? How about deficiency? How about subordination? How about inability? How about inconsistency? How about less than? How about inferiority? How about condescension? How about inequality?

What's in a name? Let's look further. Why was the term "Black Codes" used? Could it be because the codes were meant for Black people? If not, why didn't they name them

Minority Codes? And if Civil Rights were granted to Black people for the injustices perpetrated against us in the past, why aren't those rights called Black Rights? Could it be that those who wrote the laws had already figured out how they could be the primary beneficiaries of those laws, while simultaneously keeping Blacks "in our place?"

Finally, let's look at this affirmative action thing, or "affirmative access," or whatever you want to call it. Why and for whom were those laws written? Could it be for Black people? So why weren't they called Black Affirmative Action Laws? "There's nothing in a name", they said. "You know who we mean." Thirty years later we find that white females benefited most from "Black Affirmative Action".

Civil Rights, affirmative action, minority set-asides, minority and female owned business programs, small business programs, and all the other charades that are played today were brought about as a result of injustice against one group: Black people. Only now, Black people sit back and allow others not only to step right in front of us and go to head of the Civil Rights line, we also passively allow them to literally and unapologetically call us out of our name with impunity. But, what's in a name anyway, right?

A typical example of the shenanigans we see played on our people once again is taking place in Comedy Central U.S.A., Cincinnati, Ohio. The National Underground Railroad Freedom Center is being built here and was shopped as a "Black thing." Now that the Center is being constructed, and economics comes into play, the theme is "Minority" economic inclusion. That's right. A "goal" of 25% of the contracts, etc. has been established for "minorities." Go figure.

Our Comedy Central City Council (some call it *City Clown-cil*) just approved a "Small Business" program to address disparities they found in our Croson Study. The report says quite plainly that Black folks and other folks have been discriminated against in the past. What do they do about it? Well, instead of implementing a race-conscious program, they recommend and approve a race-neutral "Small Business Program" and then pat themselves on the backs for looking out for "minority" businesses. Let me reiterate. The report said, among many other things, that Black people, who comprise nearly 50% of the city's population, received 1.41% of a publicly funded highway project that cost more that $228 million! The solution: Implement a Small Business Program rather than a Black Program. Who's going to win in that game?

Whenever there's a problem the establishment thinks it can solve it by putting Black faces on slick brochures, sending Black folks to talk to other Black folks to tell us everything is fine, or by putting a Black person on television to plead their case. They are quick to use the correct name during the times they find themselves in trouble, but they gravitate to other euphemistic substitutes when they hand out the prizes.

Are you going to allow someone to call you out of your name? If so, Black people will stay exactly where we are – on the bottom rung of the economic ladder. What's in a name? Better still, who's in a name? You are. Accept nothing less than your correct name. Oh yes, those "minorities" in the abovementioned test. They are all – every single one of them – "Black" people, albeit, some with a small "b"!

Now you know why my newspaper column is called "Blackonomics" rather than some silly euphemism like "Minoronomics."

Are you a Certified Black Person?

Are you genuine? Are you legitimate? Can you authoritatively attest to your Blackness? Can you confirm it? Can you assure it? Can you guarantee it? Those terms comprise the dictionary's definition of "certify." And, there is one more definition, which I will get to later. Black business owners hear this word, "certify" many times, especially when they want to do business on some publicly funded project where millions and sometimes billions of their tax dollars are being spent. We also have to be "certified" when it comes to obtaining contracts from private corporations under the banner, of course, of "diversity," "inclusion," and other socially acceptable programs. By the way, that other definition of "certify" is: "To attest officially to the insanity of ..."

Insanity? Now that could be used to describe Black folks, especially those of us who have become fertilizer for the certification game. Someone said, "If you keep doing what you've always done, you'll keep getting what you've always gotten," and it's insanity to think you'll get something different. I agree. How long have we been certifying our Black businesses? Nearly forty years of so-called affirmative action programs and we are virtually at the same place we started back in the 1960's; some would say we are even further behind.

So which definition suits you? Should Black businesses submit to the paperwork hassles, the intrusive questionnaires, and hours of trying to justify why they should get 15% - 30% of the business, while white owned firms get virtually all of the business without having to justify anything? Should Black owned companies continue to gather at meetings, and information sessions, and "inclusion parties" in order to get their fair share of business from the public and private sectors? Can Black owned businesses, if allowed to compete on their own merit and experience, win larger contracts?

Of course, those are rhetorical questions because the opportunity to play the game by the same rules that white companies play by has been shrouded and nearly eliminated by Certification Programs and Diversity Programs and Economic

Inclusion Programs. Even in cities where the majority of the population is Black or in cities where the total population of all so-called "minorities" exceeds that of white people, Blacks and others scramble and squabble over the measly percentages allocated to the "minority." Of course, now they are also using euphemisms like "small business," "disadvantaged business," and "women-owned business."

In Cincinnati, Black people are approximately 45% of the population, and other "minority" groups make up around 10% I am told. When I was in school that would add up to 55%. Has math changed or what? Also, when I was in school, majority meant the most and minority meant less; fifty-one percent was enough to have a majority. So why are Blacks succumbing to the minority games being played on us everyday in cities across this country?

I say this over and over in Cincinnati, but it seems to fall on deaf ears. Maybe that's because some Black folks, the ones getting all of the minority portions of the business deals, just don't want our people to hear it. That's all right though; I know you are hearing what I am saying and I know some Blackonomics readers out there will stand up, speak out, and make a change.

Check this out. Even Toyota has a minority program. When Jesse Jackson threatened to boycott Toyota, $7 billion appeared and a Diversity Advisory Board was established to get more business out to minorities. The typical scenario took place. Black folks screamed discrimination, unfairness, stereotyping, and threatened to boycott, which resulted in every "minority" group getting paid. And Toyota of all companies even fell for the minority game. Hey, Toyota, you are a minority too! Why would you need a minority-diversity program to help your own people and other folks who are in the same position as you, Toyota? Aren't you in charge of things? That's like a Black company setting aside a minority portion of its business for Black people. Oops! Some of them do. But, only after they have been certified.

I recently had a discussion with a brother about the certification process and why we have to go through it. He said we have to protect against "front" companies. "You know how some of our people will let white firms use them as fronts, Jim," he responded. He was right about that, which speaks to our lack of consciousness and love for one another. It's easy for someone to exploit that by offering a few dollars to a sellout. However, while we do have work to do among our own brothers and sisters who sell themselves and their people that way, I wondered why that brother didn't mention anything about those other "front" companies known as "women-owned businesses."

We know, and have seen white women go from being housewives one day to business owners the next, and receive lucrative contracts almost immediately. Some I am sure go into business on their own, but many are put into business by their husbands and others merely to take advantage of those "certification programs" and to get a piece of the action. If you write the rules surely you know how to play by them. No one is saying anything about those "front" companies, many of which are taking business from Black folks, but we are really concerned about Blacks who are fronts.

So, are you a "certified" Black person, or are you just "certifiable"?

Section VI

Puleeeeeeze! – Let's Get Serious

"The fundamental crisis in black America is twofold: too much poverty and too little self-love. The urgent problem of black poverty is primarily due to the distribution of wealth, power, and income – a distribution influenced by the rival caste system that denied opportunities to most 'qualified' black people until two decades ago."

Cornel West, *Race Matters*, 1993

Economic Powerlessness means
Political Powerlessness
"The idea that the Afrikan American community can exercise effective power, political or otherwise, without simultaneously exercising economic power, is a fantasy... As long as the Afrikan American community is relatively weak so will be its [political] representatives, no matter how high their offices.
Dr. Amos Wilson, *Blueprint for Black Power*

We Need a Plan!

"We've got to have a plan; we've got to move this beyond conversation." Those were the words of Kweisi Mfume during the State of the Black Union panel discussion held in Washington, DC on Saturday, February 3, 2001. Among all of the comments made by both panels, those were the ones that struck home with me. For all of the things cited by the panel, education, civil rights, politics, criminal justice, faith-based initiatives, and, of course, economic empowerment, our need for a strategic plan is fundamental to our success in these areas of endeavor.

I have good news for Brother Mfume. With regard to the national consensus that economic empowerment should be at or near the top of the collective agenda of Black people in this country, and in light of the fact that the Urban League, N.A.A.C.P., P.U.S.H., et al, agree with Dr. Martin Luther King, Jr. when he said, "The emergency we now face is economic," we do have plans. More importantly, we have brothers and sisters who are actively and dedicatedly working those plans.

Before I delineate the plans, let me say that most of what I heard from the panelists, in terms of the problems we face, is grounded in economics. I do not, by any stretch of the imagination, deny that we must fight on many fronts. All of the issues discussed by the panelists, especially the education issue, are important and must be addressed by us and for us 24/7. However, I contend that if we fail to take control of a greater portion of our economic resources, we will be in Washington next year discussing the same issues and asking for "a plan" to solve our problems.

So here are the plans that are currently being implemented. I know, I know, I've said it all before, and those of you who regularly read my column will probably find this quite redundant. But, Frederick Douglass admonished us to be redundant when he said, "Agitate, agitate, agitate. So let me agitate a little more.

To Mr. Mfume and all of the others who participated on the panel, there is a plan and a movement called The MATAH Network. The founders of MATAH should have been invited to be on the panel. They would have shared not only their plan but their movement as well.

There is a plan called Powernomics, established by Dr. Claud Anderson, who should have also been on the panel. This man has had a plan for years; it seems most of our people have not been listening – or, at least not following his plan. And where was George Fraser, the Networking Guru, who recently released his SuccessGuide Millennium noting the achievements of Tavis Smiley and Tom Joyner? This brother is doing what many of us only talk about and is helping his people replicate his success. He has a plan and has worked his plan – everyday for the past 15 years.

There is also Mrs. Ernestine Henning, who founded the Richard Allen Foundation, and has also established Visions 2000, an economic power movement that will do more than give report cards on hotels owned by others. It will increase Black ownership of hotels, as several have suggested Black people should pursue, and it will create investment opportunities for Black people in Black owned income-producing assets. This kind of plan and follow-up action can provide secure futures for our children. You know, the way the other folks do it. I would have loved to have seen Sister Henning on that panel.

Then there is Muhammad Nassardeen, who founded Recycling Black Dollars in Los Angeles, California. He would have made an excellent panelist because he has what Mr. Mfume called for: A Plan. Mr. Nassardeen has been working his plan for many years; have we overlooked him in our zeal to assist our people with economic freedom?

Oh yes, one of my favorite plans is the R.E.A.C.H. Program, operated by Bishop Luke Edwards in Eutaw, Alabama. Started in the 1970's, this plan is still working and would have made an exemplary topic for the panel discussing the State of the Black Union. We could all learn a great deal from Bishop Edwards and his plan, especially the part that moved brothers and sisters from being welfare recipients to becoming entrepreneurs and landowners.

I am sure there are other plans and activities around the country, in addition to the ones I have cited, which merit our attention and our support. The brothers and sisters who have established these movements and who live their plans everyday should always be included in panel discussions and forums such as the one held in Washington. I hope Tavis Smiley and Tom Joyner will somehow see this article or some other information on these plans and programs and get these people on their shows and on any future panels they put together. These two brothers have the eyes and ears of millions of Black people. Wow! I shudder to think what an impact they can have on their listeners by giving them this kind of information.

Wouldn't it make a lot of sense for us to take the successes we have among our people and build upon them? There were several successful programs represented on that august panel of brothers and sisters. Replicate them also. As we all know too well, talk alone is very cheap. We must have some real action as well as talk, and I hope we will see it very soon.

As I said, we have some very good plans, and most importantly we have action attached to those plans. It would be great if our national organizations would support and help implement these plans, especially since they do not have plans, as Mfume told us at the end of the State of the Black Union forum. Please spread the word; maybe they will get it one day.

Kwanzaa – *Celebration or Practice?*
(Written for Kwanzaa 2002)

Every December we gear up to celebrate Kwanzaa. Each of the seven social and spiritual principles (Nguzo Saba) of Kwanzaa are held in veneration and we see many African Americans setting aside certain times in their homes to stress Unity, Self-Determination, Collective Work and Responsibility, Cooperative Economics, Purpose, Creativity, and Faith. Since 1966, when the first celebration of Kwanzaa was held, Black people in this country have steadily increased the visibility and importance of this celebration. Let's take a closer look.

Unity   Now there is a word we love to scream and celebrate in our communities all of the time. Unfortunately, it is just a word, and while a lot of brothers and sisters are down with the word, they are not down with the practice of the word; they are not willing to do what it takes to have unity. Beginning on December 26th we will hear the Kwanzaa call for "Unity." Will this be the year that we finally achieve the unity we celebrate?

Self-Determination   What a concept! Our forefathers and mothers, despite their meager resources and violent constraints, practiced this principle. That's how they built their own towns, started and supported their own businesses, paid for their children's education, and built their own economy. And then came "dis-integration." I don't know about you, but where I live some of us still allow our fate to be determined by other folks.

Collective Work and Responsibility   What a principle that is! Said another way, "Working together to take care of our responsibilities," makes it even plainer for me. There are many things we can do together to make our individual lives better, and we certainly should be doing more of those things. Why aren't we? Many of the problems we face on a daily basis are the result of our not working together – collectively – to take care of our own responsibilities. If we would simply apply this principle of the *Nguzo Saba*, we would be well ahead of the game.

Cooperative Economics   That's what this column has been about for nearly ten years now. Yes, I have written thousands of words on the subject, but even more importantly, I have also practiced what I have been preaching. Hardly a day goes by that I don't spend a dollar at a Black owned business, advocate for a Black businesses, promote a Black business, help a Black business, encourage Black on Black spending, and actually live the fourth principle of Kwanzaa. Isn't it amazing that with all of our economic and intellectual resources we celebrate *Ujamaa* much more than we practice it?

Purpose   Have you ever wondered what your purpose is on this earth? Have you wondered also about our purpose as a people, brought or maybe even sent to this foreign land from a land that has everything a person could ever need, enslaved and subjected to the worst treatment of a people in the history of the world, and surviving to become the most educated and affluent group of Black people in the world? Why did it happen? What are we suppose to do with what we learned? How are we to channel the tremendous strength of a people who would not be denied, who could not be wiped out, who multiplied, as the children of Israel multiplied, in spite such horrific treatment? What is our purpose? Is it to celebrate *Nia*, or is it to find our purpose and actualize it?

Creativity   We celebrate the genius of our people by doing what Brother Amos Wilson referred to in his book, **Afrikan-Centered Consciousness Versus The New World Order.** He said we spend a lot of time bragging about the pyramids our ancestors built, but we refuse to build some pyramids of our own to honor the work of our forebears. Our creativity in 2003 should be couched in making this place a little better for our having been here. We must create something lasting, something sustainable, for which we can be not just remembered but revered.

Faith   The final but the most important principle. Without faith in God, faith in ourselves, and faith in one another, we will not achieve the other principles, which is at the root of our problem in this country. We have been lulled into a slumber of complacency, thinking we have it made as individuals, and have devolved into a collective state of distrust for our brothers and sisters. Our faith must convince us, once and for all, that we are all we have when it's all said and done. Our faith must push us toward God and away from "The Man." Our faith must keep us grounded when things get tough and allow us to rely on one another for the uplift of us all. But we must always remember: "Faith without works is dead." What are those works? The other six principles of Kwanzaa, that's what.

As we participate in our Kwanzaa celebrations, let's commit to the **PRACTICE** of Kwanzaa – all seven principles of Kwanzaa – all year long and for the rest of our lives. Here's how. Let's designate 52 days for each principle (52 X 7 = 364 with one day off). Kwanzaa is more than a mere celebration; it is a way of life. Anything less is just hype.

Happy Kwanzaa, Brothers and Sisters – All Year Long!

Is a Flag More Important Than a Life?

With all of the uproar and righteous indignation we heard from organizations and individuals all over this country regarding the Confederate Flag controversy, and the ensuing and successful boycott of the State of South Carolina's travel and tourism industry, you would think there would be even greater outrage at what is going on in Cincinnati. Roger Owensby, a young Black man who was not even wanted by police, was beaten and choked to death by two white police officers. Timothy Thomas, a 19 year-old Black man, wanted for outstanding misdemeanor traffic violations, was shot and killed by a white police officer. More than a year has passed, and none of the three police officers has been disciplined by the city administration.

But wait, there's more. The two officers in Roger Owensby's case, one of whom said after beating the young man, "We kicked his ass," were let off by the criminal *injustice* system. A jury of two Blacks and ten whites was divided along racial lines and consequently declared "hung" (What a term!). The prosecutor, Mike Allen, refused to retry the officer who applied the illegal chokehold (they euphemistically called it a "head-wrap"), even though he personally promised the parents he would do so, because he felt he could not get a conviction. As Gil Scott-Heron once said, "It was only murder."

The officer who shot Timothy Thomas, Steven Roach, after being found not guilty, was given a job as a gun-toting police officer by the Cincinnati suburb of Evendale, as his reward for being "one of the five best police officers" on the Cincinnati police force, according to his former chief, Tom Streicher. Again, no discipline has been doled out to any of these officers.

My question is this: If we can boycott the State of South Carolina for flying a confederate flag on its State Capitol Building, not to mention the other states and cities that have been boycotted for social and political reasons, i.e., disrespect for Nelson Mandela, Pete Wilson's (former governor of California) stand against affirmative action, and the King holiday controversy in Arizona, aren't the lives of two Black men worth at least the same thing?

Cincinnati has been in the eye of the storm since April of 2001. People all over the world know what happened in this city. In the South Carolina case we had the national leadership of the N.A.A.C.P., Martin Luther King III, and many others who called for Black folks to stay out of South Carolina because of the flag issue. But where is that same outcry in response to the killing of two Black men, the overall absence of justice, and the disrespectfully blatant economic disenfranchisement that pervades the City of Cincinnati? Is a flag more important to our people than the lives of two Black men?

There is opposition to economic sanctions by some Black people, just as there was in South Carolina. While I respect their opinion, I wholeheartedly disagree with it. The rationale for their opposition is that sanctions will hurt Black people because they will lose their entry-level jobs at hotels and Black businesses will suffer because conventioneers will not be available to spend their money with them. The same rationale was given in South Carolina, but the boycott, nevertheless, went on and on and on. I understand it may even be ratcheted up because the flag now flies in a higher position than it did prior to being removed from the Capitol.

To sum it all up, and since we just celebrated Martin Luther King's birthday, I think it would be appropriate to allow our dear brother's words to reverberate. At the National Association of Black Journalists conference last year, Harry Belafonte cited the last thing Martin said to him before he left on that fateful trip to Memphis. He said they discussed the next level of the protest movement: Economic empowerment. He also said, Martin shared his concern that black people were about to integrate into a burning house.

Martin's final speech gives us great insight into what he thought about fighting for that next frontier called economic empowerment. Most of us only read the last couple of paragraphs of "I've been to the mountaintop," but we should read the entire speech. Here is an excerpt that discusses MLK's directions on the power and righteousness of withholding our dollars from those who treat us unjustly.

"...Now the other thing we'll have to do is this: Always anchor our external direct action with the power of economic withdrawal...We don't have to argue with anybody. We don't have to curse and go around acting bad with our words. We don't need any bricks and bottles, we don't need any Molotov cocktails, we just need to go around to these stores [and tell them]...our agenda calls for withdrawing economic support from you. And so, as a result of this, we are asking you tonight, to go out and tell your neighbors not to buy Coca-Cola in Memphis. Go by and tell them not to buy Sealtest milk. Tell them not to buy...Wonder Bread. Tell them not to buy Hart's bread.

As Jesse Jackson has said, up to now, only the garbage men have been feeling pain; now we must kind of redistribute the pain. But not only that, we've got to strengthen black institutions. I call upon you to take your money out of the banks downtown and deposit you money in Tri-State Bank--we want a bank-in movement in Memphis... Put your money there. You have six or seven black insurance companies in Memphis. Take out your insurance there. We want to have an insurance-in; now there are some practical things we can do. We can begin the process of building a greater economic base. And at the same time, we are putting pressure where it really hurts. I ask you to follow through here."

A flag or a life? You decide.

Another "Victory" for Black Folks?

After receiving an e-mail regarding the Danny Glover – MCI affair, I just had to write about it. The e-mail stated: "Urgent Alert - We Celebrate a Victory." A message from MCI to the TransAfrica Forum Board Chairperson stated, "Our contract with Danny Glover runs through January 2004 and we intend to honor our contract." The e-mail went on to say, "This morning we confirmed that the message above is the official position of MCI. To put it in another way, we won!" I then sent an e-mail asking the sender, "What did we win?"

A boycott against MCI was threatened by Joe Scarborough for casting Danny Glover in its commercials. Additionally, a group of Black folks threatened to retaliate against MCI if Glover was let go. Subsequently, Scarborough announced on his show that his pressure and his threat of a boycott of MCI had worked. He said they had officially cancelled Glover's appearances in their commercials; MCI also said Glover would be paid for the balance of his contract.

That announcement came after the Black group served notice that they would drop MCI if Glover were let go and not allowed to speak his mind on issues such as racism, George Bush's policies, and Fidel Castro. I posed the question at that time, "Who will win this latest battle?"

I thought Scarborough had won, that is, until I saw the e-mail saying "we" had won. Do you want to know who really won? MCI won. As usual, as in the battles with Pepsi, CompUSA, Revlon, and the long list of infamous transgressors against Black people, we call for apologies; we start "call-in campaigns," or another *let's-show-them-how-much-money-we-spend-on-their-products* campaign. The offending company comes up with an "act" of contrition, mounts a public relations campaign, or makes appropriate apologies, all the while cutting a deal on the side with folks like Scarborough and O'Reilly to keep them happy. So, I ask again, "What did WE win?"

Remember Fire Marshall Bill on the show, In Living Color? He would scream, "Let me tell you something!" While we are busy trying to prove how much money we spend with those who offend us, we could be redirecting a great deal of that money toward ourselves. All CompUSA had to do was apologize and hand out 10% off coupons, and we ran right back to them, instead of supporting a Black owned computer company. Hotels that offend us get bad "Report Cards" from the N.A.A.C.P.; so we end up staying in the ones that get C's rather than D's, instead of getting more Black owned hotels. MCI did its thing and now we're screaming victory because they said, "...we will honor our contract..." with Danny Glover. (The last time I checked, folks were legally bound to "honor" contracts. Is that still the law in this country?)

Let me tell you something else! Why don't we all just switch our telephone service to MATAH Direct? What's that? It's a long distance service that has the best rate and gives money back to Black folks through the MATAH Network, the only Black owned and operated distribution channel in the country. You want to win? Redirect your money rather than give it back to those who offend you. You want to win? Support companies that support you, not those that merely hire a Black actor to do a commercial. You want to win? You want to DO something? You want to take some action rather than declare empty victories? Switch to MATAH Direct. That will really prove to MCI and everyone else that we are serious about our economic freedom and that it's not even about them; it's about us. Apologies are highly overrated.

And while you are at it, why not purchase some other products, all made by your brothers and sisters, from the MATAH Network? You are buying the same products from someone anyway, and using them in your homes everyday. Switch. Buy some Grenada Nutmeg Oil from MATAH, and start relieving pain externally rather than popping so many pills and destroying your kidneys and liver. Switch.

That e-mail I cited went on to say, "This effort in support of Danny [Glover] is a reminder that in a society that professes democratic values, we all have a right, and in fact a responsibility, to express our views and be heard." That is so right, and that's exactly what I am doing. I have a responsibility to my people not only to talk about economic freedom but also to show how it is obtained. That's the real victory we should be seeking; and the latest melodrama featuring MCI will not take us there. As a mater of fact, by the time you read this article that tempest in a teapot will be long forgotten. As Justin Wilson used to say, I guarantee it."

Another victory for Black folks? I don't think so. It's just another in a long and exasperating line of shortsighted solutions to long-term problems. Danny Glover, of whom I am a big fan and admirer, will be just fine. He will continue to speak out on relevant issues regardless of what MCI or anyone else does; he's a man, a strong Black man, and he is not afraid to stand up for that. We cannot afford to allow the threat of a Joe Scarborough and a resulting capitulation by MCI to get us off track and make us think we have a victory. This is a money issue; let's deal with it with our money. Switch. Then we can claim the real victory.

The New Pepsi Challenge

Russell Simmons called for a boycott of Pepsi Cola because Pepsi *dissed* Hip Hop personality, Ludacris, by pulling his appearance in Pepsi commercials and opting for the Osborne's. You may also remember that Fox News' Bill O'Reilly used one of his tirades to pillory Pepsi for using Ludacris and said he would not buy Pepsi until they removed Ludacris from their advertisements. Looks like Pepsi is in a no-win situation, doesn't it? Will O'Reilly get his way, or will Pepsi bend to Russell Simmons' request for an apology and a reinstatement of Ludacris in its commercials? The plot thickens.

It was ironic that just before BET News did the story that featured Simmons at the press conference announcing a boycott of Pepsi Cola, BET (Owned by Viacom) ran a Pepsi commercial featuring three or four young, Black, hip-hop-looking brothers, dancing as usual to a funky beat and drinking Pepsi. At the end of the commercial, one of the young brothers said, "You know how we do." As I watched this strange juxtaposition, I wondered if the airing of that particular commercial was pre-planned for that particular time.

Here's my take on this. Russell Simmons has demonstrated his ability to rally the troops in the Hip Hop world, especially around social and political issues. He is one of the most articulate and tenacious brothers on the scene today. He is also a millionaire many times over, having done tremendously well in his own personal economic empowerment. It will be interesting to watch, for instance, how much money Pepsi dangles in the faces of young brothers and sisters, such as those in the commercial to which I referred, to get them to repel Simmons' message.

As to the boycott of Pepsi, I have no problem with it. I do have a problem with Simmons calling for a boycott of Pepsi, which simply says, "Don't buy Pepsi Cola," but does not say, "Here's what you can buy instead. And guess what, we have a Black owned alternative." Russell may not know it, but there is a Black owned soft drink company in Elyria, Ohio (near

Cleveland), called New World Beverages, started by Larry Jones, that we could be pushing our youth (and our adults) to support as Hip Hop withdraws its dollars from Pepsi.

I also have a problem with calling economic sanctions and settling for social solutions, e.g., apologies, as remedies to the issues at hand. We have seen it many times, and it makes no sense to stop spending your money with others, and then as soon as they apologize for their transgressions we return with our money in hand to continue building their wealth.

Is it reasonable for Black folks to concede and go back to business as usual after we get an apology? Is it reasonable for us to call a boycott against Pepsi and tell them it will be lifted if they re-insert a rap artist into one of their commercials? I am sure Ludacris has more than enough money and does not need Pepsi's. (But I do understand that a little more won't hurt him.) I am also certain that most Black people can do without Pepsi and many other products, and have the ability to mix and sell soft drinks, as well as hundreds of other products.

So, I say to Brother Russell Simmons, please tell the Hip Hop community to take the money they withdraw from Pepsi and spend it with Black owned businesses. Tell them to emulate you and other young entrepreneurs who made millions by owning businesses. Tell them to invest in the Black owned soft drink company. Tell them that our economic freedom is worth much more than mere apologies and empty platitudes. Tell them, as they come to the Hip Hop Summit in Atlanta, to pool their money and build an economic foundation, in addition to using their voting power. Tell them, Brother Russell; tell them.

To the young brother in the Pepsi commercial who said, "You know how we do," I say to you, "*They* know how *you* do." They know that you will buy their products and compete to be in their commercials, even in spite of what Russell Simmons is asking you to do. They know that your group spends millions per year on soft drinks and other items they make and sell. They know that you, young brother, are a threat to their sales if you are an educated consumer, and if you are on the road to your own collective economic empowerment via business ownership. They also know that if you geared more of your interests toward being producers rather than consumers, they could no longer just use you to dance in their commercials. Who knows? They might even offer you a few distributorships.

To Pepsi, I say, I don't envy your position. O'Reilly obviously carries a lot of weight. After all, he scared you into taking Ludacris out of your commercials by threatening a boycott. Now Russell Simmons has called a boycott, and he has a great deal of clout too. This looks like a new Pepsi Challenge to me.

The Shortest Boycott in History

Well, that didn't last long, did it? What ever happened to the boycott of Pepsi Cola called by Russell Simmons on behalf of the Hip Hop Action Network? Since it was only a short while ago, I am sure you remember the reason for the boycott and the subsequent "deal" made by Simmons, Pepsi, and Ludacris. The deal called for three million dollars to go to the Ludacris Foundation in exchange for an end to the boycott that, according to unofficial online polls, would not have been supported by a majority of Pepsi drinkers due to "brand loyalty and disagreement with Simmons" on the issue. Where are the Montgomery boycotters when you need them?

Some say Simmons sold out Hip Hop for $3 million. Some say Simmons used the threat of boycott to leverage support for his own venture into the lucrative soft drink industry. Others say Simmons was taking a stand in support of those he represents: the Hip Hop generation. I don't know what Simmons' motivation was, so I will not comment on that. I do know that sometimes the tactics we use to achieve "economic progress" versus what we receive in return for our threats and saber-rattling make little sense.

I can't say it better than someone named "B Easy," who wrote an outstanding response to the Pepsi boycott issue on the www.sohh.com website, a top-of-the-line Hip Hop site, from what I could see.

B Easy says, "We didn't solve the problem by getting money. Solving the problem is boycotting Pepsi and letting them financially feel what happens when you disrespect Hip-Hop. This is about integrity and respect and you can't put a price tag on it."

Makes "cents" to me, B Easy. Tell us more.

"Imagine how the Hip-Hop community could have been galvanized as a force to be reckoned with. How American youth could have felt the power of their dollar and their voice," he continued.

Hmmm. I see what you mean, B Easy.

"Instead [of our seizing this opportunity]," B Easy continued, "the Hip-Hop community sits once again as lame consumers ready for any corporation to market to us any way they see fit. *(Hey guys... just add a Hip-Hop soundtrack to the commercial... they'll buy it.)*"

That's what I've been telling our people for years now. What are your final thoughts on this issue, B Easy?

"The only one to benefit from this boycott fiasco was Pepsi, Rush Arts, and whoever's down with the Ludacris Foundation. Pepsi gained our silence. And Russell gained a measly $3 million for Rush Arts to add programs to schools," B Easy lamented.

As I said, I can't put it any better than that.

We have been down this boycott road before, many times. There are several boycotts in force right now, the one against the City of Cincinnati included. What amazes me is the reaction, even from some of our brothers and sisters, when Black people call for a boycott. White folks say it's not the right thing to do; the Mayor of Cincinnati called the boycotters, "Economic Terrorists." Some Black folks got on that same bandwagon and rebuked their own people for using a last resort tactic to address wrongs committed against us.

But check this out. White folks call for boycotts all the time and nothing is said. France has lost, at last count, some $300 million in business because of a boycott called by white talk show hosts and others. A boycott of Pepsi was called by Bill O'Reilly before Simmons did so. Another "conservative" talk show host, Joe Scarborough, has suggested a boycott be instituted against MCI because Danny Glover "called George Bush a racist."

It's a veritable boycott feast when it comes to complaints by whites. Let Blacks call a boycott and all hell breaks loose! Thus, we have the shortest boycott in history in Simmons' boycott of Pepsi Cola, because white folks and some Blacks did not approve of it, and finally, the *coup de grace*, the finishing blow: Pepsi promised to pay a little money.

A group of outraged Black folks in Florida are now calling for a boycott of orange juice, amusement parks, and other Florida products because some 12,800 high school seniors are not likely to graduate. The reason: a culturally biased test.

When a Black State Senator was interviewed on a television news show, the white host said first off, "I don't think a boycott is the way to solve the problem." Don't you get tired of that kind of double standard?

Boycotts are no fun for either side, and it's nice when they are short, as long as the offended constituents come away with a real benefit, not only for one or two persons, but also for the widest range of those offended. You know, the ones who were willing to make the sacrifice.

While the Pepsi boycott was probably the shortest in history it would not have been so bad if there were something to show for it right now other than a *promise* of $3 million, over a three-year period from Pepsi. I have to go with you on your assessment, B Easy. You should consider writing a column on economic empowerment. Know what I'm sayin', dog?

What would we do without white folks?

Remember the e-mail that posed the question, "What would this world be without Black people?" It was really a history lesson on all of the things Black people invented, and suggested that if Black people had not been here our traffic lights would disappear, many of the machines we depend upon would not work, and many other conveniences we enjoy everyday would not be here. It was a nice reminder of the importance of Black people to this country. However, even though Black people invented a great deal of the items we use today, with a few exceptions of course, they could not get patents on their inventions, or they were simply *relieved* of them by white people.

Now, let's take a look at what Black people would do without white people. First of all, some of us would simply throw up our hands in exasperation and call it a day – no, we would call it a life. Some of us would feel so bad, so lonely, so dispossessed, so depressed that we would not know where to turn. "What are we going to do now?" some would ask. Others would lament the loss of all of those stores and all of those products and services they are so use to purchasing. Some would cry, "Where will we buy our clothing, our cars, our houses, and our food?" "For whom will we work? What about our jobs?" Others would just go insane trying to figure out how they would get their banquet tables sold for their annual dinners and soirees. What a sad day it would be for many Black folks.

On the other hand, rather than complaining and crying, some Black folks would immediately get to work on those issues. Some would say, "Let's do for ourselves." Others would rally the people and call for new businesses and new products and services and efforts to support our people. Some Black folks would even have the audacity to think they really could run major corporations, industrial farms, airports, states, and even this country. But then, what other choice would we have?

What would you do without white people? Would you suffer from a lack of the essentials of life? Would you wilt under the pressure of having to figure out this thing called life all by yourself? Could you successfully navigate through the swirling waters of life's uncertainties? Could you survive? Marcus Garvey told us we are living on borrowed goods, and we must get something of our own. So instead of us wondering what this country would do without Black people, just imagine what we would do without white people.

Suppose they closed all of their supermarkets to us, could we feed ourselves? Imagine them denying us the right to use their banks, would we pool more of our money and start more Black banks? If whites said we would no longer be allowed in their department stores, would we create our own? You get the picture I am sure. What would we do?

It's nice to call for "Black-Out Days" and "Stay Home From Work Days" and "Don't Spend Any Money Days," and all of the rest of the Black absentee efforts we hear about. But what would we do if there were a "White Out Day?" Maybe even a "White Out Month?" Would we panic? Or, would we finally start doing more for ourselves? Would we finally start preparing an economic future for our children, the same way other groups in this country are doing for their children?

You know, sometimes I wish it were so. Maybe if white folks stopped doing what they are doing for us, we'd be more inclined to do more for ourselves. Maybe if they would back off a bit and we would step it up a bit, better relationships would exist between the two groups, because there would be more reciprocity, more leverage available to Black people, and a greater likelihood of positive responses from white folks when we really do need their support. Maybe, if Black people would get our economic act together by recycling our dollars, supporting our own businesses, and building income-producing infrastructure, maybe whites would be knocking on our doors asking to play ball with us.

What would we do without white folks? The same thing our fathers and mothers did before integration; that's what we'd do. We would develop economic enclaves, second to none in this country, by committing to the principle of self-reliance.

Yo! Let's keep it real.

Did you notice the article in the Wall Street Journal (July 2003) that discussed the millions of dollars being made by a certain brand of liquor because a famous rap artist mentioned it in his rap song? Here's a quote from that article: "Listening to Busta Rhymes's hit song 'Pass the Courvoisier,' Anne-Sophie Louvet cringes at the thumping rap music and says she doesn't understand the lyrics. But what the shy French grape-grower does understand is she owes a debt of gratitude to American hip-hop artists." My first thought was, "I wonder how much Busta's contract is worth for such a fantastic deal for that brand."

I also thought about Run DMC, and Grand Puba, and Heavy "D" who did the same thing for brands like Adidas, Hilfiger, and Fila, respectively. And what about all of those videos with Bentleys and Escalades in them? Man, those rap artists must be making a killing, I thought. But are they?

Then there is our man Kobe Bryant. Yeah, he was making a lot of jack for Nike but when he got in trouble, Nike *swooshed* as far away from Kobe as they could get. Seen Kobe eat any Big Macs or *obey his thirst* lately? Here is a brother who spent $4 million on an "apology ring;" I just have to believe a Black salesperson got the commission on that rock. You think?

Would you like to venture a guess on how much money Black rap artists, athletes, and entertainers have garnered for companies owned by everyone but Black folks? How is "keepin' it real" related to creating even more wealth for everyone else while, at the same time, denying your own brothers and sisters the same opportunity to reap the economic benefits of your success?

Where I live, Black professional athletes come to town and buy million-dollar homes. When they leave they sell those homes. Who do they use as their real estate agents? You know who they are. Well, at least you know who they aren't. If these athletes and entertainers used Black agents to purchase their homes, not to mention hiring Black business agents as well, the Black economy would be in much better shape. If all those "homeboys" who tell us "How I'm Livin'" by showing off their fine cribs with their chinchilla bedspreads, game rooms, their gold and platinum "grills," and all five or ten of their cars, if they are really keepin' it real, they are at least seeking out Black folks with whom to do business.

After all, if you rappers, et al, want to spend your money on things that generate commissions, like purple diamonds and "cribs," please consider using Black salespersons, Black agents, and Black accountants, attorneys, etc. Don't be another O.J., who didn't figure out how much he needed his own people until he found himself in deep trouble. If you want to keep it real, you have to understand the real world, not just what happens on your block or in the "hood." And then, you must act upon that knowledge by doing something more than merely enriching others through your desire for their baubles, bangles, and beads.

I hope Busta Rhymes read the Wall Street Journal story, and I especially hope he noticed the attitude of the lady who was so happy about the increased sales of Courvoisier; "Anne-Sophie Louvet 'cringes' at the thumping rap music..." She couldn't care less about his music, but she loves the money he's making for her.

Keepin' it real? Yes, that's what those to whom we give our money are doing. Their reality is business, commerce, and being on the supply side of things rather than always on the demand side. We demand and they certainly do supply. Just look at BET now. Despite the fact that its programming wasn't too much better before Viacom bought it, BET is now a 24/7 video playin', booty-shakin', gangsta rappin', playa pimpin', comic viewin', how I'm livin', basketball rim rattlin', network, with a little gospel music on the side, that is only interested in getting two things: Black folks' money and our full attention. And if you switch to Viacom's other network, MTV, you'll see much the same thing, more geared toward whites with a little Snoop Dogg "hissel, dissel" thrown in to add more flava.

I know, I know, I am not up on the latest lingo, but at the end of the day, the real deal is this. Corporations that really don't care about us are exploiting us, and we allow it to happen with impunity. Black rap artists, entertainers, and athletes control billions of dollars, not to mention what their supporters spend for the products they endorse. If we are going to keep it real, we must be smarter than we have been. Not just those three groups but all of us, no matter how much or how little money we have, all of us must change the way we do business – with others and with ourselves.

No offense to the brothers and sisters who are doing well and making millions; I rejoice in your prosperity. But, use a little sense with your dollars. At every available opportunity, let your dollars work to the benefit of your people for a change. That's what keepin' it real is all about in this country.

Is the "Black Economy" an Oxymoron?

Although the dictionary calls it *archaic,* the "management of a household" is one of the definitions listed for the word "economy." Another definition is "a saving or attempt to reduce expenditure." Yet another is "a system of interacting elements, especially when seen as being harmonious." And still another definition for economy has to do with "the production and consumption of goods and services of a community regarded as a whole." As I look at those descriptions of an economy, only the last one partially applies to Black Americans collectively, and that's the "consumption" part.

The U.S. Census 2002 statistics for businesses will be available in the third quarter of 2004. Every five years a survey is done to determine how many businesses there are in this country, who owns them, how many persons they employ, and what their annual revenues are. The figures for 1997, while lauded for the increase in the number of Black owned businesses, revealed decreasing revenues for Black businesses, relatively few employees, and a vast majority of them in the service industry.

The 1997 census revealed total receipts for Black owned businesses to be a little more than $71 billion which, when juxtaposed against an aggregate disposable income during that period of approximately $400 billion, illuminated a dearth of business ownership and a glut of consumer spending. Other statistics disclosed low savings among African Americans and a grossly disparate median income and net worth when compared to other ethnic groups.

As we enter 2004, we already know our disposable income is more than $700 billion and forecasted by the Selig Center to exceed $900 billion in 2008. The 2002 U.S. Census data will likely reveal a bump in business receipts, but the total will probably still be less than $100 billion. Median income, net worth, and savings disparities will likely stay the same and the mythical Black economy will trudge along like a brand new, twelve-cylinder, state-of-the-art, top-of-the-line automobile running on only six of those cylinders. We will definitely look good, but we sure won't be *doing good*

That's essentially how we are as individuals. We look real good, but when it comes to how we are doing, that's another story. Maybe one of the reasons for that can be found in some of our consumption statistics. The Selig Center reports that Blacks spend more on telephone services, children's apparel, electricity and natural gas, and guess what, footwear.

I could do an entire commentary on those expenditures, especially the shoes, but it's fairly obvious what impact they have on our households and our disposable income. We have multiple cell phones, we buy the latest fashions for our children, we keep our homes and apartments very warm, and we have the latest gym shoes, three or four pairs of them.

In his book, Black Bourgeoisie, E. Franklin Frazier stated, "[Black] business enterprises come within the definition of small businesses; in fact, they fall within the lowest category of small businesses. When the first study was made of Negro business in 1898, it was found that the average capital investment for the 1,906 businesses giving information amounted to only $4,600.00. When the latest study of Negro business was made in 1944, it was revealed that the average volume of business of the 3,866 Negro businesses in twelve cities was only $3,260.00."

In 1997, the Census data indicated Black-owned firms' average receipts were $86,500 compared to $891,000 for all firms. Was Frazier correct in his assessment of what he deemed as the *mythical* nature of Black business? Was he correct when he suggested the Black middle class was also a myth? He made a lot of folks angry when he wrote, "Negro business ... has no significance in the American economy, [and] has become a social myth embodying the aspirations of this [Black Bourgeoisie] class." As we look at today's statistics we must reconsider Franklin's position, because the numbers reflect the same conditions he discussed in 1957.

Frazier was decrying our definition of "middle class" as one that embodies high incomes and material possessions, e.g., the mink coats, diamonds, and Cadillacs to which he referred, instead of business ownership and economic growth. While we consider the trappings of the good life as "wealth," sold to us by everyone else of course, we are mired in a dysfunctional – and maybe even *mythical* -- Black economy.

Much of our economic pain in the 21st century is the direct result of our failure to develop a real Black economy, our failure to take care of our "household," our failure to save more of our money, our failure to work harmoniously, and our failure to produce goods and services commensurate with our percentage of population and income. Additionally, we have failed to work together for the uplift of the masses, sharing our resources with one another and helping one another as we make our way individually.

The so-called "middle-class" Blacks have distanced themselves, not necessarily physically but mentally, and as Frazier wrote, they have been obsessed "with the struggle for status." And many of the less fortunate among our people spend too much time being jealous and envious of our brothers and sisters who have achieved at higher levels. The result is an oxymoronic Black economy.

Section VII

It's the Doing That Counts

*"Be ye doers of the word and not hearers only, deceiving
your own selves"*
James 1:22

*"There are [Blacks] who are willing to worship the
pyramids of 4,000 years ago but will not build pyramids
in the present so their children may see what they left
behind as well." We have a leadership who rallies the
people to look at past glories but leave their children
neglected; who will make great analytical and oratorical
dissertations on the inadequacies of Eurocentric education
and yet will not contribute one penny of their money or
their time to the construction of their own schools."*
**Dr. Amos Wilson, *Afrikan Centered Consciousness
Versus the New World Order***

Hearing But Not Doing

On June 24, 2003 Ken Bridges would have been 54 years of age; he was killed on October 11, 2002, by a sniper in Virginia. Brother Ken, co-founder of the MATAH Network, was cut down in the prime of his life, as he was On His Way To Freedom. His earthly flame was extinguished as he reveled in his latest and greatest business accomplishment, on his way to economic freedom, not leaving his people behind but taking them with him. Ken died as a result of some very strange circumstances and twists of fate. His demise reminds me of other brothers – strong brothers who loved their people and tried desperately to lead them to economic freedom.

Booker T. Washington died 88 years ago, at age 58, after he contracted some strange affliction. Marcus Garvey passed away 63 years ago, at the age of 53; certainly doing everything he could to lead his beloved people to economic freedom. Malcolm X died 38 years ago, barely 40 years old, after he had made a shift in his thinking and demonstrated his willingness to resist the continued psychological enslavement of his people. Martin Luther King was assassinated 35 years ago, at the tender age of 39, when he decided to take the path to economic freedom and show us the way as well. All of these strong Black men, and others of course, died on their way to freedom, but they left a legacy here for us: Their words. Just consider what Amos Wilson, dead at 53, left us in his 850-page volume, **Blueprint for Black Power**.

They repeatedly told us what to do, how to do it, when to do it, and even why we should do it. They talked until their voices rasped with pain; they wrote down their words for us to see and to ponder; they did radio and television interviews for posterity; and their lives have been chronicled biographically and autobiographically for the world to review. Did we hear them? Did we follow their instructions? Were we merely hearers of their words rather than doers of their words?

It seems we wait for years before we even appreciate the words of our fallen leaders, especially those who promoted economic empowerment. Some of us are just now recognizing what Booker T. was trying to accomplish with his National Negro Business League. Marcus Garvey was vilified by some his own people, the elitist Negroes of his time, but now we hear so many of us invoking the name of Garvey, and saying his strategy was the right thing to do. MLK is probably the most quoted of the freedom fighters, although many of those who quote him have reduced his life and mission to two one-liners. (It's funny how they never quote his statements on economic empowerment) The Biography of Malcolm X has now become a household item, and today millions parrot his words.

We certainly heard the words of these giants, but did we heed them? The answer: a resounding "No." Yes, we celebrate their birthdays and get real excited about their words. Take the MLK holiday, for example. We gather by the thousands, hear nice speeches, and then leave without even collecting one dollar from each person in attendance – to start <u>doing</u> some of the things MLK advocated.

Ken Bridges, yet another strong Black man who left us much too soon, also left his words. It has been less than a year since his departure. Are we going to wait 30 or 40 years to realize that he was also a giant, that his message was vital to our survival in this country, and that he loved us so much that he devoted his life to help lead us to economic freedom? I certainly hope not. We cannot afford to keep wasting the lives of our warriors, reducing them to a few sound bites and quotes. Are we going to do what he told us?

We have not done what Booker said; we have failed to follow the prescription Marcus left us; we have squandered Malcolm's directions; we've not followed Amos' Blueprint; most of our politicians don't have one Maynard Jackson vertebrae, much less an entire backbone; Martin's words still ring loud and clear; but our actions are far from reciprocal.

Here are some of Ken Bridges' words:

"Our ability to obtain our true freedom is directly related to the level of consciousness that we have and continue to have... and our willingness to redirect a greater portion of our consumption spending toward ourselves."

"We can shape our condition, including true freedom, if only we would think that we can be successful in our quest for freedom."

"As of today the concept of white supremacy has been eliminated from my focus other than to point out that it exists in the minds of most people of African descent, and raising our consciousness is the only way to eliminate it."

"Let's go get our freedom, brothers and sisters!"

"The non-MATAH, the 'need-to-grows', will continue to make buttprints instead of footprints when it comes time to run for freedom."

"Our problem is that we have been programmed to hate everything African about ourselves."

Want more? Do what Ken asked us to do as a critical part of our quest for economic freedom. Get involved with the MATAH Network and don't just read Brother Ken's words; do what he says. And while you're at it, make a commitment to purchase some of the products, all made by your brothers and sisters across the country, from MATAH. Did you know that Black people spend nearly $1 billion per year on laundry detergent alone? Did you know that you can buy a Black-manufactured laundry detergent from MATAH? So, whom are you paying to wash your clothes?

We must be doers, not just hearers. Ken, and our many ancestors that preceded him, will be proud.

Forty years [after his death], it's easy to quote Malcolm and put him on a postage stamp—now that we've killed him. Martin Luther King Jr. was ultimately abandoned by the civil rights establishment for his stand against poverty and war. Today he has a national holiday, and even conservatives have to honor him—now that he's no longer here to shame them. Ditto for the Black Panthers. Everybody says their dad wore a black beret—now that J. Edgar Hoover isn't alive to tap their phones.

Progressive vision almost always lacks mass appeal. While possibly enjoying a bit of rebellious sheen, prophetic insight is decidedly uncool; it involves the sacrifice of family livelihoods, the sullying of reputations, and, at worst, death. Only the afterglow is romantic. Everybody says they would have fought with Nat Turner—now that none of us are slaves.

Excerpt from: **Compa$$ionate Capitali$m**, *by* **Ta-Nehisi Coates**
January 7 - 13, 2004
Village Voice

Revolution or Evolution?

You would think that since the end of slavery and through the ensuing years Black people in this country would be further along in our economic evolution than we are today. You would think there would be no need for the economic empowerment messages that other columnists and I write on a regular basis. You would think Black children of the 21st century would be sitting pretty right about now, considering all we have been taught and all we have been through in our economic struggle since we were fired – I mean freed.

As I read the powerful words of our ancestors, both men and women, I hear the very same messages coming from them over 100 years ago. I hear them saying to our people who lived during that time, "Let's build our own businesses," "Seek for ourselves," "Save our money and work together." "Be producers." It goes on and on.

The question that arises is: Why haven't we heeded the messages of our ancestors? We are still trying to implement some of the economic principles they lived by many years ago. They had far fewer resources than we have today; they were quite limited when it came to transportation, communication, and education. Yet they developed and followed principles that if practiced today would propel us to true freedom.

A collective effort that should have been a natural evolution from generation to generation, among Black people, has now become a much-needed revolution. Don't get me wrong. Revolution is all right, but our economic destiny should not be in such bad shape that it now takes a revolution to correct it. Our economic demise is the direct result of a lack of evolution. If we had followed the natural path of economic growth for Black people in this country, from the early 1900's until today, we would have evolved into one of the most powerful groups in the entire world. All we have instead is the dubious recognition of having an annual income that, if we were a country, would make us the tenth largest in the world.

Revolution or evolution? We always seem to gravitate toward revolution – and, admittedly, in many cases it has been very necessary. But as far as economic empowerment is concerned, we now need a *revolution* simply because we failed to have an *evolution.*

There was a time, Dr. John Sibley Butler's "Economic Detour" premise notwithstanding, when Black businesses flourished, even without access to the general market. Entities such as the National Negro Business League, the Universal Negro Improvement Association, and other Black business organizations not only helped create new entrepreneurs, they also stimulated a Black business psyche that encouraged our people to support one another, to do for ourselves, and to work for our economic self-sufficiency. We were producers and landowners; we developed expertise in all fields of endeavor; we created jobs for ourselves; and we circulated our dollars among our own people.

I hear so much talk about an "economic revolution" for Black people. Unfortunately, "revolution" in this case deals more with "revolving" than it does with "revolt." It simply means that we are getting back to a point where we were before, as in a circle. Are we running in circles when it comes to economic empowerment? I truly hope not. Economic revolution must be conceived and grounded in "overturning" our situation, not "returning" to it.

I know we all understand that Black business is not a revolutionary idea. We should also understand that it is, in fact, an evolutionary construct that moves from an infancy stage through various growth periods and cycles, and eventually becomes a Johnson Publishing Company. The evolution of Black business development should have moved from the models we saw in Durham, North Carolina, Tulsa, Oklahoma, and other cities, to a $500 billion dollar business segment rather than the current $90 billion segment we have today.

Revolution or evolution? Because we walked away from our brothers' and sisters' businesses when we "won" integration, the proper evolution of our businesses was stymied and, in some cases, halted. Now we are faced with starting an economic revolution. We must transform and transport our minds to a place where some of us do not even want to be, despite the fact that we were all there once before. We already had what we are now trying to win back. Evolution would have maintained what we had, but now it will take revolutionary thinking and revolutionary action to cause us to work together for true economic and psychological freedom.

Revolution or evolution? We can have both. We should have both. Strong Black owned businesses still exist in this country, despite the buyouts we have witnessed in recent years. Evolution is paramount to their existence. Revolution is necessary for those of us who are consumers, small business owners, and advocates. We must change the way we do business. Specifically, we must change the way we spend our money. If we have revolution and evolution, Black people will make the progress we must make in order to gain a much higher level of economic freedom.

NOBCChE – The Secret is Out

When Chris Kinard and Dr. Robert Ford called me about coming to the annual conference of the National Organization for the Professional Advancement of Black Chemists and Chemical Engineers (NOBCChE - pronounced No-be-shay), my first thought was, why? Chemistry? Engineering? "Oh nooo," I thought, "I don't know anything about Chemistry and Engineering." My tentativeness was allayed when they asked me to lead a panel discussion on entrepreneurship. You know me; just say the magic word, "Entrepreneurship" and I'm there. Man, am I glad I accepted that assignment!

The 30th Annual Conference of NOBCChE was held in Indianapolis, Indiana, April 13-18, 2003. This year's theme was "Advancing Science & Technology through Innovation and Creativity." It was an absolute pleasure to see so many Black scientists, engineers, chemists, university professors, and businesspersons on hand. It was especially pleasing to see 100 or so college students from across the country as well as the high school students in attendance. But, back to why I was there.

I served as moderator for NOBCChE's Entrepreneurial Forum, whose theme was "Creating New Opportunities." Considering that the U.S. chemical industry is being negatively affected by growing competition from emerging global markets, it is incumbent upon workers to consider other options. Certainly entrepreneurship is one of those options, and NOBCChE brought a strong, enlightened, and experienced panel together to impart much-needed information on how to get started.

There was the *energetic* entrepreneur, Brenda Truedell-Bell, owner of Khem-Sci Research and Development Company, Indianapolis; the *insightful* entrepreneur, John Thompson, Thompson Distributing Company, Indianapolis; the *innovative* husband and wife entrepreneurs, Andre and Sherry Warren, owners of WLS Enterprises, Inc. Indianapolis; the *young and relentless* entrepreneur, Dr. Barry Self, Southeastern Dental Research Corporation, Port Allen, Louisiana; and then there was the *trailblazing* and *tenacious* entrepreneur, William "Bill" Mays, Owner, Mays Chemical Company, Indianapolis. What an august group of entrepreneurs!

In addition to being very intelligent (What else did we expect? After all, they are Chemists and MBA's), this was a group of entrepreneurs *par excellence* who were ready, willing, and quite able to share information on the opportunities and challenges of business ownership.

Brenda Truedell-Bell, after working for Eli Lilly as that company's first Black female Chemist and obtaining four patents on antibiotics, started a research company that specializes in nutraceuticals for children's health. She gives credit to Dr. George Washington Carver, for her inspiration and guidance. Brenda is a dynamo, always pressing forward in her business and helping children at the same time.

John Thompson, the pragmatic, bottom-line oriented, go-getter, is in the business of buying businesses. He shared his experience and expertise in an area of entrepreneurship that is too often overlooked by Blacks in our quest of business ownership. John's practical advice on how and when to purchase an existing business surely gave the attendees something to think about as they explore business options.

The tag-team of Andre and Sherry Warren, relatively new entrepreneurs, disclosed some of their "secrets" on *How to Succeed in Business and Stay Married*. They talked about one of the principles of what our ancestors called Ma'at: Balance. Parents of a young daughter, two full-time careers, and a brand new business are enough to make the best of us lose it from time to time. But the Warren's, while they do face challenges, have figured out how to take full advantage of their individual talents and strengths, and how to balance the many tasks they face on a daily basis. They designated a special corner in their 19,000 square foot warehouse as their daughter's homework and play area, setting the stage for another young entrepreneur a few years from now.

The young Dr. Barry Self was quite impressive. He definitely has a grasp on how to get things done. Having listened to and followed his father's advice, Barry has done a tremendous job working on his vision. He shared his trials and his victories, and he provided examples of how determination and commitment to a sound, well-researched, and well-planned business concept will lead to success. Barry could have given up and taken a more comfortable road in life, but he chose the entrepreneurial path instead and is making the best of it.

Finally, the venerable William G. Mays, Chemistry major, MBA in Marketing and Finance, having worked for Procter and Gamble and Eli Lilly before starting Mays Chemical Company over 20 years ago, willingly shared his wisdom with the attendees. What impressed me most were his candor regarding his business and his understanding of the oft-quoted Luke 12:48, "To whom much is given, much is required."

Mr. Mays extolled the virtues of striving for the top, where there is "plenty of room," unlike at the bottom, where "it's very crowded." He warned future entrepreneurs about failing to prepare, educationally, emotionally, and financially for the venture at hand. He substantiated what I tell my students, "Nobody is going to finance your dream for you." You must bring some of your own money to the table.

Mays shared insights on political involvement by entrepreneurs, saying business and politics are "different sides of the same coin." He also discussed the importance of providing a working atmosphere in his company that inspires and supports entrepreneurial ventures by his employees, which was validated by Andre Warren, who currently works for Mays Chemical, and John Thompson, who used to work there. Bill Mays is a Black businessman with a commitment to help others. What a combination for our collective success.

Thanks, NOBCChE, for your progressiveness and for inviting me to be a part of such an outstanding conference. Maybe I will see you in San Diego in 2004. (For more information, see www.nobcche.org)

Black Talk Radio – Is it talk without action?

As we await the FCC public hearing on further deregulation within the radio and television industries, and what move Michael Powell will make this time, I wonder what will happen to Black radio, specifically Black Talk Radio. You may not know it, but there are only a few Black owned radio stations that can be characterized as "Talk" Stations. One is right here in Cincinnati, Ohio, WDBZ, The Buzz, which carries our show, Blackonomics, each week. Considering the dearth of Black Talk Radio throughout this country, what should we do, if anything, in light of the impending expansion of a playing field already filled with heavy hitting media giants?

In light of its stark resemblance to an oligopoly, where a handful of owners virtually control the airwaves, radio in general and talk radio specifically should be at the top of the list when it comes to empowering Black people. Sharing ideas and establishing relationships through which to build and leave an economic legacy for our children and their children, could be greatly enhanced via Black talk radio. The question is: Do we use it for that purpose?

As we assess the current landscape, we see one company that owns 1200 radio stations, some of which are piping in music 24/7 to Black youth. We also have other conglomerates saturating the airwaves with white talk show hosts who could condense all of their shows to one because they all say the same things. You know what I mean, the political rhetoric abounds throughout the day; it's like the hosts all read the same notes and rehearse their lines together. You know exactly what you are going to get from them, but then again, who's in control of the media?

As far as Black talk radio is concerned, we do get a variety of opinions. But unlike the rallying cries I hear on those "other" stations, calls to action against events or persons that rub the host the wrong way, or calls for collective political action against an "enemy," much of our Black radio talk is just talk – talk without action. I don't mean to use a broad brush with that statement; I only want to sound the alarm.

The next round of deregulation could mean an even further decline in Black ownership of radio outlets and, more importantly, a decline in Black talk radio. I contend that Black folks do not have the luxury to squander a significant portion of our precious airtime dealing with ridiculous and petty issues. Sure, we need a laugh every now and then; sure, we need escapes from reality ever so often; sure, some of us could even use a little idle gossip here and there. But while others are busy capturing the minds of our children, and many of our adults, by gobbling up as many radio stations as possible, we are on Black radio often complaining about what someone said on a white owned station or, even worse, castigating one another.

Ownership and control of income-producing assets are keys to the economic growth of a people. In addition, ownership of communication outlets, vehicles through which messages are transmitted that affect what we think and how we act, are of primary importance. Why would anyone want 1200 of them if they were not important, not only as moneymakers but as programming tools? In a war, the first thing you do is cut the communication lines of the enemy. Black lines of communication are not being cut as much as they are being bought and controlled, but the results are the same.

Brothers and sisters, we have many hours of Black talk available to us across this country, although not necessarily transmitted via Black owned stations. Nonetheless, don't you think we should use what we have to create positive action among people, when it comes to economic empowerment? Don't you think we should be paying more attention to the FCC, Michael Powell, and the upcoming public hearing that is, incidentally, not covered very much in the dominant media? (I wonder why.)

Don't you think we should make more forays into the communications arena, especially Black talk radio and turn it into a positive movement for Black folks? Other groups have done it. Why not us? Other groups are not afraid to speak on behalf of their people. They make no apologies for it, and if you call some of their radio talk shows they will tell you where you can take your opinion. Simply put, they have an agenda; they work everyday to maintain the power status quo.

Don't you think we could use more action to go along with all our talk? Airtime is precious, and the capability of speaking to thousands of our people via a Black talk radio program should, at every opportunity, call for and move our people to responsive action.

The next time you call in to your favorite talk show, try to say something that will stimulate Black folks to act on the basic principles of economic empowerment. Let's turn Black Talk Radio into Black Action Radio.

Well Done Beats Well Said Every Time

You know, we talk a real good game when it comes to economic empowerment. We talk about what "we need to do," what we should do, what we can do, and even what we will do. We get together, usually in someone else's hotel or meeting place, and discuss our economic plight and how we are going to finally change things when it comes to our economic destiny. We are tired of the white man running things and keeping us out of the game. We are really upset, this time, and we are going to leave this meeting (this time), go home, and put into action the things we discussed. Yes, this time we will do it!

Haven't you seen it all before? Haven't you heard it all before? Aren't you tired of the emotionalism, the feel-good speakers, the rap and clap sessions, and the sheer madness of having chicken dinners every year, in hotels owned by the very people with whom we are angry? Aren't you finally ready to *do good* rather than to merely *feel good*? I know I am. No, I have been for a long time.

When I speak at various gatherings I usually say, "I did not come to make you 'feel' good; I came to make you 'do' good." Because well done beats well said every time. We can spend the rest of our lives *getting ready to*, *fixin' to*, and *being about to*. Just look at our past and see how much time we have wasted gettin' ready to overcome rather than overcoming. We are still singing, "We <u>Shall</u> Overcome." When?

As quiet as it's kept, we will overcome when WE decide to overcome. As our dear Brother, Amos Wilson, wrote in his book, **Afrikan-Centered Consciousness Versus the New World Order**, "Recognize that power ultimately has to do with a relationship between people and that the white man's so called power is to a large degree based on the nature of the relationship he has with the Black man. We empower him by the nature of our own behavior and attitudes as a people. He cannot be what he is unless we are what we are."

Brother Wilson continues, "We waste a lot of time trying to transform them (whites) when through transforming ourselves they will be transformed automatically. The power is in our hands." Don't you agree with Amos Wilson, especially when you consider how much time we waste *gettin' ready*?

When it comes to economic empowerment we have wasted at least thirty-five years, if not more. The night before Dr. King was assassinated, he was instructing us on what to do economically in order to change the relationship we had with those oppressive people in Memphis, and I am sure he was speaking to the rest of us as well, no matter where we lived. Since that fateful night on April 4, 1968, instead of continuing on the path he discussed, we decided to take that other road – that road called political empowerment.

Thirty-five years later, we have thousands of Black folks in public office, and we get so excited and hyped about that next election. But we have spent and continue to spend little time doing anything about our collective economic empowerment. Politically, we are living large, or some would have us believe. Economically, we are no further up the ladder than we were in 1968. As a matter of fact, according to a report by the Urban Institute, Black households were better off in 1968 than they were in 1995. (You may notice I always refer to economic empowerment in the plural rather than the singular.)

We have had thirty-five years of leadership that has talked from time to time about doing something about the collective economic plight of Black folks, thirty-five years of leaders getting their own individual *economic thang* together, thirty-five years of speeches, threats, protests, scandals, and rip-offs, but virtually no progress on building an economic legacy for our children, virtually no ownership and control of income producing assets, and virtually no means even to provide the very basics of life for our children without depending on the very people about whom we complain.

Yes, well done beats well said. We had better get about the business of doing more business with one another, like the Vietnamese are doing in their newly found nail salon businesses. We had better start supporting our businesses a lot more than we do now. We had better start teaching our children about entrepreneurship. We had better move from the demand side of the tourism industry over to the supply side. We had better start pooling our money and get into the businesses that supply our sustenance. We had better take a breather from the partying, the conspicuous consumption, and the emotion-laden get-togethers, and we had better start <u>doing</u> things that will strengthen our economic future.

Don't just talk about economic empowerment; be about economic empowerment. Give and buy Black. Because, well done beats well said every time!

MATAH - Taking it to the Next Level

During the weekend of August 22, 2003, I had the honor, privilege, and pleasure once again to serve as M.C. for the annual MATAH Conference, which was held in Philadelphia, the home of the Ken Bridges family. As many of you know, Ken was one of those killed during the sniper attacks in the D.C. area; Ken was also a co-founder of the MATAH Network, along with his partner, Al Wellington. Jocelyn Bridges, Ken's "Queen," and all of the Bridges children were in attendance as well, not only to celebrate the life and legacy of Ken Bridges but also to kick off a new era in MATAH's revolution and evolution. They, along with hundreds of other conscious, loving, and determined brothers and sisters, were there to take MATAH to the next level.

The conference kicked off with meetings of the MATAH Holdings, LLC and MATAH Investment Club, LLC. (That's right. You can invest in MATAH) We then moved to the formal part of the meeting with a welcome and libations from Anthony Phillips (Philadelphia) and Brother Heru and his Queen, Sister Gloria (Columbus, Ohio); Pastor Joseph Parks, from Winston-Salem, North Carolina, gave the invocation. We then issued a challenge to the MATAH to move to the next level and after that, as they say, "It was on!"

Dr. Therman Evans, a minister and medical doctor, gave one of the best speeches I have ever heard. This brother is outstanding, and if you ever have an opportunity to hear him speak you should definitely take advantage of it. Dr. Evans talked about bees and squirrels and how they, with their miniscule brains, have enough sense to take care of themselves, in an orderly fashion. He admonished us to do the same for ourselves. I'm telling you, this brother threw down the gauntlet in a big way. When the tapes and CD's are available, you just have to get them.

Other speakers included Jackie Mayfield, Founder and President of Compro-Tax, a brother who has created franchise opportunities for some 90 (and counting) entrepreneurs. We were graced with an uplifting message from Brother John

Raye, television legend and sales guru, who spoke on the topic, "The power of commitment," and we heard from MATAH's new Vice President, Charles "C.J." Johnson, who shared strategies for taking MATAH to the next level.   Gaston Armour, from Chicago, Juanda Honore from Los Angeles, and Ashiki Taylor from Atlanta, all MATAH regional sales reps, shared insights on their particular areas of expertise and how they have helped grow the MATAH Network in their respective regions.

We heard two gifted ministers, Dr. Carroll Johnson, Bibleway, Baltimore, Maryland, and Dr. John Mendez, Winston-Salem Ministers' Conference, both of who are absolutely sold on MATAH's One Church – One Channel Program, founded by Father George Clements.   They took everyone to church as they emphasized good stewardship via the MATAH Network.   Their message, along with Evans' message, should be heard by every minister in the country, especially our Black ministers.

Tom Pope, the powerful, informative, and fearless radio talk show host, heard on the Powernomics Radio Network, also lauded MATAH and threw out the caveat that talk is cheap. The real test, Pope shared, is what we do when we leave the conference.   Tom had not planned to speak, but we were all very happy he did. Thanks for the booster shot, Tom!

I don't have enough space to tell you everything that took place at the conference, nor do I have the space to cite everyone who participated. Suffice to say that it was certainly inspiring and refreshing to be in the midst of such love, consciousness, and understanding of what we must do to take our brothers and sisters to the next level.

As I sat and listened, I wondered, as I usually do, why more of our scholar warriors, our entertainers, our business owners, and our national opinion leaders do not speak out in support of such a natural economic strategy, the same strategy every other group uses to get ahead in this country: redirecting a greater portion of our spending toward one another. While I have to assume we are all reading the same economic book, I guess they're just on a different page – and that's all right. We all need one another.

Finally, there are three more persons I must mention. First, on a sad note, we lost another strong MATAH brother during the conference. Billie Joe Smith, known as the "Big Guy," died in Toledo, Ohio. Like Ken and Brother Sepet, Billie Joe died on his way to freedom. Please pray for his family.

The other person I must note is a man's man, a conscious brother, a humble, charitable, loving, family-oriented Black man with a heart as big as the outdoors. MATAH Chairman, Dr. Walter P. Lomax, received the Ken Bridges Legacy Lifetime Award for his commitment, support, and dedication not only to MATAH but also to his family, his business, and to his people. I could write an entire column on this brother, but I will simply say, "Thank you, Dr. Lomax, for your generosity, your grounding, and your understanding of 'To whom much is given...'" May God continue to bless you and your family.

Last but not least, there is my sister, Jocelyn Bridges. I will not even attempt to describe what I felt when she spoke at the end of the conference. Ken is smiling and Ken's love still flows through you, my sister. Your strength and continued determination to go on are indicative of what the MATAH is all about. You have decided to take it to the next level, and we must do no less as well. Take it to the next level. Get involved with MATAH!

The Black Capital Network

Kudos to Sister Jennifer Parker and, of course, her excellent support staff of volunteers, for conducting one of the best economic empowerment conferences I have ever attended – and I have attended quite a few. Jennifer is the brainchild of The Black Capital Network (*www.thebcn.com*) and has diligently labored to bring her vision of economic prosperity for African Americans to fruition. She "stayed the course," as George Fraser would say, and presented the second annual Black Capital Network conference. She and her husband, Mel, held on to their commitment, continued to make the sacrifices necessary to accomplish their goals, and they brought an outstanding event to the people of Buffalo, New York, on November 1, 2003.

I had the honor and pleasure to conduct a Blackonomics workshop during the conference, but my excitement is grounded in three other aspects of the BCN: I was thrilled to see the turnout of participants; I was impressed at the variety of vendors and, not only their willingness to support the BCN but also their reciprocal commitment to recycling Black dollars; and I was especially pleased with the outstanding speakers Jennifer brought to the conference. I often talk about how even I need an economic empowerment "booster shot" from time to time to keep me going. Well, I certainly got that and more at the Black Capital Network Conference.

Being in the company once again of Brooke Stephens, financial author (*Wealth Happens One Day at a Time*) and lecturer, listening to Brother Melvin Gravely, entrepreneur, author (*When Black and White Make Green*), and lecturer, hearing real solutions for accessing capital, seeing the New York activist and legend, Dorothy Pittman Hughes, (*Wake Up and Smell the Dollars – Whose Inner City is it Anyway?*). in person, and just being in close proximity to so many accomplished entrepreneurs and fantastic brothers and sisters was, indeed, a privilege and an honor for me.

Then there was Simon T. Bailey. The author of Simon Says...Dream – Live a Passionate Life, Bailey took the conference by storm, or should I say a "Whirlwind"? This brother delivered an outstanding speech. If you have not heard Simon or read his work, somewhere down the line there is a treat waiting for you, because sooner or later you will come in contact with this brother, who is one of the nation's most sought-after speakers.

Weaving metaphors, life-lessons, homespun yarns, common sense, metaphysics, and stark realities into a tapestry of positive, results-oriented, and very practical strategies for success, Simon T. Bailey was a joy to behold. He is a fresh face on the scene and surely someone to watch as he humbly makes his way to the top, but reaches back to help someone else as well. We should listen to what Simon says.

All in all, the Black Capital Network was a veritable potpourri of excellence, comprising local business owners and corporate representatives with national authors and entrepreneurs. The event ended with a book forum, sponsored by local attorney and author (Fighting for Your Life), John Elmore, and The Weddings of Color Expo and Fashion show. The forum featured local authors and was moderated by Yvonne Rose, co-owner and Editor of Amber Books, Phoenix, Arizona, the nation's largest African American self-help and career guide publishing house.

The Weddings of Color Expo and Fashion Show highlighted wedding gowns by New York designer, Therez Fleetwood. Ms. Fleetwood is also the author of the new best-seller, The Afrocentric Bride, which features the most beautiful and culturally sensitive wedding gowns ever made. Check out Ms. Fleetwood's gowns and her book; you will be very pleased with what your see.

Now what is the bottom line of all of this? Meetings and conferences are held by and for Black people in this country virtually every week. But, as I told my audience, it's not just the meeting that's important; it's what happens after the meeting. My challenge is always centered on the "doing," the positive action that emanates as a result of the many meetings we have. As for as economic empowerment conferences are concerned, it's one thing to practice it during the conference, at the vending tables, in the workshops, and during the book signings, but it's a different thing to leave the venue and really get involved in day-to-day economic empowerment. It's another thing to make it a habit to support Black owned businesses, to grow and expand our businesses via strategic partnerships, cooperative purchasing, and mergers. In other words, it's one thing to talk about it and another thing to DO it.

While I thank Jennifer Parker and everyone else who attended the conference, I encourage us as well to follow up and follow through on what we learned there. I pray that we will do what we say, practice what we preach, and walk our talk when it comes to economic empowerment and entrepreneurship. We cannot afford to keep going to meetings only to return home and do nothing with the information we gleaned from those meetings. Let's get busy y'all.

Kwanzaa 2003 – What do you have to celebrate?

For nearly forty years Black people in the United States have celebrated the seven principles of Kwanzaa. Established by Dr. Maulana Karenga in 1966, Kwanzaa is an African American and Pan-African holiday celebrated by millions throughout the world African community. Kwanzaa brings a cultural message which speaks to the best of what it means to be African and human in the fullest sense. Our obvious support and celebration of this occasion suggests our commitment, not only to the principles of the Nguzo Saba, but also to their fruition. Thus, we ask you: What Kwanzaa success will you celebrate this year? What have you done during the year that qualifies as a celebratory event during Kwanzaa?

Have you achieved Unity among the people in your locale? Are you unified to the point that you love one another more and support one another more? Do you have proof that you have unified around some pertinent issue or cause? If so, then let the celebration begin.

How about Self-Determination? That's one of my favorite. What have you done in your city to demonstrate your commitment to determining the future of your children? Are others still controlling your destiny? Or, have you taken it upon yourself to build and support your own institutions, open and grow new business, and create your own jobs? Maybe you have accomplished other things that will determine your future. If so, Congratulations!

A few years ago I worked on the design and execution of an event in Cincinnati called Ujima-Cincibration, which some of you probably attended. The intent of the affair, conducted each year, was to celebrate what we had accomplished during the year vis-à-vis our *collective work and our responsibility* toward one another. The event survived for four years and failed primarily because the premise upon which it was founded was ignored by those who subsequently managed it. If we work collectively on community projects such as neighborhood clean-up, elderly assistance, and tutoring, imagine the things we could celebrate on December 28th for Ujima.

Now, here's my favorite: Cooperative Economics. Have you done anything cooperatively this year to increase the economic viability and stability of your community? Have you pooled any of your money to finance a project or to form an investment group to assist micro businesses? Nuff said on that one.

What have you done to build and develop your community in order to restore our people to their traditional greatness? In other words, what is your purpose, and have you actualized that purpose? If you have, then you definitely have something to celebrate.

Created anything lately? What has been the level of your creativity this past year? Is there anything, not necessarily something material, that you developed in your community? Maybe it was a new financial institution, or maybe it was a new resolve and commitment to do better than you did the previous year. Creativity covers a multitude of endeavors. What did you create?

Finally, how much faith do you have in the things you are celebrating? How much faith do you have in yourself? How much faith do you have in the Creator's ability to carry you through in times of struggle? Are you one of "little faith," or is your faith sufficient to support you in your quest to fulfill the other six principles of Kwanzaa?

On December 26th of every year, after forty years of celebrating, we should be able to look back and revel in the things we have accomplished through our celebration of Kwanzaa. What will you see when you look back this year? If nothing is there, if nothing is there but a mere celebration, then you have work to do, so that this time next year you will have some tangible accomplishment to celebrate.

Aren't you tired of mere spoken words? Aren't you just a little weary of empty rhetoric, events based on words followed by little or no subsequent action? Wouldn't you like to see us, after forty years of celebrating Kwanzaa, be able to point to something we built and sustained because of our celebration of values we hold so dear? I know you would.

Here in Cincinnati, we have the Sankofa Educational Enrichment Program, headed by Sister Kimya Moyo. Each year they celebrate the principles of Kwanzaa by recognizing seven individuals who best represent each principle. In 2004, at the organization's annual event, Ms. Kenya James, Black Enterprise Magazine's Teenpreneur of the Year, will be the keynote speaker. They also "look back" every New Year's Eve at what they accomplished in relationship to Kwanzaa, and they look forward and plan activities for the coming year.

Please get started now on what you will celebrate during next year's Kwanzaa. And let the celebration never end!

Section VIII

What Is Your Money Saying?

"Being poor doesn't always mean being without resources. Anacostia is one of the poorest neighborhoods in Washington, D.C., yet the total income of all its households is $370 million per year. Most of this money quickly departs in the hands of landlords, business owners, and bankers who live in more upscale parts of town.... The principal affliction of poor communities in the United States is not the absence of money, but its systematic exit."
Michael Shuman, *Going Local*

Thorstein Veblen, Economist, coined the phrase "conspicuous consumption" (1899) to designate the act of purchasing and using certain goods and services, not in order to survive, but rather to identify oneself to others as having superior wealth and social standing.

Spend, Spend, Spend!

That's the rallying cry of our politicians with George W. leading the way. They know, as many others do, that the economy begins and ends with consumption. They know that unless we, the consumers, do not spend our money, this economy will collapse. They know they have to put a good spin on the current atmosphere in this country, especially since September 11, 2001. They know they had better make us feel better about the economy, about our future, and about this country, or we will withhold our dollars and bring this country to a screeching halt, something Bin Laden with all of his dastardly deeds could never accomplish.

As we hear and see these messages coming from our political and business leaders, it should give us a hint as what Black people can and should do to build an economy for ourselves. Spend, spend, spend; only spend at Black owned businesses. If it works for a multi-trillion dollar economy, it will surely work for what currently stands at a $700 billion economy – the black economy.

We should, we must, start our own rallying cry to spend as well, but with Black businesses. We must use the same promotional strategy that our national leaders are using to get our brothers and sisters to understand that buying from Black businesses is the key to our collective prosperity. I am so glad the President and others finally let the secret get out. They told us, as I have been writing for years, and many other brothers and sisters have been saying for decades, that the only way we can build and maintain an economy is to trade with one another.

While the national call is for consumers to spend their money on American goods and services, resulting in a *circle the wagons* mentality among many consumers, Black people should once again, as in the days of segregation, do the same thing. There's just one hitch. We should not continue to go out and spend our money with those who care nothing about us, those who hold us in disdain, and those who continue to suck the life-blood (our dollars) from our neighborhoods.

Don't you think it's time we stand up and follow the directions of our national leaders? Wouldn't it be a good idea for Black people to get on the bandwagon that Bush is pushing? I know I would love to see us spending more, buying more products and services – from Black people. Just imagine the boost to the economy it would have – our economy. Picture the patriotism of an army of Black consumers spending just another 10-15% of our $700 billion with Black businesses.

Let's look at the connection between spending and economic freedom. If at least a portion of the latter were not dependent upon the former, we would not hear the calls to spend, spend, spend coming from the power structure. Thus, it follows that the economic freedom of Black folks is directly related to how we spend our money.

National leaders are asking us to spend, despite the fact that thousands of employees are being laid off and executives are getting millions of dollars in raises and *golden parachutes.* To add insult to injury, Blacks do not own the businesses to which this spending spree is being directed. What else do we need as proof to move us toward mutual support and cooperative economics? By the way, won't we be celebrating Ujamaa very soon? It is a shame we do not practice it and the other six principles of Kwanzaa 24/7. But I digress.

Here's what's up. Brothers and sisters, we do not own 30 supermarkets in this entire country. If a national calamity beset the U.S., unless white folks, Arabs, and Indians share their food with us, we will be up the proverbial creek without a paddle. We own very few banks, therefore our need for funds during such a time would be a very low priority to those who do own and control the majority of the financial institutions in this country. We own one national channel of distribution, The MATAH Network, and if we are faced with developing new ways to earn a living by creating our own products and services for our people, how will we gain access to those products and services as well as to Black consumers without a channel of distribution?

This is my plea to Black people in this country. Don't take lightly the things you see happening around you.

Understand that if we do not follow the basic tenets of economic survival, you know, the way the Arabs have done in Dearborn, Michigan, the way the Vietnamese have done in Westminster, California, and so on, we will be left wanting, left begging someone else to take care of the necessities of life for us. Sure, you may be well-off, but what about your people?

Please act upon that understanding – that reality – by spending a greater portion of your disposable income with your brothers and sisters. Our very lives, our children's lives depend upon it.

Let's Set Some Economic Goals

In a conversation with Brother Ashiki Taylor (The MATAH Man, as he is called in Atlanta), as we discussed goals, a thought arose that prompted this article. That thought was centered on the establishment of an economic goal for Black people. We get hyped about attaining goals in sports, for instance, by reaching the goal line in football, by getting to the goal on the basketball court, by setting a goal for homeruns, steals, and such in baseball, and if you like soccer and have heard that announcer yell GOOOOOAL!, you know exactly how exciting reaching the goal can be. These goals are all set in an effort to do what? To win the game! So, what should our goals be for winning the economic game?

Before we set a goal we must know where we are. So, I took a look at the U.S. Census report on businesses and, without getting too technical or statistical, decided to share a few items from that report. The 2002 statistics are not yet available, so we had to use the 1997 report for this article.

Blacks owned 823,000 businesses and generated $71.2 billion in revenues. If we project those figures into 2003, we could justifiably estimate the number of Black owned business to have increased by 200,000 but with revenues of only $92 billion. I say this because, according to Black Enterprise Magazine, the 2002 revenues for the top 100 Industrial/Service firms and the leading 100 auto dealerships were $20.9 billion. Also, because a 1992 report by the Department of Commerce noted that 56% of Black-owned companies had revenues under $10,000 and only 3,000 Black businesses had more than $1,000,000 in annual sales.

A consistent and interesting side bar: As the number of Black owned businesses increase, their revenues do not follow suit. Between 1992 and 1997 Black business ownership rose 26% compared to just 7% for all U.S. firms. However, revenues for those Black owned businesses increased by 33%, below the 40% increase for all other firms. This begs two questions: What are African Americans doing with our billions in annual income? Are other groups supporting our businesses the way we support theirs?

Facing numbers like those, coupled with our percentage of population, which happens to be around 13%, don't you think it would be great if we established and worked toward an economic goal that not only reflects our percentage of population but builds an economic foundation as well?

While we could compare Black business to Jewish, Hispanic, and Asian business, we won't. It's been done many times and has been used to justify our economic position, by suggesting that we are not "entrepreneurial" and other ridiculous myths promulgated by the establishment. I suggest you read Dr. Juliet E. K. Walker's "The History of Black Business In America," as well as Dr. John Sibley Butler's "Entrepreneurship and Self-Help Among Black Americans" to get the real reasons for our being behind in business ownership. Additionally, this is not about other groups and what they have accomplished. This is about us, Black folks; and it's about what we must do for ourselves to create a firm economic base for our children.

So what should our goal be? Let's look at this thing on a local level rather than on a national level. In cities like Detroit, where the Black population far exceeds 50% and, unfortunately, the majority of the economies in most of the Black neighborhoods are controlled by East Indians and Chaldeans, Koreans, and everyone except Blacks, we should have a goal to increase our percentage of business ownership. In cities like Atlanta, where Blacks control most of the politics, how about establishing a goal to control more of the economics as well? In Memphis, Tennessee; Richmond, Virginia; Winston-Salem, North Carolina; Jackson, Mississippi; Birmingham, Alabama; and I am not about to leave out Cincinnati, Ohio; why don't we establish an economic goal, to control a certain percentage of our dollars?

Since we comprise 13% of the nation's population and only spend 5%-7% of our annual income with Black businesses, we should see the value and the need to make significant changes in the way we do business. We should work locally by setting a goal, based on our percentage of population, to increase our spending with Black businesses.

In those cities where we are in the majority, let's do even better by not settling for "minority" status and being relegated to the smaller percentages of economic benefits derived from public development projects. In cities where we have smaller percentages, such as Portland, Oregon; San Diego, California; Seattle, Washington; Tucson, Arizona; and Los Angeles, California, let's work even closer together to increase our spending with one another and to increase business development and growth.

Let's set goals on a local level to capture, control, and retain, at a minimum, a relative share of our dollars and a greater portion of our local economies. How? Make it a point to switch from the products you are currently purchasing to those products made by Black people; many are distributed via the MATAH Network, if you didn't already know that. Insist on, and be prepared to fight for, equitable distribution of public funds and projects. Stop allowing others to set "goals" for Black people under the guise of Minority Programs. Set your own economic goals and work toward them everyday.

Another Year, Another $700 Billion

You have heard it before. You probably hear it every year. The day after Thanksgiving is the biggest shopping day of the year - the beginning of the "holiday" season when more money is spent than any other time of the year. Another year, another $700 billion, and counting. What did you do with your share?

Each year I hear our people complaining about how much we spend and I hear some of them planning "no-buy" campaigns for this time of the year. Well, how about planning and implementing a "buy" campaign this year? How about a real "Buy Black" campaign this year, starting right now?

You know, it's not about showing "them" our economic impact during the holidays (they already know what it is); it's about showing ourselves. It's not about doing negative things against someone else as much as it is about doing positive things for us, especially when it comes to spending our dollars. So, what do you say? Will you make that commitment? Will you follow through on it? Surely there is something among the hundreds of items on the MATAH Network, all made by Black folks and some of which you use everyday around your home, that would make excellent gifts for your friends and family.

So why not make a purchase from your brothers and sisters? Why not contribute to your own economic freedom? Let's make a statement that will positively affect our people and lessen our priority on making economic statements that negatively affect "them." I know it's a small step, but isn't it worth it? We have to start somewhere. Why not start by Giving and Buying Black?

This is a "no-excuses" immediate way to show not only the world, but also our people, just how strong we can be if we simply support one another to a greater degree than we do presently. This is an excellent way to show that we are not selfish with one another, not envious of one another, not afraid of our brother or our sister having a dollar more than we have. This is an opportunity for us to demonstrate the principles

Kwanzaa and not just celebrate them. This is a time when Black people can take charge, take control of what's in our pockets and purses and make a grand economic statement with a portion of our $700 billion – for and among ourselves. How? We do it by buying more from our own people and circulating our dollars a lot more, thus positioning ourselves to face the New Year with a new resolve, to use more of our money for our benefit.

Let's not look back at next year and only be able to say, "Oh well, another year, another $700 billion." Can you imagine the positive economic impact we would have if we simply redirected another 10% of that $700 billion toward our own businesses? That's $70 billion, brothers and sisters! Surely we can afford it and surely we could use it in our coffers for a little while longer than a weekend. Think of the jobs we could create for our people. Think of the new businesses we could establish. And, think of the folks who currently get our money, without having to reciprocate in any meaningful way, think of what they would be saying – and doing – to get us to come back and spend more with them. I don't know about you, but those thoughts make me feel wonderful.

Please consider what I am saying and take action, positive actions this year and beyond, to change the way you do business, change your spending habits, and change our economic position in this country. Plan to make regular purchases from Black owned businesses, and just as we are so committed to keeping Dr. King's dream alive, let's go one step further with this dreaming issue. Let's _live_ his dream by empowering ourselves economically

I guess I'm at the point of begging now, so I'll shut-up. Peace, love, and blessings.

Money Talks – Especially Black Money

You've heard the saying, "Money Talks." And it's true. You've probably also heard the saying, "Money Talks and (you know what) Walks." Money definitely talks, but, have you ever wondered what money says when it talks? Have you thought about the facts that point out, quite graphically, that when money raises its head, or is put on the table, or is taken off the table, the attention of those affected by it dramatically increases? Obviously, understanding its power and the role it plays in this economy, money speaks loudly and clearly, and Black money speaks even louder. But what does it say?

We know from past experience when we have grievances, if we resort to economic retaliation we can get things done. Why? Because Black money speaks louder than any other. $700 billion can get pretty loud, and those who are getting the lion's share of it right now pay close attention to what it is saying. They sit up and take notice when we resort to withholding our money from their coffers. Just look back in history and you can see what I mean.

Now look at what happened on what is affectionately referred to as *Black Friday* in 2002. Walmart had $1.43 billion in sales. In the aggregate retailers enjoyed a 12% increase in sales over the previous period. Total sales reported were $7.2 billion – on one day! How loudly did Black dollars speak to the retailers on that day? And what did those dollars say? I am sure whatever they said at the malls and other stores, it was sweet music to the retailers' ears.

The only language that gets things done in this country is the money language. How else could executives of major corporations steal so much of it and get off with what amounts to a disciplinary hearing and a warning? How could we now be faced, once again, with going to war under the guise of "national security" when it's really all about oil? Whatever happened to Miss Martha Stewart? Didn't she commit a crime? And what about the stock market? Now there's a good one. They tell us that insider trading is illegal, and they expect us to believe they don't tell their friends and relatives that a deal is about to go down. C'mon. As I've said before, why do you think those folks on that balcony at the stock exchange always clap at the end of the day – regardless of a loss or a gain?

Why do you think the call went out from George W. and the gang to spend more money immediately after the World Trade Center tragedy? Why would he wipe out a budget surplus to give the proletariat $300.00 - $600.00 in advance tax refunds, thus, putting us back into a deficit? Of course, we know the richest folks received the greatest benefit from that so-called tax cut. Have you given much thought to the executives from Tyco, Enron, WorldCom, Arthur Andersen, Halliburton, General Electric, and all the others who have pilfered billions from their stockholders? That's money talking, folks, and it's speaking loudly and boisterously.

Now what about Black money? Well, I see a great deal of it in the hands of brothers and sisters who seem to have plugs in their ears, unable to hear what their money is saying. I see the Hip-Hop crowd doing voting summits but not economic summits, despite their collective worth of billions of dollars. I see many of our Black athletes and entertainers, also large and in charge of billions of dollars, spending, spending, spending rather than investing in their own brothers' and sisters' businesses. And I see millions of everyday brothers and sisters spending their share of our $700 billion haphazardly, aimlessly, and unashamedly on the trinkets made by everyone else except Black folks. It is obvious they are not listening to their money.

Black money is talking and saying positive things to white owned businesses, Asian owned businesses, Arab owned businesses, and the many others that Black consumers support. Our money is saying nice things like, *"Hi, how are you today? I hope you are doing well, sir, and I trust that I can help make your day much better by soothing your mind and fattening your bank account. You know, we really love you so much and we want you and your children to prosper, and always feel secure in your knowledge that we are here for you. All you have to do is make something and we will purchase it. So, don't you ever worry about anything; we will be with you and we will support you. Have a nice day."*

Yes, money talks, and Black money talks even more. Its soothing voice and its comforting and reassuring smile make non-Black business owners feel real good. But do you know what Black money is saying to Black folks? It's simply saying, **"Good-bye!"**

Let's Stop the Bleeding

In our so-called "Black communities" there is a crisis of monumental proportion; a crisis that if not checked will prove to be our demise. Dr. Claud Anderson, author of Black Labor, White Wealth and Powernomics, has been traveling the length and breadth of this country admonishing us to wake up and change our ways before it's too late. Anderson has not merely been telling us what we should do; he has an action plan for us to follow.

It's the same way with others, such as Ken Bridges and Al Wellington of the MATAH Network; Conrad Worrill of the National Black United Front, a little known brother named Kenneth Price, author of the soon-to-be released book, The New Urbanomics. We have brothers and sisters like Bishop Frank Stewart, Julianne Malveaux, Ron Daniels, Brooke Stephens, William Reed, Dr. Rosie Milligan and Charles Ross, who are sounding the alarm AND offering positive steps for our economic progress. It's not that we are on life support yet, but we are losing a great deal of blood, which if left unchecked will prove to be fatal.

The folks I noted above comprise a cadre of individuals whom you do not hear or see a great deal of in the media, especially the dominant media. Have you ever wondered why that is? The folks above are not afraid; they are not ashamed of being Black; they are not hiding behind organizations and in corporations; they are strong and unwavering in their message of economic empowerment. They are our Emergency Medical Technicians, the first ones on the scene to stop the bleeding and take us to a place where we can be treated and recover from our wounds.

Yes, we are bleeding profusely brothers and sisters, and we must stop the bleeding, not with a band-aid but with stitches. Our dollars are flowing out of our neighborhoods. The professionals call this phenomenon *float* or expenditure leakage, which translates into what the experts at the Brookings Institution call a "market opportunity to provide competitively priced goods and services to inner-city consumers." A 1999 report issued by the Center on Urban and Metropolitan Policy, written by Robert Weissbourd and Christopher Berry, cited some glaring and, quite frankly, embarrassingly stark statistics that portray Black people as nothing more than "economic opportunities" for others.

Please note the report was not casting aspersions on Black folks, rather it was simply pointing out some facts about inner-city neighborhoods and their consumers and suggesting ways that businesses and government entities could better serve the residents as well as their own interests. It stressed investment opportunities within under-served neighborhoods and was positive in its approach to suggesting ways to effect much needed change.

Nevertheless, my take on this issue conjures up visions of massive hemorrhaging, and it very strongly suggests that we need to stop the bleeding. Take this example for instance. The report compares one of Chicago's Southside neighborhoods, South Shore, to the affluent northern neighborhood of Kenilworth. It states, "...urban neighborhoods like South Shore in Chicago have more buying power than the wealthiest of suburbs. South Shore's median family income is $22,000; Kenilworth's is $124,000. But South Shore packs $69,000 of retail spending power per acre, nearly twice that of Kenilworth's $38,000."

What does that mean? It means inner city residents, despite their tremendous resources, are virtually bleeding to death. The *float* referred to in the report is literally millions of dollars going out of the neighborhood, which in turn, according to the report, also negatively affects employment for those living in the neighborhoods. It states, "For business, this translates into lost sales, or what marketers call 'float dollars.' For inner city residents, these are 'float jobs,' as crucial dollars that could employ local residents and fuel the neighborhood economy are spent elsewhere."

We are bleeding brothers and sisters, and we must stop the bleeding before we die. As I said, we have EMT's ready, willing, and able to apply the tourniquets and even to stitch up our wounds. It's up to us, however, to access their expertise, to follow their instructions, and to take the prescriptions they write for us. If we are going to stop the bleeding, if we are going to put an end, once and for all, to the preventable loss of life blood – our dollars – from our neighborhoods and turn them into real communities, we must make the changes being recommended by our economic leaders.

We must consider our "spending power per acre" as cited in the Brookings Institution Report, just as others are considering it and gaining a stronger economic foothold in the billions Black people earn and spend each year. We must redirect a greater portion of our income back to ourselves via our own businesses, and we must develop a culture of wealth retention, a culture of collective economic empowerment among our people, regardless of where we reside.

So, put the band-aids away. Get out the sutures. Let's stop the bleeding.

The Power of Wealth versus the Power of Income

In his fantastic book, Black Wealth through Black Entrepreneurship, Robert Wallace says, "...it becomes painfully obvious that the basic problem facing the [B]lack community is that it lacks significant power to have a direct and sustained impact on its own destiny." The key word in his statement is "power." Notice the title of Brother Wallace's book includes the word "wealth," not "income," and if you have read the book you also noticed Wallace's instruction to us when it comes to capturing real power.

Too many of us spend most of our time bragging about the tremendous so-called "spending power" of Black folks in this country. We quote the information from the University of Georgia's Selig Center and take pride in the fact that we have an annual income of $700 billion. Did you know that the term "Black spending power," as used by the statisticians, simply means "disposable income"? Yes, Black people have $700 billion per year in disposable income, and as Sister Shahrazad Ali says, "Black folks have the most disposable income because we dispose of most our income."

So, what is the difference between income and wealth? What is the difference between income and wealth when it comes to power? Well, the bottom line to wealth is net worth. Check out a person's net worth and you can see how wealthy he or she is. The latest statistics show Black families have a net worth one-tenth of that of white families – and even less than that of Asian families. Need I say more?

The next time you see the statistics on Black Buying Power, stop and think about the word "power" and what it means in that particular context. Power for whom? Yes, it's Black Buying Power, but it's power for those who receive some 95% of our $700 billion everyday. It is power for others to purchase fine homes and cars. It is power for others to build their own communities. It is power for others to send their children to college. It is power that is transferable – the best kind of power – to the progeny of others, thus allowing them to maintain their collective hold on the economic system of this country.

This is why I use the term "Black Buying Weakness." If we continue to give our power to someone else through our conspicuous consumption of their products and services, we will continue to have billions of dollars in aggregate income and only thousands of dollars in individual family wealth. Additionally, we will continue to have the power of income rather than the power of wealth, which only allows us to our pay bills, continue to work on the proverbial *plantations*, purchase all of our needs and wants from the proverbial *company store*, and create the power of wealth for others.

The systems of sharecropping and dependence upon the company store, as coalminers had to do during the 1940's and 1950's, are being continued today when it comes to the enormous amount of income and the relative miniscule amount of wealth among Black people. We could never catch up back then, and we will never catch up now, if we continue to depend upon income rather than wealth.

The power of wealth manifests itself in ownership and control of income-producing assets and infrastructure such as banks, hotels, manufacturing facilities, real estate, distribution channels, and other wealth-builders and wealth-retainers. The power of income manifests itself, via the transfer of that income to others, in ownership and control of assets by those from whom Black folks must purchase our very sustenance.

If we allow that system to continue, by pouring the vast majority of our income into the vast pools of wealth owned by others, we will always be on the bottom of the economic heap. Yes, some of us will still have the latest cars, fine homes, stock portfolios, and high positions (jobs) in corporate America, but collectively we will remain an income-rich and wealth-poor group of Africans in America.

We must take stock of our economic position in this country by understanding that income is not wealth. It's not what you earn; it's what you keep. You shouldn't work for money; money should work for you. Credit is a good servant but a poor master. Poor people pay interest; rich people earn interest. Don't have champagne tastes with a beer budget.

Stop ending each month with more month than money. The clichés go on and on. But you get the picture, I'm sure.

Please start redirecting more of your income toward your own people, just like other groups do. And the next time they count how much money we have collectively, they will add a footnote that says, "Black spending among Black owned businesses has increased significantly, the result of which is an increase in the net worth of Black families as well as an aggregate increase in Black wealth."

The power of income or the power of wealth. Which would you prefer for our people?

Wealth-Building Takes Backbone

Too often we sit around and commiserate about our economic plight. In essence, what we are doing is wishing it were not so. If we are ever going to start building our own wealth, instead of building it for everyone else, African Americans must stand up and get busy. Wishing just won't make it so. It will take dedication, commitment, and just plain old-fashioned work by Black folks if we want to change our economic condition in this country and around the world. And it must begin with the understanding of the importance of building and retaining wealth among Black people.

Robert Taylor, the founder of the Better Life Club, says, "Wealth-building must be number one on every black person's agenda because economics is the foundation of social life...The simple fact is that virtually every problem we face as a people either had its origin in poverty or poverty makes the problem worse. Education, political empowerment, and pride are all needed, but none of them represent the fundamental need of our people."

Taylor went on to say, "We must produce more than we consume and earn more than we spend. Otherwise, growth and wealth building are impossible...if we remain weak economically, it will make little difference how educated we are or how many politicians we have. In capitalist America, you cannot build wealth and financial security with just a job. You must own... businesses to generate profit income and invest to generate interest income." He ended his statement by quoting Newt Gingrich, whom Taylor says, "I do not like very much." He says Gingrich told a reporter, "If black people want more respect, they should get more money."

Maybe since a white guy uttered those words Black folks will feel more compelled to act on them. After all, we have heard these same words from our ancestors for years and years. While there have been times in our history that we followed their instructions, our current actions, collectively of course, are sadly and sorely lacking. We sure like to brag about our past and the successes of our brothers and sisters, for instance, Black Wall Street in Tulsa, Oklahoma, Hayti in Durham, North Carolina, Allensworth, California, Mound Bayou, Mississippi, and many more. Don't you think it's time we renew what they accomplished? Isn't it time for us to start more of those economic enclaves?

Wealth-building is vitally important to any group of persons, especially in this country, and even more important is the retention of that wealth within the particular group. Black people not only built this country, we have built communities for other groups of people in this country – and we continue to build them today by buying everything anyone makes or does. We have paid more college tuitions for youth from other communities than we have for Black youth. We have bought more homes and cars for others than we have for ourselves. We have grown and sustained the businesses of others to a far greater extent than we have our own. As Newt suggested, we had better get busy, folks.

Solution. Robert Wallace, in his book, Black Wealth Through Black Entrepreneurship, says, "Without a doubt, the best way for us to accumulate wealth quickly and increase the circulation rate of our dollars within our community is through the rapid formation of businesses in our community. To accomplish this, we must start directing a greater number of our young people through the entrepreneurship channel. This will not only benefit the African-American community, but the overall American community."

We must also release ourselves from the psychological enslavement that keeps us from supporting our brothers and sisters in business and understand that it is only common sense for people of a particular group to support those within that group. Just watch the Jewish people, the Arab people, the Chinese people, the Vietnamese people, the Indian people, the European people, and other groups. They show us everyday that no matter what the situation, they will always support the interests of their people over the interests of others, especially Blacks.

We have no choice but to stand up for ourselves and do for ourselves, and that takes strength and an attitude of fearlessness and love for one another. When Marcus Garvey rallied 50,000 people around an economic cause, they shouted, "Marcus gives us backbones, not wishbones." The last time I checked, if you want to stand tall and stand straight, if you really want to build and retain wealth among African American people, a backbone is required.

Use Our Spending Power to Empower Ourselves

The news keeps coming out every week. Black folks' so-called "spending power" is on the rise, and corporate marketers are devising more ways of taking advantage of this "new found" treasure. The latest news comes from an article in Black Enterprise Magazine (2003), **Black Spending Power Tops $630 Billion** - Advertisers respond to the steadily increasing economic clout of the African American consumer, by Tamara E. Holmes. I call it "Black spending weakness," but let's take an in-depth look at our so-called "spending power."

Way back in 1986, I worked for a Black-owned marketing firm in Chicago, and I remember doing a sales presentation to executives of a certain company that would, if approved, give our firm a contract to promote that company's products. Of course, we specialized in marketing to the Black consumer. I will never forget the attitude of one of V.P.'s of that company. He was just passing time listening to us, probably just waiting to get back to his desk and file a report that said he had spoken to a Black company, thus, having done his affirmative action thing for the year.

I will also never forget one of the questions he asked, as well as the implication of his question. He came with the preconceived notion that his company had no reason to advertise or spend dollars on a Black consumer marketing campaign, despite the consumption index of his products by Black people being three times the average amount. Why? Well, his question will enlighten you. He asked, no he suggested through his question, that Black people don't read anyway, so why should he do more advertising and marketing. He also implied that since Black people already spend large sums of their money on his products and continue to be the loyal consumers they are, it would make no sense for him to spend money for something he is already getting free.

And you know what? He was absolutely right. I was mad, but he was right. I got no contract, and he continued to get millions of dollars in sales from Black consumers.

According to the article in B.E., "Black people's spending represents the margin of profitability for a number of consumer products. African Americans have the capacity to use their spending power to influence corporate decisions on employment, investment, and purchasing practices that would benefit the black community, including black businesses." Oh really? Then why aren't we using that power?

The article goes on to say, "More than $1.5 billion is being spent on advertising targeting African Americans by national advertisers," says Ken Smikle, president of Chicago-based research and information company Target Market News. "Marketers are getting more and more intelligent every day." Did it take them 20 years to gain such knowledge about their Black consumers? And, when you compare a measly $1.5 billion to Blacks' $630 billion (and even more by some reports) you have to like the return on their investment.

Another interesting point made by Smikle is, "One of the indicators of how well we're doing and how important that growth is to African Americans can be seen in the increase of dollars contributed to political organizations, political parties, and political candidates." My question: "How many dollars are going into Black business development, entrepreneurship, and other economic empowering activities?"

Ken Smikle also points to Russell Simmons' threatened Pepsi Cola boycott as proof of how seriously companies take the importance of black spending power and political and economic clout. The boycott was averted after PepsiCo agreed to donate millions to youth organizations around the U.S. Questions: How many millions? Donations to what organizations? Has anyone followed up to see if those donations have been made yet?

My final question: What are Black people getting for our $600-$700 billion in "spending power?" First of all, the only way we can have real power is to use it. Otherwise, words like "potential," "latent," and "dormant," will continue to dominate when it comes to African Americans and our so-called power. How do you know you have power if you don't do something that exhibits that power? I strongly contend that "Black Spending Power" is a misnomer, an oxymoron. How can we be a powerful people simply by spending? As the B.E. article implies, our power lies in the act of not spending.

Amos Wilson, in his book, *Blueprint for Black Power*, cites the words of Thomas R. Dye, *Power and Society*: "Economic power is the power to decide what will be produced, how much it will cost, how many people will be employed (and laid off) what their wages will be, what the price of goods and services will be, what profits will be made, how these profits will be distributed, and how fast the economy will grow."

Brother Wilson adds, "In capitalistic America the foundation of economic power is private property whose ownership not only refers to real estate but also to the ownership of 'the means of production,' of accumulated capital, wealth, [and] surplus production." How can we have power by spending our money – on someone else's stuff?

Black spending "power"? I don't think so. But we could change things by spending more of our money among our own businesses, building them up, creating new jobs, and controlling a larger piece of the overall economy. Power is only power for those who use it. Everybody else is using our so-called spending power, brothers and sisters. So, in order to prove we have power, we have to use that power to empower ourselves.

Turkeys' Day
(November 2003)

By the time you read this article many of you will have eaten enough, in one day, to feed one of those starving children for a week, and some of you will have gone out and spent your hard-earned money on things you did not need just because the advertisers told you the biggest shopping day of the year is the day after Thanksgiving. You will have taken advantage of the big sales and all of the bargains, thus, continuing the trend of enriching others by creating wealth for them, while maintaining the current level of economic enslavement that exists among African Americans. Oh yeah, and we will inevitably hear the post Thanksgiving fallout about Black Friday and how we should have spent our money at Black owned businesses and vendor marketplaces.

I have written several articles on this subject and decided to curtail my pre-Thanksgiving pleadings this year. It seems to do no good at all to suggest that we incorporate a daily, year-round, sustainable economic strategy rather than get all bent out of shape when Thanksgiving and Christmas roll around. I suppose that's too easy and we definitely like things to be difficult, don't we? For instance, I have pushed and advocated for a mindset, a collective consciousness, among Black folks that would create in us a daily "habit" of seeking out Black businesses and mutual support.

If we could ever get to that state of mind we would not have to revisit the annual flawed strategy of waiting for the holidays to react to our economic plight in this country. We would not need Black-Out Days and other superfluous efforts that only last for short periods of time and have no sustaining effect on those we are attempting to hurt. As a matter of fact, we get so hung-up on hurting others and often neglect the fact that we should be helping ourselves.

With all of that said, I am suggesting that we are the real turkeys in the economic scenario of this country. They carve us up and divide us up every year – as a matter of fact, they do it all year long. They stuff us with advertising and marketing campaigns, rub us down with the *oil of credit*, tie our legs together in order to keep us contained, and then they bake us all day long in their *oven malls* until we are done, I mean really done. Then they feast on us for the following four weeks or so, as turkey stew, turkey sandwiches, turkey soup, turkey hash, and turkey salad.

They slice us, dice us, fry us, mix us up, and stir us up in an effort to keep that turkey flavor flowing for as long as they can. And we accommodate them by continuing to buy, buy, and buy all year long, all the while neglecting our own economic survival.

Yes, we are indeed their Thanksgiving turkeys, brothers and sisters. We are also their Christmas presents. When are we going to wake up from our fantasy-land economic delusions? Black people in this country are the economic fodder for everyone else's wellbeing and prosperity. We complain, march, and come up with strategies and tactics that do no more than make us feel good about getting an apology from those who economically exploit us.

Our so-called leaders tell us when to be angry, what to be angry about, and at whom we should be angry. They even tell us when it's time to stop being angry, but they seldom tell us anything we can do to economically empower ourselves to the point where it would no longer matter who calls us a name or fails to give us good service at their restaurant.

What brand of leadership serves its own people up for Thanksgiving dinner? I often say that we have enough intellectual capacity to do great things for our economic future and that of our children. The message from our "leaders" should be couched in economic freedom, self-reliance, and empowerment, rather than feeding us a steady diet of mere "feel-good," "you can do it," and "you're a winner," speeches and strategies.

They should be teaching us how to move beyond the rhetoric to real action and progress from year to year. They should, in addition to the registering to vote campaigns, teach us what Booker T. Washington taught us: How to register our dollars all year long. They should show us the way to economic freedom; they should lead us there, and they should serve us, as Carter G. Woodson wrote, with their expertise in business, finance, and entrepreneurship.

Every Thanksgiving and Christmas, we are marinated, basted in our own savory juices, and cooked to perfection until the meat just falls off our bones, not unlike the dollars that fall out of our pockets and purses. We traipse to the stores, plop down the green, and return to our abodes to complain about how miserably "they" treat us.

This year, as we move through another holiday season that used to be a Holy Day season, let's resolve to change the menu and take turkey off the tables of the corporate hordes. And let's stop allowing our people to be consumed and digested, only to be excreted upon when the New Year begins. I apologize for the graphic language, but this is just that serious, brothers and sisters. We're supposed to <u>have</u> the meal, not <u>be</u> the meal. It's called "Turkey Day," not "Turkeys' Day."

Section IX

Education and Entrepreneurship

"I have spent 2 1/2 years in a major research effort concerning the economic viability of the inner city. The problems in the inner city are not there because of lack of effort. They are there because we are using the wrong model... the only way to solve the problems of the inner city is by building an economic strategy... we need to create the conditions to develop profitable businesses there."

Dr. Michael E. Porter,
Harvard University Business School

"Without a doubt, the best way for us to accumulate wealth quickly and increase the circulation rate of our dollars within our community is through the rapid formation of businesses in our community. To accomplish this, we must start directing a greater number of our young people through the entrepreneurship channel.

Robert Wallace,
Black Wealth Through Black Entrepreneurship

"Let's be judged not by the color of our skin but by the content of our business plan."

Fred Terrell, Owner, Provender Capital

Wanted: Entrepreneurship High Schools

"When I saw how learning about entrepreneurship increased my students' self-esteem, confidence, math and reading skills, and prospects for the future, I wanted every young person to learn about it." These are the words of one this country's leading experts on youth entrepreneurship, Mr. Steve Mariotti, author of **The Young Entrepreneur's Guide to Starting and Running a Business**, and Founder of the National Foundation for Teaching Entrepreneurship (NFTE). Mr. Mariotti goes on to say, "I firmly believe there should be a national effort to teach every young person the fundamentals of starting his or her own business."

I agree with Mr. Mariotti. And like him, I also chose to do something about it. To paraphrase the words of Pastor David Lane, of the Berkeley Heights Church of Christ in St. Louis, some of us see a problem and say "somebody" should fix it "someday." "Well," Lane said, "Somebody is not in the phonebook, and someday is not on the calendar. I am the somebody and someday is today." Mariotti knew he was that somebody, so he took the bull by the horns, after teaching in some of New York City's toughest schools, and began his quest to teach entrepreneurship to students who had become disinterested in traditional high school. In 1987, he continued to follow through by founding NFTE (pronounced "Nifty")

As I listened to Pastor Lane, I thought about myself, and related to his words in very personal way. I saw a need for a Black Chamber of Commerce back in the early 1990's and, knowing that somebody had to start one someday, I chose to be that somebody and that someday came on June 14, 1996. In April 2000, I began to see more clearly the need for entrepreneurship training in our public school system here in Cincinnati. That was the beginning of yet another venture that I was unsure of how to bring to fruition, but I knew that somebody had to do it someday. Today, we are well on our way to opening a brand new entrepreneurship high school in Cincinnati in September 2002.

In his speeches, George Fraser always says, "When the student is ready, the teacher will appear." I had no idea how to get it done, but I knew the students were ready, and I suppose I had to be one of the teachers. The Cincinnati Public School Board, the Superintendent, and the general public were the ready "students." The "teachers" came in the form of many interested supporters excited about this new opportunity for our children. The "teachers" came in the form of public and private sector individuals enthusiastic about the new school and offering their help on every level. Again, the school will open this year (2002), and the students, with the involvement and support of their parents, will have an opportunity to become college-bound entrepreneurs.

Our new school is the result of a lot of hard work and determination by too many people to mention in this article. Thanks to the initial financial support from the Bill and Melinda Gates Foundation and subsequent support from the Cincinnati Public School System, the entrepreneurship high school, the first of its kind, opened new doors for our children.

Most reasonable people in this country would certainly agree on the importance of business ownership in the stabilization of communities and the very critical area of wealth-building and wealth-retention in those communities. In my entrepreneurship classes, I always stress the fact that small businesses support this country, even more than larger enterprises, by creating most of the job opportunities and most of the individual wealth we see today.

Our youth, Black youth, must have that same opportunity. How do they get it? They get it through education that is centered on the practicality and reality of ownership and control of income-producing assets, and by being job makers rather than, or at least in addition to, job takers. Entrepreneurship is the key to our children's future; see that they learn it.

Having before them striking examples of colored men who could find no employment in the United States, the free Negroes began to realize that their preparation was not going hand in hand with their opportunities.
Dr. Carter G. Woodson, The Education of the Negro

Demopublicans, Republicrats, and Entrepreneurs

An article in Fortune Magazine (May 2, 2003), written by David Dent, inspired this column. It is an outstanding article, which probably will not be read by many of our people, so I thought I would use it as an example of the issues about which I write and speak. The following quote from one of my "mentors," Dr. John Sibley Butler, says it all: "I tell my students, I'd rather you be a capitalist pig than a Senator." That comment brought to mind and, quite frankly, verified for me even more the vital need for Black people to start and grow businesses.

In addition, the article reminded me that during the past forty years our people have been led down the proverbial primrose path of "politics only" by some of our Black leaders, and we continue to pay the price for having neglected to lead some down the economic path, as well as to keep those who were in business in the 1960's on that path. Oh we were just so happy we could finally "play" politics that we turned our backs on economics and our own businesses. We then ran off to support those we had complained about for so many years, purchasing from them and creating even more wealth for them and their children. It was "Civil Rights," y'all, not "Civil Privileges!" It's certainly not a privilege to spend your money with someone else; it's a right, a choice.

With our newfound privileges, and some of our leaders telling us it was the road to freedom, we began to elect thousands of Black folks to political office. We also chose our side once again. Just thirty-five years prior to gaining our civil rights we were arguing about the fact that most Black folks voted Republican. Now we argue about Black folks, for the most part, voting Democrat. And the beat goes on. Instead of getting on both sides, it's always been an all or nothing scenario when it comes to Black politics, which has hurt our efforts to have any meaningful economic clout in this society. Some one said there's not a dime's worth of difference between the two political parties. So why do Blacks put all our eggs in one political basket? Better still, why not start our own party?

I will let Gwen Day-Richardson, owner and operator of CushCity.com, an Internet-based bookstore, tell you. The Fortune article cited Richardson's break from both parties, and her resorting to the only thing that leads to political clout, the only thing that gets politicians to listen, the only thing that drives politics: Business.

Richardson said she worked for the Democrats and became disillusioned and "fed up" with what she perceived as a lack of their support for the business community. She switched camps and went to the Republicans, only to be "paraded" around as a poster child for inclusion and used as an example to prove the GOP was not a racist party. No win at all in either one of those scenarios for Richardson, or for any of us for that matter. So this sister left both wings of the political bird and answered the entrepreneurship call.

I just love the way Brother Fred Terrell, founder of Provender Capital, stated his position in the article as well. He said, "[Entrepreneurship] is a way of continuing to advance [the Civil Rights] movement." Big "props" to those who championed the cause for voting rights and other social fairness issues; we should respect them and hold them in high esteem. But what good will their sacrifices bring if we simply continue to be content with getting more and more Black people elected, and ignore the value of business ownership? What good will it do if we do not cause a resurgence of Black owned businesses, the way it was in 1910, according to Dr. Butler, who said, "In 1910 Black Americans were more likely to be self-employed than any group in America."

That's where we need to be. That's where we must go. That's where we must turn our attention – right now! We have squandered at least 35 years, as if we were not already far enough behind, when it comes to economic empowerment. The establishment conceded political gains to Black folks in the 1960's; the same way politics was the concession in South Africa when Mandela was released from prison.

The establishment understands where the real power is, and they know it is not in politics, especially if the group in political control has no economic base. In South Africa we see 15% of the population controlling 85% of the economic resources, while Black folks now occupy high public offices. In this country, well, you know the deal; we still own around 1% of the economic resources, just like we did in 125 years ago. But, we have elected more than 10,000 Black folks to political office.

What's the lesson here? While some of our leaders failed to keep us on the economic path back in 1965, and although we are even further behind, we have no choice but to follow the examples of our sister, Gwen-Day Richardson, and our brother, Fred Terrell, who says he can contribute more to the civil rights movement as a private businessman running Provender Capital. We should adopt Brother Terrell's words as our mantra: "Let's be judged not by the color of our skin but by the content of our business plan."

A Grand Time with Granville and Other Friends

The last three weekends in May 2003 will always provide fond memories for me. I had the pleasure of visiting three cities and speaking to my brothers and sisters about two of my favorite subjects: Economic empowerment and entrepreneurship. It is always good to see and be among relatives I have never met before, and it's especially good to bring the message of empowerment and true freedom to our people. So, for three straight weekends I basked in the sunshine of Black men, women, and youth, evangelizing the word of economic freedom – and the pleasure was all mine!

I started with a speaking engagement at the Africentric High School in Columbus, Ohio, at the invitation of Brother Richard Lundy, Director of the Kemetic Institute. It was refreshing, first of all, to see an African-centered high school, and then to be among conscious brothers and sisters who would carry on the message of economic empowerment beyond the walls of that particular venue.

My next stop on the speaker circuit was Baltimore, Maryland, at Sojourner Douglass College, for the Reality Speaks Series, sponsored by Brother Jabari and the Conscious Views Bookstore. Once again, it was fantastic to meet more of my long lost relatives, and to top it all off I shared the stage with one of this nation's greatest entrepreneurs: Mr. Ray Haysbert, former owner of Parks Sausage. What a thrill it was to see him again, and then to hear him speak to the audience in support of my message on economic empowerment; that made my year!

Then came the final weekend of my "Whirlwind" tour. Brother Michael Artson, President and CEO of the Granville Academy of Northern Virginia, invited me to speak at the Academy's graduation ceremony. In case you haven't heard of Granville Academy just pick up a copy of Black Enterprise Magazine (June 2003) and see the feature on Kidpreneurs - Youth Entrepreneurship.

Granville Academy was started in 1983 by William Granville, Jr., a brother from the "hood" of Trenton, New Jersey, who decided, with a little nudge from one of his teachers, to change directions in his life before it was too late. After retiring from a very successful career as a senior executive for one the world's largest companies, Mobil Oil, Brother Granville went to work again, this time doing what many of us just talk about. He set out to "give something back" by repaying the support and time his teacher invested in him. Granville established the academy to train inner city youth in the dynamics of business and entrepreneurship.

Twenty years later Granville has 12 chapters along the east coast from Waterbury, Connecticut, to Tampa, Florida, and in Cleveland, Ohio. Bill Granville started the Academy with his own funds and continues to "invest" in his people by instilling in our youth what many of us only celebrate once each year: Kujichagulia, Ujamaa, et al. Bill Granville, currently attending divinity school to pursue his *third career* as a minister, also founded a charter school in Trenton, New Jersey, which serves K-12 students. He says, "Our goal is to open a charter school in each of the states where our affiliates operate." And wouldn't you know it, he's still not satisfied. He told me he is working diligently to start a Black College somewhere in New Jersey as well. Here we have a Black man, and I do mean a "Man," who did quite well as a highly paid executive in corporate America, passing on his knowledge, his financial resources, and his example to our youth.

I was especially excited about the fact that entrepreneurship is being taught at Granville, along with technology, of course. It was a pleasure to see Michelle Artson, who will attend Delaware State University, Bill Granville's alma mater, present her prize-winning business plan to the audience. The other students participated in various aspects of the ceremony and demonstrated their skills and talents in several areas of endeavor. You would be hard-pressed to find a better group of young people than those at Granville Academy.

Yes, I had three great weekends during the month of May 2003. Granville Academy was the icing on the cake. Thanks to my brothers, Richard Lundy, Jabari, and Michael Artson for your confidence and support. Thanks to those of you came out to hear the message. And, thanks to the young brothers and sisters who will be well prepared to receive the baton and run swiftly toward the goal of economic freedom and independence.

To all of our people, young and "seasoned," to Brother Ray Haysbert, to my sister entrepreneur, Jernay Freeman, who made a special trip to Fairfax, Virginia for the Granville affair, and to all the parents who came out in support of their children, "Thank You." You are the reason I do what I do.

To the readers of this column, I simply ask you to support these organizations with your money and your time, and support those organizations in your respective cities as well. When we get the spirit of entrepreneurship and true economic freedom into our children, they will be armed for the struggle ahead of them; they will have the ultimate fighting weapon not only to survive in this country, but also to thrive.

Smart Bombs and Dumb Children

Hey, whatever happened to George Bush's education mantra, "We will leave no child behind"? Oh I almost forgot. He has something much more interesting occupying his time right now. Maybe he'll get back to the children when his war is over. But maybe by then there won't be enough money left to assure that even one child gets ahead, let alone none of them being left behind. Priorities come into question here. Do we prefer "Smart Bombs" rather than smart children? It looks like George Bush does, considering his budget requests for the war in Iraq and its subsequent "clean-up" and "reconstruction."

Yet another "Gotcha" has been played on the people by George and his merry men (and woman). I always wondered why old Dick Cheney left a $36 million job for the job of Vice President. Now I know. The Kellogg Brown & Root unit of Halliburton has pulled up to the national gas station and said, "Filler up, George," and he has accommodated. Cheney must be a soothsayer; he resigned from Halliburton just in time, didn't he?   Yeah, just in time to make more "smart bombs" with which to decimate Iraq so Halliburton could waltz right in and make billions cleaning up the mess.

Meanwhile, leaving no child behind has faded into virtual oblivion, conjured up every now and then in our memory of a compassionate conservative who, during his inaugural address, looked us in the eye and said, "America, at its best, is compassionate. In the quiet of America's conscience, we know that deep, persistent poverty is unworthy of our nation's promise. And whatever our views of its cause, we can agree that children at risk are not at fault." Well, it may not be their fault, George, but they will certainly be the ones to pay for it.

Marian Wright Edelman, Founder and President of the Children's Defense Fund, wrote an article (May 2001) titled, "Does President Bush Really Mean to Leave No Child Behind?" She noted, "The president has said that education is his highest priority yet that is not reflected in his budget. For every $1 he has proposed to invest in education, he has proposed to invest at least $40 in a tax cut that will leave millions of children behind and widen the gap between the rich and the poor." Marian is the real soothsayer, folks.

What we have now is a country that is willing to sacrifice its children's education for more smart bombs. Many of us, including our compassionate President, are willing to accept smart bombs and dumb children, smart bombs and poor children, smart bombs and hungry children. At this point in the "Leave No Child Behind" charade, the Bill and Melinda Gates Foundation is doing more than our government to help our children get a good education! But I keep on forgetting, we are at war and Bush needs $75 billion to pay for it. What could I have been thinking?

At a time when a large percentage of our children are functionally illiterate, many of them dropping out of school for various reasons, displaying the lowest of social and interpersonal skills toward their classmates and their teachers, and then ending up in prison, you would think the "Leave No Child Behind" cry would get top priority. But remember back in the 1980's when Reagan and Daddy Bush were in the Big House ("Wars" on crime and drugs)? And remember what Master Clinton did when he moved in ($20 billion for new prisons)? According to an article in Time Magazine titled, "...And Throw Away The Key", by Jill Smolowe, (February 1994), the spending priority during that period centered on prison-building, private as well as public. Are things getting clearer now?

While telling us more money does not make a better student, our prison-crazed leaders were spending billions on new prisons that were equipped far better than our schools. Their obvious reasoning was that more money made better criminals. How ridiculous was that? But just look at what we have today. The stock market loves the prison industry. How can you do better than owning hundreds of acres of land, complete with a prison facility, and to top it all off, it comes with its own group of slaves? What a deal, huh? In that Time article Robert Gangi, Executive Director of the Correctional Association of New York, warned, "Building more prisons to address crime is like building more graveyards to address a fatal disease."

A new era is now upon us. The moneychangers have subscribed to the notion that building more smart bombs is more important – and more profitable – than building smart children. Remember the old Doritos commercial on television? I can see some Jay Leno impersonator in Washington saying, "Go ahead, use as many as you like; we'll make more." Well, we are also making dumb children. But who cares about that? We'll just put them in our nice private prisons – and throwaway the key.

I can hear the conversation now:

"Hey George, pass me another billion dollars; the American people won't miss it," Cheney says to Bush.

As he accommodates the request, George asks, "What ever happened to my 'Leave No Child Behind' policy, Dick?"

Cheney responds, "We didn't leave any children behind, Mr. President; they are all tucked away in comfortable state-of-the-art prisons. How about we send them some nice smart bombs for Christmas?"

Rebuilding the Entrepreneurial Spirit

The latest statistics from the Department of Commerce, just as in 1992, show Black business start-ups on the rise. The count now exceeds 850,000. On the surface this increase in the number of Black owned businesses from 1987, when the number was purported to be approximately 425,000, makes for good copy in the newspapers and other publications. It even makes many of our people feel good about our progress when it comes to business development, and that's a good thing, of course. However, the complete story is not disclosed merely by looking at the number of Black owned businesses. We must look also at the revenues of those businesses.

In 1992 the interesting small print disclosed by the Department of Commerce indicated that 56% of the 627,000 Black businesses in their report had annual revenues of around $10,000. Ten years later the USA Today reported that in 1982 Black owned businesses led other ethnic groups in revenues. Now, in 2002, Asian businesses lead the pack with $336,000 annually, followed by Hispanic businesses with $155,000, and bringing up the rear are Black owned businesses with a meager $86,000 in annual revenues. I said it recently and I say it again. Black people have an annual aggregate income of nearly $700 billion, yet our businesses have average annual revenues of $86,000. You do the math on that one.

I think we have been led by and we have come to be content with mere numbers when it comes to Black owned businesses. The larger the number grows, the better off we are made to feel about our situation. But aren't revenues more important, or at least just as important as the number of Black owned businesses that exist in this country?

The success of Black business must not only be couched in how many there are, which is still far too few, relative to our approximately 40 million in population. Black business must also be associated with growth and revenues. In other words, we must assure Black businesses not only survive but thrive. Too often we talk about the survival of Black owned businesses, neglecting to acknowledge the fact that unless a business grows it will not survive. Growth is also change; it's being able and willing to adjust to the up and down world of economics, social upheavals, and customer preferences.

So what we need in this country is not only an increase in the number of Black owned businesses. We also need different kinds of businesses, especially those upon which we depend for our sustenance, i.e., supermarkets. We need business growth, business support, business training and education, business investment funds, partnerships, alliances, cooperatives, and control of vertical business chains within industries that Black folks dominate. (Dr. Claud Anderson has been telling us this for years.)

We must also have a distribution system that we can control and not be subject to the whims, greed, and unfairness of non-Black distributors who realize that once we obtain distributive control of our products we will be well on our way to economic freedom.

Finally, we desperately need to rebuild our entrepreneurial spirit. Just as our ancestors demonstrated long before they arrived on these shores, during slavery, and after they were so-called freed (I call it fired or, at best, laid-off), we must return to that same spirit of independence and interdependence, despite being told we are free. Rebuilding the entrepreneurial spirit will take us where we must go in order to survive and thrive in this country – this capitalistic country.

Everyone should know by now that jobs are steadily disappearing, or at least leaving this country. We must be *job makers* in addition to *job takers*. We must instill in our children the entrepreneurial spirit, which will give them the security of knowing they can take care of themselves in this society and not have to depend upon the largess of government or layoff-prone corporations.

Let's get busy. Let's start new businesses, but let's also support them to a much greater degree than we do now. Let's get together and strengthen our businesses by forming strategic alliances with one another – as well as with others. And let's teach our children the value and benefits of being an entrepreneur. Catch the spirit of entrepreneurship. Our ancestors will be proud, and so will our children.

Somewhere Lorraine Hansberry is Smiling

Young, Gifted, and Black, vivacious, a smile that can light up a stadium, determined, tenacious, intelligent, and she's an entrepreneur too! This young lady has achieved far beyond her 14 years, having already made an enduring impression on adults and other young people, and she continues in the tradition of Madam C.J. Walker, Mary McLeod Bethune, Maria Stewart, and Ida B. Wells, just to name a few. She understands and readily acknowledges her debt to her ancestors and her elders, those who paved the way for her and those who taught and continue to teach her. She deeply loves and respects her great-grandfather and gives all due credit to her mother for home-schooling her and allowing her the leeway to explore the possibilities.

Who is this amazing young lady? It's Miss Kenya Jordana James, Teenpreneur of the Year for Black Enterprise Magazine, the 14 year-old *phenom* seen on Oprah and across the country at various venues, speaking at conferences and conventions, and doing her entrepreneurial thing in her home-base of Atlanta, Georgia. Kenya will quickly tell you that she is from the Big Apple, New York City, and she has the spunk and grit to prove it. I have never seen a more determined and dedicated young person in all my years.

I asked Kenya to come to Cincinnati to speak to the students at our entrepreneurship high school, which is funded in part by the Bill and Melinda Gates Foundation, with administrative support from the KnowledgeWorks Foundation. She graciously accepted our invitation, despite having to be in San Francisco the next day to speak at the annual meeting of the California Black Chamber of Commerce. Brother Aubry Stone and his excellent staff at the Chamber worked out the transportation arrangements and we were in business.

Not only did Kenya spend several hours with the students doing two presentations, answering their questions, and taking photographs with them, she also spent an hour on a local radio talk show, Sister Speak, here in Cincinnati. She was absolutely great in both instances. She took calls and inquiries from listeners and responded with the aplomb of a seasoned adult. What can I say? Kenya James is fantastic!

Let me not forget about Kenya's inspiration, her mentor, teacher, guidance counselor, and mother, Karen Mason, also an entrepreneur. President of the Destiny Agency, a Marketing and Events Planning firm in Atlanta, Karen is a fine example of what a caring and concerned mother does for and with her child. Of course, the two of them travel together, and hearing the interplay between them, as I drove them from Dayton, Ohio to Cincinnati, was inspiring and refreshing. They really love and respect each other.

Kenya takes college courses at two Atlanta Universities, reads constantly, discusses various authors and their writings, and even recommended several books for my 10 year-old daughter to read. She and her mother have read many of the same books, which gives them an even greater opportunity to engage in conversation with each other.

Kenya founded, owns, and publishes Black Girl Magazine, but got started in business by baking and selling cakes. She has since graduated not only to publishing but also to owning a line of clothing called Modest Apparel, which she started because her mother would not allow her to wear certain things. She has a couple of other business ventures going as well, and on top of all of that she plans to become a doctor. Talk about a full plate. We adults should never complain again about being too busy.

I leave you with two thoughts. First, we must support this young lady and her business endeavors. Subscribe to Black Girl Magazine (www.blackgirlmagazine.com) and, for you business owners out there, purchase advertisements in the magazine. There are certainly more than enough business owners who will read this article who should run their advertisement in Black Girl Magazine. It is a family-oriented publication, with a very positive message. Please subscribe and advertise – now!

Second, let's not succumb to the temptation of raising the bar even higher for Kenya James simply because she is doing so many great things right now. We must not put that responsibility on her shoulders. She is only 14 years-old and, in her own words, "I'm still a child; I like to do crazy things every now and then. I like to hang out with my friends sometimes." In other words, admiring adults like me must be careful not to elevate Kenya to a level where she constantly feels obligated to be the "perfect child," irrespective of our high praise for her. True, she is operating well above average, and truly deserves our accolades, but let's always give her the space and time she needs just to be a kid.

I hope and pray that by writing this article I did not go against my own advice, but I am sure Kenya and her mother will understand and appreciate my enthusiasm for exactly what it is: Nothing but love for both of them.

Thanks, Kenya. You are definitely Young, Gifted, and Black, and I am so very proud of you.

Bill Gates - The Real Education Czar

On September 18, 2003, Bill Gates announced a $51.2 million donation from the Bill and Melinda Gates Foundation to help start 67 small high schools in New York City. The grants will go to seven non-profit organizations that work with New York City's public school system.

Gates pointed to dismally low graduation rates as evidence of the failure of traditional high schools, a problem that is even worse among poor, Black, and other minority students. Gates feels strongly that the answer is not smaller classes, but much smaller schools, and his approach has been shown to reduce violence and increase achievement among various student populations.

Gates says he wants to "create an environment where there's a strong relationship between the students and teachers," and he doesn't want students to "get lost" the way they do in larger high schools especially in urban districts. "The smaller schools allow teachers and staff to know their students better," Gates says. "When a kid walks down a hall and encounters an adult, that adult will know their name and ... be able to talk to them about their progress."

A small high school is "the way to take what is really the weak link in the education system -- high school -- and bring it up to a new level," Gates stated. Amen to that, my brother! I am a living witness to the reality of moving from a very large high school to a very small one when I was sixteen years of age.

I moved from an anonymous environment, except for my immediate circle of friends, to a more caring environment of teachers, administrators, and students at a small school in Winston-Salem, North Carolina. It was the best thing that ever happened to me during my teenage years, and had it not been for Paisley High School, and those teachers who cared so much that they would not let me fail, I probably would have been a high school dropout.

The Bill and Melinda Gates Foundation, along with a precious few other organizations, is doing what our local, state, and federal governments should be doing. While our President, who adopted Marian Wright Edelman's mantra, "Leave no child behind," is dropping "smart bombs," Gates is helping to produce "smart children," and I just wanted to say, "Thanks, Bill and Melinda Gates."

Not only can I write about what the Gates Foundation is doing in the field of education, I can also personally attest to its commitment and dedication, having been involved with the Foundation's Model Secondary Schools Project since 2001. Our entrepreneurship school is one of eight model secondary schools across the country funded by the Gates Foundation (see www.modelschoolsproject.org). The other schools are in: Detroit; Rochester, New York; Boston; Compton, California; Cleveland, Ohio; Las Vegas; and East St. Louis, Illinois.

Education and health, the two focus areas of the Gates Foundation, are obviously vital to the well being and stability of any people. The United States and the world are blessed to have foundations and organizations whose benefactors make it their business to contribute part of their fortunes to these causes.

It is not enough just to know that Bill Gates is the richest person in the world, as Forbes Magazine points out each year. It is more important for him and others like him to make a positive and permanent impact on the lives of the poor, the underserved, and the disenfranchised. Many of our super-rich entertainers and athletes could take a lesson from such altruism and philanthropy.

We are proud and appreciative of the support of the Bill and Melinda Gates Foundation, Tom Vander Ark, Executive Director, Education, and all of the project staff who work tirelessly to accomplish the overall goals of the Gates Foundation: "Creating more small high schools and reducing financial barriers to higher education. And to increase the number of talented low-income students who attend and graduate from college."

We know that entrepreneurship is the key to wealth-building in this country, and I am thankful and proud to know that the world's greatest entrepreneur, Bill Gates and his wife,

Melinda, have chosen our entrepreneurship high school as one of the small schools supported by their Foundation. I am also even more thankful for Gates and those other affluent individuals who genuinely understand what it means to help those less fortunate – and to help them by providing programs that will last a lifetime and be passed on to future generations. Thank God they also have a firm grasp and understanding of Luke 12:48 – "To whom much is given, much is required."

Piney Woods School –
Changing America ...One student at a time.

"All children can excel if their sense of futility can be overcome, and they are given the opportunity to learn in a focused, disciplined community of caring teachers... They can learn, and we will see to it that they do."
Charles H. Beady, Jr. PhD, *President, Piney Woods School*

After several unsuccessful attempts to arrange the trip, I was finally able to get to Piney Woods School, one of this country's four remaining Black owned boarding schools, located about 21miles south of Jackson, Mississippi. Nestled among the pine trees, amid rolling hills, lakes, and farmland, Piney Woods School made me feel like I had found a lost treasure. As I walked the campus and learned about the history of this school, a deep sense of melancholy came upon me and, feeling almost ashamed, I questioned why I had not come to that magnificent, historic, and wonderful place much sooner than I had.

The Piney Woods School, a boarding school for grades 9-12, was founded in 1909. The students hail from cities from coast to coast, and they even come to attend the school from other countries such as Ethiopia and Mexico. Literally every student I met during my visit was courteous; they also demonstrated the initiative to walk up and introduce themselves to me without being prompted. That alone was enough to impress me; but there's much more.

The staff of Piney Woods is a group of dedicated, concerned, and loving teachers and administrators who welcomed me with open arms and a willingness to assist me in any way they could. They exuded a pride and loyalty that would have made the founder, Dr. Laurence C. Jones, smile from ear to ear. That same spirit obviously transfers over to the students when they arrive and as they make their way through the school year. It was pure joy to be among teachers and students who were on the same page when comes to education and had great relationships to boot. Did I mention the food was excellent?

I was taken on a tour of the Piney Woods Museum and was able to travel back more than 90 years and make my way up to the present, learning about how Dr. Jones was able to open the school, seeing his writings, photos of his friends, relatives, and former students. There are photos of the famed Cotton Blossom Singers and artifacts brought back from other countries by Dr. Jones. It was a wonderful, inspiring, and enlightening experience. I stood in the small cemetery where Dr. Jones, his wife, and others are interred, and I stood inside the former slave's house that was given to Dr. Jones to start the school in 1909.

My heartfelt gratitude goes out to Marvin Jones, Assistant to the President, who arranged for my visit Piney Woods and served as my personal escort and tour guide throughout the Piney Woods grounds. To Piney Woods President, Dr. Charles H. Beady, Jr., a man of many talents and a man who loves his work and the students at Piney Woods, "Thank you, my brother, for your hospitality and for your commitment to the vision of Dr. Laurence Jones and your predecessor, Dr. James S. Wade." You are a true role model for us all.

Now for some Blackonomics business. You know I have to write something about economic empowerment. So here it is. Back in 1954, Ralph Edwards, host of the television show, "This is Your Life," featured Dr. Jones' life. Edwards was so impressed with Piney Woods that he put out a call to his viewers to send in $1.00 each to the school in an effort to raise $1 million. Nearly 50 years later, on Blake Radio.Com, during my regular show, I put out a call to listeners. I also sent out a call on my e-mail list, The Whirlwind. Now I am issuing that same call for readers of my column, Blackonomics.

That call is for you to send $5.00 each to Piney Woods in an effort to raise $1 million! (Psst, don't tell anyone, but I think we can do even better than that.) I know if $750,000 could be raised in 1954 from an effort that went out over television, a medium only a few families were fortunate enough to have, we can surely eclipse that effort in 2003.

Wouldn't it be a wonderful Kwanzaa gift to Piney Woods, a school that exhibits all seven principles of the Nguzo Saba, if they could count a million dollars in donations from across this country by December 31, 2003? In other words, I am asking you to do this right now; don't wait, send in your $5.00 as soon as you finish reading this, if possible.

I know I sound like a *Johnny-Come-Lately* to all of those fine organizations and individuals who have already given so generously to Piney Woods, but I ask you to attribute my effort in organizing this campaign to the same kind of enthusiasm that caused you to want to help this school.   This is an opportunity for everyone to help Piney Woods maintain the same high-quality education it has provided for years, an education that results in 95% of its graduates going on to college.   Did I mention they teach Entrepreneurship at Piney Woods?

Please send your $5.00 to Piney Woods School, U.S. Highway 49 South, Piney Woods, Mississippi, 39148, and let's do something great with this opportunity.   Also, plan to make a visit to the campus and see what I mean when I say, "It was a blessing to be there." Support the Piney Woods School, as it changes America, "one student at a time."

For more information see *www.pineywoods.org* or call 601 845 2214.

Update: *Hundreds have heeded the call and sent in their $5.00 (or more in some cases). Have you sent your donation in? It's never too late to something good, you know. Do your part to make history.*

Section X

The Business of Doing Business

*"True Empowerment is Economic
...we must create a culture of entrepreneurship and
economic development where the virtues of economic
empowerment are taught at home, in educational
institutions, and churches... This culture must include
ample opportunities for aspiring entrepreneurs and
community developers to acquire the skills and ethics to
engage in socially responsible business..."*
Ron Daniels,
Social and Political Activist

*"Let's get together and get some land;
Raise our food like the man;
Save our money like the mob;
Put up a factory and own the jobs."*
James Brown,
Godfather of Soul

Business Owners, Take Care of Your Business!

I hear it all the time. "I patronized a Black owned business and was treated terribly." How about this one? "I went to that Black restaurant and the service was bad, the food was cold, and the staff was discourteous and very slow." And the grand-daddy of them all: "I tried to do business with Black contractors, but they didn't show up on time, they wanted me to pick them up because they didn't have transportation, and they wanted me to go out and buy the materials needed for the job."

I write a great deal about the responsibility of Black consumers to support Black owned businesses, and sometimes it's brought to my attention that I do not spend enough time dealing with the obligation Black businesses have to provide good products and services. Believe me, I understand and do promote quality from our businesses. I teach a course titled, Black Entrepreneurship, at the University of Cincinnati as well as a course in Business Planning, in what was the eye of the storm during the aftermath of the Timothy Thomas murder – Over-The-Rhine. In my classes I stress the obligations of business owners to their customers.

My interactions with Black business owners and prospective Black business owners include an emphasis on good service, integrity, and simply doing what you say you will do for the customer. Our businesses have it hard enough without heaping more problems on themselves by not following through on agreements, not opening on time, not showing up to do the job on time, cheating and stealing from their customers, and the list goes on. You would think they would see this and make sure their employees were always on their best behavior, carrying out the very best of practices toward their customers. You would think, considering our mental enslavement, that Black business owners would try a little harder, do a little more, and make that extra effort to please Black customers. But, we still suffer from the programming that makes us hate one another and ourselves, thus making it quite difficult to do business together.

Additionally, we think it's all right to do a brother or a sister wrong, mainly because we are not accustomed to being dragged into court and sued by our people. We sure are afraid of the white man though, and we make every effort to take care of our obligations to him, because we know what will happen if we don't. Shamefully, we go about our business ripping one another off with schemes and practices that push us further and further apart, and we wonder why we cannot "come together."

I have been cheated several times by Black business owners. I have one situation that I am dealing with currently in which a sister whom I considered a good friend participated in a scheme that included forging my name to a lease for a copy machine because her credit would not allow her get the machine on her own. I have another lien filed against a sister I worked with on a conference who refused to repay a loan I made to her. These were business transactions and there are others as well, like getting poor service from stores, contractors, and restaurants. I have been there, done that, and I have several T-shirts to prove it!

But what do we do? First of all, Black business owners, get your act together! Stop taking short-cuts, stop cheating and lying to your customers, stop ignoring what Jawanza Kunjufu in his book, Black Economics, calls the African American Creed Business Commandments (Buy the book at your local Black Book Store and read it). He points out that our customers are our most important resource and in the final analysis, if they stop coming, you go out of business. So, respect your customers above all, treat them fairly, and do what you say you going to do.

We must work very hard to bring the ultimate economic partnership together, that of Black consumers and Black business owners. Once upon a time, during segregation, we had that ideal relationship but were not allowed to have access to the general marketplace. Our access is virtually unlimited now, but we must still have a firm foundation among our own people. Can you say, "Johnson Publishing?" Our charge as business owners is to meet our consumers a little bit beyond the middle and do what is necessary to keep them as paying customers.

We can ill-afford the lack of support for one another that we see in today's Black economy, especially when you consider what little bit of an economy we have (and I am not talking about our half-trillion annual income). So let's work together to build our relationships, our love, and our trust for one another. Through business ownership and good business management we can win.

Take care of your business and your customers, and they will take care of you.

If You Can't Beat 'Em, Buy 'Em

Since the mid-1980's, that has been the mantra of big corporations. We witnessed the buyout of many companies by the giants of industry and saw when even the threat of a buyout would cause the wealth of people like T. Boone Pickens and Ross Perot to increase exponentially. We saw the same thing with Rupert Murdock, Carl Icahn, and others who made a killing not only by buying out their competitors, but by purchasing other business plums that instantly made them billionaires. During that period in the eighties you may also remember the infamous comments of Revlon executive, Irving Bottner, who stated that Black owned hair care companies would soon be bought by majority companies. (Eerie, isn't it?)

Nearly twenty years later as we look back at all of those companies, all of those millionaires turned billionaires, and all of those tens of thousands of laid off employees, the trend for future takeovers is quite evident. An analysis and understanding of this trend are vital to the survival of Black owned business in this country.

I'm sure you have heard the saying, "Draw your enemies close to you." You have also heard the tried and true saying, "If you can't beat 'em, join 'em." These two maxims are the drumbeat of the so-called new economy, except the latter saying has been changed; instead of *joining them*, now the trend is to *buy them*. Although this particular scenario has taken place across the color line, we are concerned about the obvious trend by larger companies to gobble-up major Black owned businesses.

A friend once told me that a skeptic is someone who reads the handwriting on the wall and thinks it's a forgery. That adage expresses our current economic situation, in which Black companies are being bought and sold like never before. While I understand the practicality of starting and building a business to the point at which it becomes so attractive that others want to buy it, my ambivalence about these deals is disconcerting. On one hand, it has to be difficult to turn down hundreds of millions of dollars, something to which I will never relate. But, are those millions worth the lost of viable Black owned businesses?

A better question is: Are Black businesses being bought by white companies because they are so good or because those Black businesses are capturing too much of what many are now calling the "urban market" and the "emerging market"? Are white companies pulling their enemies closer or are they coming to the realization that they cannot beat these Black businesses so they had better buy them?

Back in the 1970's and 1980's the very mention of a Black owned business being bought by a white owned company or any other company would be met with anger and resistance. But soon the handwriting on the wall became clearer and clearer, with the purchase of Johnson Products and subsequently with the fall of other Black hair care companies, magazines, radio stations, funeral homes, grocery stores, and the latest plum, the crème de la crème, Black Entertainment Television. I ask again. Why?

My contention is that business development among Black people is a very threatening prospect to some. I contend that what is projected to be more than $1 trillion in annual income by 2010, among Black people, is the very reason for much of the buying frenzy we are witnessing today. It's one thing for Blacks to have millions in disposable income, the vast majority of which is spent with other folks' businesses. But it is an entirely different ballgame to have those same consumers owning major businesses through which more and more of that income could flow. Consumerism is one thing; ownership and control are another.

As I intimated earlier, I have absolutely no idea of what it's like to be a millionaire – or even a *hundred-thousandnaire*, and I am not about to suggest that those Black business men and women who sold their companies should not have done so; I just wish Black people had bought them, which brings us back, as always, to the issue of cooperative economics.

The value of Black owned businesses can never be overstated. If the affluent among us would value business ownership as much as they seem to value having three or four luxury cars, huge houses, and closets as large as stores for their clothing, they would pool some of their money and buy the Black businesses that are for sale.

Please understand what's going on, my brothers and sisters. They cannot beat us if we work together for economic empowerment; they cannot beat us if we continue to build and grow Black owned businesses; they cannot beat us if we redirect a greater portion of our consumption spending toward one another; and they cannot beat us if we begin to exchange our businesses among our people instead of selling them to others.

Brothers and sisters, they cannot beat us – so they are buying us.

Should Black Business Owners Sell Out?

In a previous article titled, "If you can't beat 'em, buy 'em," I discussed the fact that major Black businesses, over the past two decades, have been bought by white owned companies, i.e. Soft Sheen products, BET, Johnson Products. The piece also raised a dilemma faced by successful Black business owners who have grown their companies into lucrative well-run operations. Should they sell their businesses for the millions and billions offered them, or should they maintain ownership? There are two obvious schools of thought on this issue. On which side do you come down?

I am reminded of the Soft Sheen deal that put more than $100 million in the coffers of the Gardner family. I thought about Bob Johnson's statement after he sold BET to media giant, Viacom, for $3 billion. He said, "The 'E' in BET does mean empowerment." (It sure did for him) I remembered the statement made by Irving Bottner of Revlon, who said all of the major Black hair care companies would be sold to white owned firms in a few years. That statement, by the way, has come true to a great extent.

I also dreamed, because that's as close as I will get to it, about having to make such a decision – one that involves millions of dollars going into my bank account if I sold my company. What a decision to have to make, right? So please understand that my opinion is not based on experience.

Which side of this question do I support? In general, I support holding on to the companies rather than selling them. Specifically, I think each case is different and should be analyzed as such, and a determination should be made accordingly.

As I said, I will probably never have to make the decision myself; however, my position is based on the economic environment Blacks face in this country. We own very little. The aggregate total of Black business revenues is less than $100 billion. In a multi-trillion dollar economy, that is not even a blip on the economic radar screen. Relative to our percentage of population, we need nearly $400 billion more to reach parity in business ownership. To quote T.M. Pryor, "If *the Black business establishment disappeared from the American scene this moment, the American stock market would not react one smidgen."*

I say we need all the Black owned and controlled businesses we can get. I say we need to follow the example of John H. Johnson and Joe Dudley, who have refused to sell their businesses despite the prospect of millions, maybe billions of dollars in return. I have not talked to Mr. Johnson, but I have talked to Mr. Dudley. He says he has had several excellent offers for his business, Dudley Hair Care Products, but he refuses to sell because he knows how many Black folks his business helps. Mr. Dudley says his gift from God, his business, is not just for him and his family; it's for others as well. He understands the real value of his gift: being able to help others.

Joe Dudley knows exactly how many cosmetologists benefit from his business; he knows how many salespersons make a good living by selling his products; he knows that hundreds of people working at his manufacturing plant, in his college, in his hotel, and in his administrative offices depend on his business for their livelihood. And Joe Dudley is not going to do anything that will jeopardize their future. Sure, his future and that of his family are secure, but he subscribes to that adage we so often recite, "To whom much is given..."

There are others who have held on to their businesses and are doing quite well, such as Bronner Brothers and Luster Products. There are others who have sold their businesses, such as Blue Chip Broadcasting's Ross Love, who sold several radio stations to the Cathy Hughes' dynasty, Radio One. (That was a Black-on-Black transaction. Will Cathy Hughes follow Bob Johnson's lead?)

I believe we must own more businesses in order for us to have alternatives with which to spend our ever-increasing aggregate annual income. If we sell all our Black owned businesses, we will surely continue make a lot of money, but we will end up giving all of that money back to those who own the businesses, as we go on conspicuously consuming everything they make and sell.

How can we keep talking about recycling our dollars if we do not start, grow, and maintain more businesses through which those dollars can be recycled? If we are not inclined to do that, don't you think we at least need to own ten or twenty of those Mercedes-Benz dealerships?

If we do have to sell our businesses, maybe we can sell them to other Black folks. It would have been nice for a few of our rich and famous African American brothers and sisters to have gotten together to buy BET instead of Viacom. Who knows? Maybe those Black folks would have done a better job at programming.

A New "WB" – DBWB. Now, Profile This!

With all of the "WB's" (While Black) Black folks are faced with, I thought I would ask for just one more. We get profiled for driving while Black, walking while Black, flying while Black, breathing while Black, and living while Black. There are legal fights going on around the country in response to these WB's, which I pray we will win. And while we are fighting these battles I also pray that we will be caught doing another very important WB – Doing business while Black.

Yes, let them catch us buying and selling among ourselves; let them catch us starting new businesses and supporting the ones we have; let them catch us being economic advocates for our people; let them catch us doing economic movements like the Collective Banking Group, Visions 2000, the MATAH Network, R.E.A.C.H., Recycling Black Dollars, and Powernomics; and let them catch us loving and trusting one another much more than we do now.

That's one WB we can all live with and from which we can all prosper. Sure we are being profiled while doing just about everything we do, so why not add one that we control? Why not add a new WB, one that will surely get positive attention, and one for which we will be proud to be profiled? Oh yes, this WB is one that will really turn some heads.

Now, just like the other WB's, we will have to take some risks with DBWB. We need not fear being dragged from our automobiles, or strip-searched in an airport, or being shot while reaching for our wallet, cell phone, or even our bible. But, we need not be concerned about protracted legal arguments, lawsuits, and psychological counseling either. There are risks for DBWB, but they are different.

We must risk our pride and our ego. We must risk the possibility of someone seeing us helping another brother or sister and rejoicing when they do well. We must risk the small amount of time and compassion it takes to reach back down and pull someone else up after we have made it. We must risk spending a few nickels more for a product in a Black store. We must risk discussing poor service with the manager or owner of a Black owned business, rather than walking away from all Black businesses and telling our friends that Black businesses are terrible.

In order to implement DBWB, we must risk our selfishness, our reluctance in many cases to simply be Black, our *bourgeoisie* attitudes and our woe-is-me victimization, and we must risk our love and trust. We must risk being depicted as a brother or sister who is genuinely dedicated to the cause of economic empowerment for Black people. We must risk the bleak economic future our children now face, and be willing to fight for a brighter future for them right now.

We must risk the lack of acceptance by white people who see what we are doing as a threat to their economic stability. We must risk being called out of our names, being stymied at every turn, sometimes by your own people, and we must risk our current collective status in this country and around the world.

Those are the risks we must take if we plan to get caught, "Doing Business While Black." But don't the benefits far outweigh the risks, especially when you consider the results if we fail to take those risks? I can't imagine a better WB in which Black people can engage.

We must take up a new cause, brothers and sisters. Doing business while Black is what Frederick Douglass, Booker T. Washington, Marcus Garvey, and others were talking about. They also suffered from walking, breathing, and living while Black, but they knew that by doing business while Black their people would create their own economy, build their own communities, and take control of their own resources. They knew that Black people would be producers as well as consumers. They knew their Black brothers and sisters would create jobs, be distributors, and claim their rightful place in this capitalistic society if they would only get caught doing business while Black.

Those great brothers – and sisters like Madam C.J. Walker, Mary McLeod Bethune, and Ida B. Wells -- knew what Black people should do to build an economic foundation for their children and grandchildren. We are their children; we are the reasons for their sacrifices. What are we going to do for our children? What inheritance will we leave for them?

I say, let's get busy with a brand new WB. It's called DBWB – Doing Business While Black. They may continue to profile us, but they can't arrest us for DBWB.

Four! Or Is It "Fore"?

I don't know how it's spelled, but that's what golfers say when they think their shot is headed for a fan or another golfer; they don't want the golf ball to hit someone so they yell, "Four!" Well, I am yelling "Four" now, first to all the Black golfers out there, and then to all of the others, for the opposite reason. I am yelling "Four" to get your attention, and then to "hit" you with some information that, if acted upon, could move us closer to our goal of collective economic empowerment.

My new learning during Black History Month was that a Black man invented the modern golf tee. George F. Grant, who was in fact one of the first known African-American golfers, and one of the first African-American dentists, patented the wooden golf tee in 1899! A son of slaves, he graduated from Harvard with honors. His interest in sanitary conditions led to the wooden tee because he disliked getting dirt on his hands. So, for over 100 years we have been vested in the game of golf.

Now golf has taken African Americans by storm, especially since Tiger Woods came on the scene, but even before his rise to the pinnacle of the sport, there was Lee Elder, Charlie Sifford, Calvin Peete, and Althea Gibson; and where I live there was Jimmy Woods, for whom I used to caddy from time to time. I must admit I have never played golf, as a matter of fact I really don't care for the sport (A little too slow for me), but I am interested in its economic potential for Black folks.

What I see currently is a Black man (sorry, Tiger) at the top of a sport that returns little if anything to Black folks. I see him making huge amounts of money for golf and every other company he endorses in the name of golf, but I don't see too many of our people on the supply side of the golf industry. I am told there are a couple of Black owned golf courses in this country, but beyond that, I see very little ownership and control. With Black participation skyrocketing, don't you think Black folks should own more courses, make and sell more attire, or manufacture some of that expensive equipment you *linksters* love to brag about?

With that said, I'd like to inform those of you outside the esoteric loop of golf product manufacturing and distribution about a Black owned and operated golf manufacturing firm that, according to my cursory research, makes some of the best golf clubs in the world.

Nirvana Golf Technologies, Inc., located in Pullman, Michigan, makes putters, drivers, wedges, and adds an innovative and maybe unique way of designing the clubs to really fit their owners, thus, allowing for better scores. They have two U.S. patents on the process of adjusting their clubs to a custom-fit and conforming them to USGA rules. That's all I will say on the subject of golf mechanics, because that's the extent of my knowledge of the game.

My knowledge of economic empowerment and economic freedom, however, will allow me to offer kudos to the brothers who started Nirvana in 1998. Your foray into what has traditionally been a closed venue, both on the links and in the business arena, is commendable. Additionally, I ask all of you newfound golf enthusiasts, as well as those who have been working to lower your strokes for quite some time now, to support Nirvana Golf Technologies by buying and using their equipment.

Now to the "Big Hitters." I know there are many Black brothers and sisters who are livin' large and who can invest in the highly endorsed technology invented by Nirvana. It makes sense for Black people, enamored with the sport of golf, from Tiger Woods to Michael Jordan, to Charles Barkley, to Evander Holyfield, to the hundreds of Black organizations that conduct golf outings, to the celebrities who play those tournaments, to the Black corporations that use golf as their primary recreational activity during conventions and other meetings, to assist Nirvana – and other Black manufacturers – in its quest for investment capital and advancement in this multi-billion dollar industry. (Pardon the long sentence, but I was on a roll)

I know that makes sense to you as well. It also makes *dollars and cents* for us to support one another in business development and growth. Why shouldn't we? We support all of those other companies with our stock portfolios and caches of material wealth in automobiles, clothing, jewelry, and wheel rims that keep spinning when the car stops. If we can support everybody else, why can't we do the same for ourselves?

Nirvana Golf Technologies is one of the Black owned companies across this country many of us have not heard about, but since you are reading this article, you know now. The question is: How are you going to act on the information you have? One suggestion I can offer is to pass it on, and if you are so inclined and "have it like that" call Nirvana Golf at (269) 236-6970 or go to the website, *www.nirvanagolf.com,* and consider making an investment. Whatever else happens in this country, you know we are not about to give up golf, so your *ROI* should be great!

One of the secondary definitions for Nirvana is "A goal hoped for but apparently unattainable; a dream." Nirvana Golf Technologies is real, folks, and its primary goal has been attained. We can take it even higher. Support!

Why Borrow Your Own Money?

Each year many of our brothers and sisters succumb to the temptation of borrowing their own tax refund from a company that has neither interest nor investment in their communities, except for maintaining a business there for a short period of time. Does it make sense to borrow your own money anyway? That's exactly what it is, you know. Have you seen the commercials on television telling us how we can get a quick loan after we pay someone for preparing our tax return?

Understandably there are many persons who need someone to fill out their tax forms, and those in business to render that service should be paid for their time and their expertise. However, to prey upon people with tax-refund related "quick" loans, is unconscionable. But we see it every year, and many of our people participate in these schemes to relieve them of their money.

In the first place, to break-even rather than receive a refund is what we should thrive for when it comes to OUR money. Why should we lend the government our money, interest-free, for more than one year and then turn around and borrow it from someone else? Imagine what we could do with that money during the year.

Here is just one recommendation. I am sure you can think of more. Those among us who itemize and deduct contributions could give more to our churches, for instance. Take a look at the line that says, "Federal Income Tax Withheld," and see what you paid even after you deduct your refund. If you have less money taken out of your check during the year, and increase your donations and contributions to the church and others, you could reduce the amount on that line and lower your taxable income.

We often hear about people and companies that pay little or no taxes, and we either stand in awe or complain about it. We may not be able to relieve ourselves completely of the tax burden, but we can be a bit smarter when it comes to the subject. If you don't know how the game is played, you will lose every time.

Here is some more information for you. There is a national Black owned tax preparation company, headquartered in Beaumont, Texas, called Compro Tax. Brother Jackie Mayfield started the company and decided to provide entrepreneurship opportunities for his brothers and sisters by offering Compro Tax "brokerages" in various areas across the country. Did I mention this is a Black owned company?

Compro Tax provides everything you need to set up your business, including training and computer software. That's what we should be dealing with, rather than giving our money to companies that offer us nothing in return and even rip our people off by lending them their own money. I know, I know, I can hear you now, "Those people don't have to take those loans. Don't blame the businesses that offer them." You're right. Nobody is forcing us to take these loans, but let's face it; we just love instant gratification, especially when it comes to money. Even though I think these loans are exploitative just like those rent-to-own and check cashing outlets, they will continue to exist as long as we avail ourselves of them.

I guess I am simply asking you to reconsider how you view income tax refunds. We need to retain all of the money we can, and this is a huge source of money going through Black folks' hands every year. So, you have two options. Get into the business yourself and/or seek out Black tax preparers to complete your returns. Compro Tax is an excellent resource. Check it out, and stop wasting your money.

As for borrowing your own money from a stranger – or from anyone else for that matter, it makes no sense at all. Whatever you think is so important and cannot wait is not that important, and it can wait. Go for the electronic filing and have the refund deposited into your bank account; it only takes about ten days.

But even more important is our need to learn as much about our income tax returns as possible. Seek out Black owned tax preparation experts and give them your business instead of allowing this annual windfall of tax preparation fees to leave our "communities." Let's stop the bleeding, and let's stop falling for this scam. After all, it's our money.

I got mine, you got yours. Now what?

Here's a thought. How about getting together and doing something even bigger than we have done as individuals? What a fantastic thing to do. I know Black entrepreneurs have done it before. But I dare say the latest "marriage" of Black business owners to be consummated between Joe L. Dudley, Sr., Dudley Hair Care Products, and Dr. Walter P. Lomax, Jr., Chairman, the MATAH Network, will top the list.

What we have in this case are two Black businessmen who were not afraid of looking at each other's business, appreciating each other's accomplishments, and searching for and finding a way to create a strategic partnership that not only benefits themselves but hundreds of thousands of other Black folks as well.

I wrote a piece titled, Should Black Businesses Sell Out?, in which I noted the accomplishments of Mr. Dudley; I have also written a couple of pieces noting the outstanding business acumen of Dr. Lomax, in addition to his willingness to go beyond the normal range of business and build something that will last for generations to come.

These two outstanding Black men, along with the support of their families, have struck the deal of the century, and it was disclosed at the annual meeting of the MATAH Network, which was held at The Dudley Corporate headquarters in Kernersville, North Carolina, October 24 – 27, 2002.

I can hardly confine my excitement about this history-making event. This partnership is the culmination of the two organizations exploring ways they can work together and create greater efficiencies on both sides, thus being able to deliver to us, Black consumers, more products and services at competitive prices. But even more important than that will be the substantive changes in the way we view one another and do business with one another. This collaboration will set the tone for more innovative Black business relationships, by leading the way toward what many of us merely talk about: Cooperative Economics.

Seven days a week and 365 days each year, the Dudley/Lomax partnership will practice all of the principals of Kwanzaa – as well as celebrate them. By cooperating with each other, by getting rid of the ego and not allowing jealously and envy to raise their ugly heads, by pooling their resources, by being concerned about and loving their people, by trusting each other, and by putting their money where their mouths are, Dudley and Lomax, have thrown down the gauntlet to the rest of us. They are saying when two or more individuals "get theirs" it is not unthinkable to get together and do something even greater.

Too many of us are in the frame of mind that says, "I got mine, you get yours." And even some of us are saying, "I got mine, and I'm gonna get yours too." Mr. Dudley and Dr. Lomax have done just the opposite with "theirs" by coming together and taking advantage of their collective financial and intellectual resources. Believe me; this will change that playing field we always complain about not being level. As a matter of fact, it will set the stage for making a sizeable down payment on a new playing field.

How? Well, there is yet another Black man, Joel Webbe, who recently captured a significant portion of the worldwide, multi-billion dollar Nutmeg market, the center of which is located on the little island of Grenada. Mr. Webbe is also in this circle of cooperation and partnership. He and Joe Dudley entered into an agreement that will surely propel their respective companies, along with the MATAH Network, which is also playing an integral role, to heights never before attained by Black owned businesses.

This partnership includes products, distribution, and vertical business integration, all vital ingredients for true economic empowerment. You have probably read a great deal about the importance of controlling channels of distribution, i.e., the MATAH Network, and being able to get the products out to consumers. And, of course, if you have not heard about Dudley Products and what Joe Dudley has accomplished, you must have been vacationing on Mars for a while.

Meanwhile, on a sad note, we mourn the loss of one of the architects of the MATAH Network, our dear brother,

Kenneth Bridges, who was killed by a sniper in Virginia. There will be much more to come on the work this brother completed before he met his destiny. A giant among men, and a leader this country had not yet come to know, Ken's legacy of economic empowerment will live on through his family and through those of us who will continue to run for freedom. We love you, Ken.

Congratulations Joe Dudley and Dr. Walter P. Lomax. Thank you for caring, thank you for trusting, and thank you for doing!

For as long as I have known him, Mr. Dudley has always lived out the principle of helping others. From his early days at Fuller Products, when most people were concerned with leading our internal competition in sales and recruiting, Mr. Dudley took time out to help other dealers. There is something different about him. But back then, I did not know what it was. Now, however, I know. Mr. Dudley is committed to empowering others.
Al Gaddy, *New York City. Taken from the book, Walking by Faith, Joe L. Dudley, Author*

Business in the Black

I was pleased and honored to have been invited to Memphis, Tennessee to speak at the Black Writers Conference during the weekend of April 20, 2002. I was especially pleased to be in a city that really is *on the move* and is being led by a Black Mayor who is rebuilding the city in which Dr. King was assassinated. It was a pleasure to see all of the construction projects, the highway renovation, the proposed transit system linking mid-town and downtown, the two Black owned banks, and the Black owned hotel in which I stayed. Memphis, it was a real pleasure!

Speaking of the hotel, I must mention Mabra Holeyfield, the owner, who also helped established the city's *second* Black bank and owns the 24-hour Denny's restaurant franchise adjoining his hotel. Mabra is a pioneer, a *can-do kinda brotha,* and an entrepreneur who puts his money where his mouth is and does what it takes to create and sustain economic empowerment. He and others like him in Memphis are steadily moving that city to the forefront of the national scene via collective and cooperative economics.

The Mayor of Memphis, Willie Herenton, entered into a five-year initiative with the Christian Methodist Episcopal Church and the Fannie Mae Corporation to expand home ownership in Memphis and other cities. Citing the gap between Blacks and whites, Herenton stated, "African American families continue to lag [behind] white families in home ownership – 48 percent to 74 percent nationally." He has stepped up to do something about it, and that's what political leadership is all about.

For me, to be among Black people who are about entrepreneurship, ownership and control of income-producing assets, job creation, and self-sufficiency, makes me feel very special. And it is even more refreshing to see Black politicians doing what they are saying rather than hearing them saying what they are doing. Hats off to the Mayor of Memphis and to the residents as well.

Being among the several noted authors at the writers' conference was additionally gratifying, especially seeing my talented and beautiful friend, Tajuana "TJ" Butler, author of **Sorority Sisters** and her latest work, **Hand Me Down Heartache**. Also in attendance were Gary Johnson, owner of the **Black Men in America** website; Tina Andrews, author, **The Sally Hemmings Story** and **Why Do Fools Fall In Love?**; Zane, the best selling author of **Addicted** and the **Sex Chronicles**; S. James Guitard, author, **Chocolate Thoughts**, newcomer, Ms. TJ Baker, whose words will soon be emanating from her new book, **The Teachings of Miss Ellie Ruth**," and many more.

What I saw in that group of spirited authors was a group of entrepreneurs. I saw these brothers and sisters waking up in the middle of the night to write a little more on their next book; I saw them doing endless hours of research on their particular storylines; I saw them away from home for long periods of time on book signing tours; I saw them doing the marketing, the advertising, and the selling of their books, keeping the records and accounting for all expenses and revenues. Yes, I saw entrepreneurs.

I also saw a group of Black folks who, with the assistance of other writers and publishers, could form an alliance to establish a major publishing house of their own. And then, I thought, they could use the MATAH Network for distribution of their books and other items. What a story that would be! I sure would like to see our talented brother and sister writers, and others in that field, get together with their dollars and establish a national and global publishing house, thus having the ability to retain more of their earnings for themselves. Oh well, maybe someday.

Until that day comes, and even after that, please support these and other hardworking Black authors; please support your local Black owned bookstores; and the next time you're in Memphis, drop by Isaac Hayes' restaurant in the Peabody Center. The food and the entertainment are absolutely fantastic! Thanks, Memphis. Thanks Lawrence Wayne, for the invitation. The pleasure truly was mine.

Miami Nice! The Power of Economic Sanctions

Talk about turning a negative into a positive; take a look at what happened in Miami as a result of an acrimonious boycott of that city's travel and tourism industry.

I know there are other problems yet to deal with in Miami, Florida, since Black folks called for a boycott back in 1990 for the mistreatment of our Brother and Elder, Nelson Mandela, and against police brutality. However, with the opening of the Royal Palm Crowne Plaza, the $84 million, 422-room beachfront luxury hotel, developed by R. Donahue Peebles' Atlantic Development Company, *Miami Vice* is well on its way to becoming *Miami Nice*. No, it's not perfect, but it has taken a significant stride toward creating and sharing real economic opportunities for the Black citizens of Miami.

And to think it all started with a boycott of Miami. Will wonders never cease? To think that Black folks in Miami had enough foresight, strength, and strategic thought to say, yes, we will boycott, but when the boycott ends we will have gained something other than a handshake and an apology.

They got a $10 million commitment (and follow through) from the city for a subsidy toward the development of a Black-owned hotel, you know, just like white developers get when they want to build something. They also got a new Visitor Industry Council that will allow African Americans a greater opportunity to participate in and gain a larger share of Miami's multi-billion dollar tourism industry.

After suffering a tremendous economic loss as a result of the boycott, Miami officials decided the best thing to do was to get together with Black folks and get the thing settled. Now most people, including whites, are saying how nice the future looks for all involved, economically speaking, of course. As I always say, that's what it all eventually boils down to anyway.

The Greater Miami and Beaches Hotel Association president, Stu Blumberg, understands the possibilities. He likes the idea that the Royal Palm Crowne Plaza will generate more business for Miami and for the adjacent hotel, the Loews. He knows the new hotel will help Miami attract more visitors and conventions. And he knows the project can prove to be an asset when it comes to solving some of Miami's problems in race relations vis-à-vis accessibility by African Americans to tourism dollars. He understands the economic ramifications of this new hotel.

I wonder why millions of dollars have to be lost before cities and states finally say, let's talk and get this thing resolved – fairly. It's what I have been saying about our city, Cincinnati, where there is also a boycott of the tourism industry going on, in case you have not heard. Blacks comprise nearly half of the city's population. How can the economic prosperity of half of any city's population be a bad thing? (And that is one of the demands of the boycotters: Economic justice.) Obviously, if Black folks do well, the entire city does even better, just as they found out in Miami.

I wish our city could learn from Miami and not have to repeat the same mistakes. They say the best way to learn is from the mistakes of others. But I fear we will not. We will languish in resistance and unwillingness to admit the inequities that exist in Cincinnati, and the sanctions will probably go on, as they did in Miami, for quite some time. But, I could be wrong.

Our Black Vice-Mayor and our Black Chairman of the Greater Cincinnati Convention and Visitors' Bureau are making their pitch to the Black Meeting Planners at their annual convention, trying to spread the word that things are all right in Cincinnati. They are trying to convince Black folks to come to Cincinnati and spend their money instead of asking them to stay away because there is a boycott going on here. Did I say these two persons are Black? Not to say all Blacks think alike, I just wanted to make sure I mentioned the fact that they are Black.

I wonder if our Black representatives are telling the meeting planners about the gross economic disparity that exists here. I wonder if they are telling those Black convention planners that after being thrown to the floor by a police officer, a white man was given three-quarters of a million dollars by the city of Cincinnati within a few months. I wonder if they are telling them that the parents of Roger Owensby, the Black man who was stopped (for no reason), arrested, and choked to death by white police officers, in November 2000, still has yet to receive their due compensation from the city. Just wondering.

Maybe our political leadership in Cincinnati will take a look at what happened in Miami and say, "Hey, we can do that too. We don't have to continue in acrimony and discord; we can create a positive atmosphere in our city and take a giant first step toward solving the problems we face. Let's talk to Miami officials and some of the boycotters to find out how they reached their accord." Then I was suddenly awakened, only to realize that I was just having a nice dream – a *Miami Nice* dream.

Man, it sure would be nice to be in Miami right now, sitting on the beach at the Royal Palm Crowne Plaza, and sipping on one of those tropical drinks. I know I could sleep a lot better there.

Release Yourself!

Let yourself go, please! Break those psychological chains! Go get your economic freedom! Did you know we can literally let ourselves go? We can literally write our own emancipation proclamation? We can free ourselves from economic enslavement by a very simple means.

By using tried and true measures, Black people can bring about our collective economic liberation. We can do it by redirecting a greater portion of our dollars toward our own businesses. Why are we so reluctant to do that? Why are we so reticent when it comes to our economic freedom?

A famous Black "poet" back in the 1970's noted, *"If you're feeling like sometimes you want to let yourself go. Don't fight the feeling, might not come no more."* Do we want to let ourselves go? Or, do we want to hold on to the coattail of Pharaoh and remain in economic bondage?

I recently attended the Black Business Professionals and Entrepreneurs Conference, in Savannah, Georgia, and participated in a panel discussion on Black spending power. On the panel with me was Dr. Jeffery M. Humphries, Economist and researcher for the Selig Center of the University of Georgia. Dr. Humphries authors the study to which we all refer when discussing the $700 billion in Black spending power.

After hearing Humphries disclose all of the statistics about our money, it was my turn to speak. I told the audience that it's one thing to have an annual income of $700 billion, but it is an entirely different thing to determine who gets the benefit of that money. I often refer to our "spending power" as "spending weakness" because we spend the vast majority of our money with businesses other than our own.

Thus, while our so-called power translates into power for someone else, it does little to empower Black people. We have been too busy buying homes for other people, buying automobiles from them and for them, and sending their children to college, instead of using a greater portion of our money for ourselves. The result is a perpetuation of the same scenario: Our children end up working for their children.

Can you imagine giving 95% of everything you have to someone else? Well, that's what we do with our money. You do the math on that one and see who is ahead and who will always be behind. Can't we release ourselves from that kind of slavery? Yes, we can. Here's my joke of the week: Why won't Black people purchase a laundry detergent made by Blacks instead of the detergent they have bought for years? Answer: I don't know!

Now some may say, "I didn't know I could buy Black manufactured detergent," and we know what they say about ignorance being bliss. Well, now you know. Awaken from your blissful slumber. The MATAH Network distributes the detergent, and many other Black manufactured products, and the ball is now in your court. Once you have information it's incumbent upon you to do something with it. What will you do with the information I just gave you?

If we would make this one simple change in our purchasing habits and add to that change on a regular basis by buying other products, we could beat our habit and release ourselves from the clutches of the master marketers and advertisers who tell us how to spend our money and then laugh all the way to *their* banks.

This does not only apply to detergent; that's just a simple example. We can also purchase many more products and services offered by our brothers and sisters, you know, the way Asians, Hispanics, and Jewish people do. We can also pool our resources and support one another more by investing in ourselves.

Did you see the front-page story in USA Today titled, "Asian Business Owners Gaining Clout"? The subtitle read, "Their growing success has shifted power away from Blacks." The article pointed out, "Twenty years ago, Blacks were No. 1 in U.S. minority business ownership. Not anymore," the article stated, "Now, Hispanics are first, Asians second, and Blacks third..."

The story compared the annual revenues of the three groups, which tell the whole story. Asians hit the scale with a whopping $336, 200 versus $155,200 for Hispanic companies.

Black companies come in at a paltry $86,500. Enough said. I hope.

We must release ourselves from this maddening cycle of economic foolishness. By the way, the name of that "poet" I mentioned is Larry Graham. For those of you old enough to remember, his group, Graham Central Station, recorded an *album* (not there's a word from the past) called, **Release Yourself**, back in 1974.

Here are a few more of his inspiring words. *"Don't be a fool and wait too late. Think back from then to now, how long you had to wait. This might be your last chance; this might be your first. To try and hold it in might only make things worse... Release Yourself!"*

Section XI

Home Cookin'

"Boycott apparently losing steam"

The Urban League's decision to bring its 2003 convention to Cincinnati is the latest in a series of events that threaten to break the year-old boycott against the city.
Cincinnati Enquirer, July 13, 2002

3 Days Later...

"Boycott's sting gains intensity"

Urban League joins boycott over black cop's suspension. The National Urban League announced Monday that it will not bring its 5,000-delegate convention to Cincinnati in 2003 after all. Urban League President Hugh B. Price cited the Friday suspension of Cincinnati Police Lt. Col. Ronald Twitty and the prospect of protests at affiliate offices around the nation as reasons for the decision.
Cincinnati Enquirer, July 16, 2002

On November 30, 2003, Nathaniel Jones was killed by police officers in Cincinnati, Ohio. This incident, another in a series of similar incidents between Black men and white police officers, once again made world news and pushed Cincinnati even further back toward the days when slave catchers ran and ruled the streets of the "Queen City."

While there is no need to recant everything that took place in the Jones' incident, and understanding that whatever is done in the dark will come to the light, I will simply acknowledge Mr. Jones, and remember Lorenzo Collins, Roger Owensby, Timothy Thomas, and Michael Carpenter.

In the Jones case, while all of us will form an opinion about what happened and take whatever position that suits our perspective, even after we hear the eyewitness accounts of what happened during the missing one minute thirty-seven seconds of police videotape, I'd like to offer two indisputable facts.

The first fact is that Mr. Jones was not breaking any law when he was approached by the police officers. In Ohio a citizen has a right to at least question an unlawful arrest. Why was there an attempt to arrest Mr. Jones even before the struggle ensued?

The second fact is this: In Cincinnati, only Black men have died from these kinds of encounters with white police officers. Black officers have been punched of the face and abused in other ways by Black and white citizens, but they have not killed anyone. What do Black officers know about how to diffuse a situation that white officers do not know?

In a city where the Mayor makes stupid and insensitive comments like, "The police officers were being threatened with a deadly weapon, a 400-pound man," and the President of the Fraternal Order of Police refers to Mr. Jones as a "crack-head," and when police officers can stand over a dying man and do nothing to save his life, we know we are in serious trouble, and Cincinnati is indeed in serious trouble.

A close friend and business associate offered these ominous words with respect to the death of Nathaniel Jones:

"Put your hands behind your back!"

"I can't, you're beating me!"

"Put your hands behind your back!"

"I can't, I'm too big."

"Put your hands behind your back!"

"I can't, you're breaking my arm!"

"Put your hands behind your back!"

"I can't breathe; you're on top of me!"

"Put your hands behind your back!"

"I can't…. I'm dead."

There is irreverence for Black life in Cincinnati; a pall hangs over this city that if left unchecked will eventually destroy what little positive reputation it has. Even sadder is the fact that many Black people who reside in this town do not speak out when their brothers are shot down in alleyways like rabid dogs, or shot in the back of their heads while sitting in their cars; there is no righteous indignation by the so-called righteous Black folks when brothers are choked to death by police officers or beaten before their very eyes on television.

All we seem to be willing to do is march in protest and complain about these things on talk radio, that is, until someone gets paid to quiet the rabble-rousers. We are reluctant to fight this fight with our dollars, the only weapon we have plenty of and the only one that this society fears. I submit that if we stop firing our dollars at certain corporate tycoons and start firing them away from those who mistreat us and away from those who oppress us and who say nothing when they see an injustice, a great deal would change in this city and in this country.

How silly we Black people must be? How childlike? How easy a prey for corporate profiteers? That we will allow murders of our men, abuse and rape of our women, and brainwashing of our children, and yet continue to give our money to those who perpetrate these crimes against us, borders on insanity, and it is definitely the poorest example we could portray to the world and to our youth.

I pray we will do what is necessary to stop this madness, but I also fear there will be another Nathaniel Jones in Cincinnati, Ohio. To support that statement I offer the following excerpt from a report in the Cincinnati Enquirer, in the aftermath of the Jones case.

The headline reads: **"[Cincinnati] Council votes yes on Tasers, no on police CPR retraining."**

Council voted 6-3 at its final meeting of the year to ... buy Tasers for the Cincinnati Police Department. "To say that we are going to Taser people, but we are going to think about whether we are going to give CPR doesn't make sense to me," [Councilman Chris] Smitherman said. "If we are going to start Tasering people, we have to make sure our police are equipped across the board."

Councilman David Pepper (Son of Procter and Gamble Chairman, John Pepper) said the issue was not one of Tasers versus CPR. "My hope is that we can do both," Pepper said. "We looked closely at Tasers and we need to look as closely at CPR."

Will someone tell me why a City Council would have to "look closely" at a proven life-saving technique, namely CPR, before it approves the use of it? See what I mean?

Cincinnati – A Real-Life Cartoon

"[Cincinnati] Boycott starting to hit home; Talks take on urgency."
Acknowledging that a boycott of downtown Cincinnati has started to hurt,
business and civic leaders are talking about how to blunt its impact. Mayor
Charlie Luken on Thursday offered to meet with one of the boycott groups
asking entertainers to avoid performing in Cincinnati.
March 15, 2002

His overture came the same day that comedian Bill Cosby rejected the mayor's
request to pay some of the plaintiffs' legal fees in the recently settled racial
profiling lawsuit. Response from Bill Cosby's attorney: *"Mr. Cosby is*
particularly distressed that your request was made public in what can only be
described as an inappropriate and heavy-handed attempt to pressure him into
providing the requested funds."
April 19, 2002

By now, most of you have heard about the beatings,
shootings, and choking of Black men by white police officers in
Cincinnati, Ohio, and the subsequent boycott against the city's
travel and tourism industry. You have seen the recalcitrant
Mayor of the city do all he can to dismiss those who have the
temerity to stand up and say enough is enough. You have seen
the "Leading Blacks" do whatever they are told by the power
structure in an effort to head off their people at the pass and
disrupt the righteous and justifiable protests over criminal
injustice and economic disparity. You have seen it all right
here in Cincinnati, Ohio. But wait. You have not seen it all.

The National Urban League recently announced that it
would hold its 2003 Convention in the "Queen City," despite
the call for and support of economic sanctions against
Cincinnati by Black folks all over this country. You are
probably aware of those who refused to come to Cincinnati
until police brutality and "economic apartheid" are
discontinued. The National Progressive Baptists, Bill Cosby,
Whoppi Goldberg, Ed Gordon, Smokey Robinson, the Black
Airline Pilots, and the list goes on and on. You probably know
as well that a major public relations campaign is up and
running to get Black folks, specifically, to come to Cincinnati
and spend their money – because "Cincinnati's on the move," as

the slick brochure says. When you think about it, water going down a toilet is on the move too, isn't it?

You probably have not heard about the latest turn of events that took place just one day after the Urban League said it would come to Cincinnati because things were "turning around." The highest-ranking Black police officer in Cincinnati, Lt. Col. Ron Twitty, was summarily stripped of his police powers and put on suspension. Why? Because his police car had a dent in it, and the Chief of Police, Tom Streicher, had some concerns about how it got there, despite seeing the report that was filed by Colonel Twitty. Let me say that again. There was a dent in the Colonel's police car; the Colonel was stripped of his police powers and suspended.

The juxtaposition of the two press conferences, one held by the Urban League and the Mayor saying things were turning around and Cincinnati is improving, and the other press conference held by the Chief of Police and a few of his staff, which included – wouldn't you know it – one silent, do-nothing Black subordinate at the table with him, expressing their grave concern about a dent in an automobile, was too much to take. I surmised it was God doing the Mutombo finger-wag at Cincinnati, telling us, "No, no, not so fast Cincinnati. Things have not yet changed, in fact, they are worse. You still have a lot of work to do"

If this kind of blatant, disrespectful, insulting, and embarrassing attack can be made on a 29-year police veteran, a Black man who has fought for the police department and supported it through the controversies of the past couple of years, a man who has ten pages of commendations in his personnel folder, a man who is next in line to be the Police Chief (uh-oh, I think I said something there), if they will do this to him, what can the rest of us expect? And the Urban League thought things were getting better.

The latest chapter in the recent history of Cincinnati and its heretofore very well kept secret policy of *contain and control of Black folks* is, for those of us who have been asleep, a wide-eyed indication of why there is a boycott of this city. While I do not revel in the economic sanctions and I do not and would not celebrate another man's demise, economic or other wise, as Chris Rock once said about O.J., "I understand."

When economic sanctions are imposed on a business or a city we should understand that people have reached their Fannie Lou Hamer boiling point. Sanctions are last resort reactions to a myriad of mistreatment, disparity, and unfair practices. They are the only weapon in a capitalist-dominated society that have any real long term result, albeit, both positive and negative. I understand the boycott because I have seen, up close and personal, the games people play, the buyouts of Black "leaders," and the puppet masters pulling on the strings of the Black puppets, making them dance to their music.

I understand because I see our brothers and sisters suffering from the results of oppression, neglect, and disrespect in this city. I understand because I have seen and continue to see billions of dollars being spent on economic development projects in this city with only stated "goals" for participation in those projects for "minorities." I understand because I have seen too many broken promises, too many back room deals, too many Black men mistreated by police, and too many white officers (and a few black ones too) get off without even a slap on their hands.

To sum it all up, three days after the Urban League's announcement to come to Cincinnati, Hugh Price announced they would not come. One of the reasons given was the Twitty decision. The other was the boycott and the potential disruption it would cause to the Urban League and its mission. God does indeed work in mysterious, and many times comical, ways. Stay tuned to Cincinnati, because contrary to the words of Bugs Bunny, that's NOT all, folks!

Irony of Ironies

Truth is nowhere to be found, and whoever shuns evil becomes a prey. The Lord looked and was displeased that there was no justice. **Isaiah 59:15**

What would you think if you read the headline of your local paper and it said, "One man commits misdemeanors and gets death; another man commits murder and gets misdemeanors"? I am sure you would think it was a mockery, a travesty, a miscarriage of justice, and every other negative you could come up with, right? Well, guess what! It very well could be the headline in the local newspapers in Cincinnati.

You remember Timothy Thomas, the unarmed young Black man who had outstanding misdemeanor warrants, who was killed by a white police officer in Cincinnati. While we still do not know the "official" reason for the killing, one thing we do know is that Brother Thomas had misdemeanor traffic tickets. We know he ran from the police. We know that he was killed. We know the alleged initial statement by the officer was that Thomas "reached" for something. We know that was a lie.

Officer Stephen Roach, the policeman who shot Thomas, now faces two separate indictments, both misdemeanors. He is charged with negligent homicide and obstructing official business, both of which are misdemeanors and carry a maximum of nine months in jail. However, a person found guilty of these charges, if he or she does not have a previous record, is not likely to go to jail, especially if he or she is white.

Yes, irony of ironies. If this does not convince you of the gross, in-your-face disparities that exist in our criminal "injustice" system, I don't know what will. Even though a few years ago a national commission told the country these disparities exist, we still kept our heads in the sand. Denial of the information from that commission will get you exactly what we have here in Cincinnati: A Black man who failed to buckle his seatbelt, and ran from the police because he had misdemeanor charges, ends up murdered by a white officer who gets charged with two misdemeanors for his actions.

And some white people are still asking, "What's the problem?" "Why are Black people so angry?" "Why are Blacks marching and obstructing business in downtown?" Why are Black people not satisfied with officer Roach's indictment?" "Don't Blacks understand that if they prevent the downtown and Over-the-Rhine businesses from making money they will eventually move? "Don't they know that the tax base will be eroded if these businesses are not allowed to continue to make money?" "What about the jobs these businesses provide?" What will happen to those employees of the bars and the restaurants and the antique shops and all of the other effected businesses?"

The list goes on and on, but I think you get the point. The hue and cry regarding the after effects of the Timothy Thomas murder did not go up until the businesses began to lose money. The Mayor of Cincinnati really got upset when one of downtown Cincinnati's major events, Jammin' On Main, was cancelled. By the way, it is a predominantly white attended event. All of the bands that play in the event are white as well.

The gnashing of teeth did not really start until the specter of more dollars being lost raised its ugly head. Major corporate leaders called for meetings with city officials to put an end to what they perceived as the real problem. They were faced with losing money, and they were not about to take that lying down. It's funny how money always seems to creep into the picture at times like these.

So now the irony of ironies in our injustice system has evolved into a money issue – as I knew it would sooner or later. The cat is out of the bag, as they say. I don't know what the next chapter of this unbelievable story will be, but I assure you it will be interesting. The Mayor has formed a commission, but strangely enough there has been no allocation or even mention of money for the group, as if mere talk will solve the problem.

Yes, it will be very interesting, but I doubt if Cincinnati or any other city can top the latest irony we witnessed when Prosecutor Mike Allen announced his indictment of officer Roach for the murder of Timothy Thomas. Stephen Roach received misdemeanor charges for murder. Timothy Thomas received murder for misdemeanor charges.

A Tale of Two Timothy's

Here we go again. The rich and powerful are coming to the rescue of the poor and downtrodden after the rebellion that was caused by the shooting of Brother Timothy Thomas. Let me say first that I hope and pray something positive takes place – something that will indeed provide benefits to the people who are most adversely affected by the economic injustice we see in this town. I also hope and pray that those lurking in the shadows of profiteering, selling out, and taking personal advantage of our brother's death will refrain from their usual tactics of merely looking out for themselves.

Now, with that said, let's get to the news. To recap, Timothy Thomas was shot and killed by a white police officer who, we are told, checked the "Black" box on his police application. Maybe Cincinnati doesn't have 25% Black officers after all.

Mr. Timothy Thomas, after fleeing from police officers, and I emphasize, "after" not "while" fleeing, was shot for reasons that have not yet been fully disclosed. We do know that he had some pretty *serious* outstanding warrants – for traffic violations and for not wearing his seatbelt. We know that he died in a place where many of us would not even walk. I was with the Cincinnati Black United Front members during our cleanup of the site where the brother was slain, and I saw the filth, smelled the stench, and imagined what it must have been like for young Timothy as he took his last breath, lying in broken glass, trash, and garbage.

This brother died in a place not fit for a rat to die in, a place where people discard their unwanted items, a place where things rot away, and a place where things (and in this case a person) end up being tossed haphazardly away without regard. Juxtapose that environment where a Black man died against what we will see next month when a white man will die in sterile comfortable surroundings. There is another Timothy, named McVeigh, who will be put to sleep without pain or discomfort.

Timothy Thomas failed to put his seatbelt on; he did not pay his traffic fines; oh yes, he also had the temerity to run from the police, maybe because he feared for his life. Running from police for many young brothers has become a form of self-defense. No crime there. Timothy Thomas killed no one, robbed no one, sold drugs to no one, and he was killed and died in a rat-infested alley, as he tried to make it back home to his three-month old son. Unfortunately, they will never see each other again, at least not on this side of heaven.

Timothy McVeigh, on the other hand, killed 168 people and injured thousands more, both physically and mentally, with his dastardly act. He planned his crime and carried it out with a calculated and cold preciseness that would leave any reasonable person in chills. This Timothy said the children who died in his hell on earth destruction of that federal building were merely collateral damage. He did what he did because that's what he wanted to do. Now he will die, years after being proven guilty, and he will die now only because he asked to die.

Timothy Thomas did not ask to die, although some say he did because he ran from the police. He was shot down like a rabid dog in an alley only used for shortcuts and garbage.

Timothy McVeigh will drift off comfortably into slumber, made a martyr by some, and may cause through his death even more chaos and acts of violence by those who support him and his cause.

Timothy Thomas' death was horrible and agonizing. He has also become a martyr of sorts, and his death has already caused acts of violence, and it may cause even more. But he had no cause; instead, he has become a cause.

This tale of two Timothy's is a microcosm of what is taking place around this country. Black men are being killed in unthinkable numbers because of ridiculous, fabricated, and untruthful reasons. White men wield knives, guns, swords, and other weapons at police officers, but they don't end up dead.

Black men wield bricks, wallets, cell phones, and sometimes they reach to unbuckle their seatbelt, only to end up executed on the spot because of their threatening gestures and movements.

This tale of two Timothy's reminds me of what Dickens wrote regarding the best of times and the worst of times. The movers and shakers (the aristocrats) of Cincinnati are enjoying the best of times, while the poor and neglected (the paupers) suffer fro the worst of times. There is neither bread nor cake to eat, and the storming of the Bastille has begun. The king (Mayor Luken) has opened his court to hear what the rabble has to say. The guillotine has been raised and some heads will roll in the city administration.

We will soon see the results of all of this action. I just pray that we will not simply return to business as usual, and I hope everything that is done by those who now want to fix the situation will have a direct benefit on the people, the young men and women, who raised the consciousness of this city in the first place. If this is just more window-dressing, we will surely see more of what we have witnessed over the past week. Timothy McVeigh will be remembered for what he chose to do with his life. Timothy Thomas should be remembered and memorialized for what he will not be able to do with his.

Rest in peace, my young brother, Timothy Thomas.

Grand Slam

The headline in the Cincinnati Enquirer read, "Larkin Hits First Career Grand Slam." Barry Larkin, the great shortstop for the Cincinnati Reds baseball team had, after more than 6,000 at-bats hit his long-awaited and prized grand slam home run. Congratulations, Barry!

The headline made me think once again about the tragedy that took place in Cincinnati nearly two weeks before Larkin's historic feat, and it once again made me ponder the lack of involvement by the Black players on the Reds, two of who are from Cincinnati. I marveled at the thought of seeing Barry Larkin and Ken Griffey, Jr., also a hometown guy, lead the charge to have all the Black players – and some of the whites if they chose to – protest the shameful killing of Timothy Thomas by refusing to play in their first home game after the shooting and the street rebellion.

Wow! What a grand slam that would have been. Barry Larkin would have hit the home run of his life, one he would have cherished as much or more than the one he hit this week. Ken Griffey, Pokey Reese, Dimitri Young, et al, would go down in history for standing against wrong and injustice. Speaking of justice, David Justice could have done the same thing; he's from this area too.

I think back to the Elian Gonzalez standoff in Miami. The Cuban baseball players boycotted one game in support of little Elian, and he was not even being threatened with death, much less having been shot down in an squalid, dark, rat-invested alley like brother Timothy Thomas. Why, or should I say "how" could these millionaire Black athletes not take it upon themselves to make a statement like the Cuban players did for their compatriot?

Yes, Larkin could have hit his first grand slam on the first night the Reds were back in town after the violence occurred. Instead, he and all of the other Black players chose to play in conditions so frigid they had to wear ski masks and other clothing to keep them warm. Maybe God sent the cold to remind us of how cold we are when it comes to our fellow brothers and sisters. Whatever the reason, the coldness was demonstrated by the Reds – or should I say, "the Blacks," on that abnormally cold evening in Cincinnati.

This is not an indictment of Barry Larkin and Ken Griffey, or any of the others. Rather, it is yet another call to consciousness. Our Black athletes and entertainers have a tremendous opportunity to make grand statements, to hit grand slams, with their influence and their collective actions in the public eye. A protest by the Black players on the Cincinnati Reds would have shown this country a picture it desperately needs to see. More importantly, it would have given Black America a huge lift, especially within the ranks of our youth.

Our Black entertainers could do the same thing, for instance, by standing on stage at the upcoming Cincinnati Music Festival and declaring their outrage at what is taking place in this city. They can make a statement of support for their brothers and sisters here who are fighting for social, economic, and justice on all levels. Wouldn't that be something to behold?

Now, for all the Black conventioneers, conferees, event attendees, and visitors to Cincinnati, you can also play a role in this debacle. You bring millions of dollars to our city, the vast majority of which goes to non-Black owned businesses. Make it a point to seek out Black owned businesses in which to spend your money while you are here, please. As a matter of fact, the Blacks in Criminal Justice annual conference will be here in July. I hope and trust they will make a statement as well and maybe adopt a formal position against what is happening in Cincinnati.

You see, there is something for everyone in this tragedy. From Ken Griffey, to Barry Larkin, to Pattie LaBelle, to Frankie Beverly and Maze, (Remember "Ain't gonna' play Sun City"?), to visitors and conferees. We can all hit grand slams for our people by simply standing against wrong and standing up for what is right – unapologetically and unwavering in our resolve – no matter the small sacrifice each of us must make.

As hard as I try, I cannot begin to understand what goes through the mind of a millionaire whose family is financially secure for life and even for generations to come. I will never be in that position, but I rejoice in the success of Black people who are. Maybe I am not aware of what they have to lose if they stand up for their brothers and sisters. Maybe I am just naïve about their particular situations. Or, maybe I am right in my position. Maybe, if all of us would elevate our consciousness, our love, and our trust for one another, we would be much better off collectively.

I would like to see all Black athletes, entertainers and others make a collective statement about what is happening not only in Cincinnati but also across this country. That's the kind of Grand Slam I would love to read about.

Where have you gone, Jim Brown, Bill Russell, Muhammad Ali, Tommy Smith, John Carlos, and Curt Flood? Please come back and teach our young how to stand up and be Black.

Economic Terrorism

The boycotters have also roundly criticized Mr. [Charles] Luken for using his position to denounce the boycott as "economic terrorism." They said the remark was hypocritical for a mayor who has accused his opponents of name-calling. Feb. 16, 2002

The recent economic sanctions called by Black groups in Cincinnati, and now supported by other white and Black groups, have caused quite a stir in the Queen City, and that's putting it mildly. Public officials are gearing up an advertising and promotional campaign to deflect the criticism of Porkopolis' lack of justice for the police officers who killed two Black men and the absence of economic inclusion of Black people in billions of dollars in public economic development projects. Those on the opposing side say until Cincinnati brings about justice in those two areas the sanctions will continue. The Mayor of Cincinnati, Charlie Luken, calls this "Economic Terrorism."

Let's go back and look at what brought all of this to Cincinnati. While we are familiar with the incidents that took place in April of 2001, maybe most do not know what happened in November of 2000 when Roger Owensby was choked to death by police officers. Since that time, none of the officers involved in both of the deaths has been disciplined by city officials, not to mention the courts.

In addition to these incidents, back in July of 2000, several downtown restaurants closed their doors when the largest festival in the city came to town along with thousands of Church of God in Christ conventioneers. The festival attracts thousands of Black patrons and of course the church members were Black as well. Subsequently, in response to the closings, a boycott of the restaurants was called and a group called the Cincinnati Black United Front was established.

Moving on to 2002. Several activist groups have decided that the only way to get the attention and an acceptable reaction from the so-called powers-that-be is to call for economic sanctions against this city's travel and tourism industry as well as its entertainment industry. This action has widened the chasm between Blacks and whites, and it has ratcheted-up the discussions on both sides of the argument to make the point that I always make: It's always all about the money.

The National Progressive Baptist Conference, a Black organization and the largest convention scheduled for this city in 2002, recently agreed to come to Cincinnati despite the call for sanctions. They say they are coming to "heal" the city. Bill Cosby, Smokey Robinson, (and maybe Wynton Marsalis) have cancelled their scheduled appearances in Cincinnati. More to come, I am sure. But everyone must decide within himself to support the sanctions or to fight against them. I don't think there is any room for neutrality here.

The Mayor of Cincinnati has called the sanctions "Economic Terrorism" (I suppose that means those who support the sanctions are terrorists), and he says the only way to "overcome" is for people to come downtown and spend money. Every time he mentions the conventions and the entertainers coming or not coming to this city, he ends his comments by noting the economic impact of the group or individuals schedule to visit the city. It seems he couldn't care less about life or justice or anything else except the economic impact of Black conventions and entertainers.

Thus, he uses the vilest of contemporary terms, "Terrorism" to describe a peaceful, nonviolent means of direct action and protest against what many Black people in Cincinnati, and some white people, feel is flagrant, arrogant, pompous, and condescending mistreatment of nearly 50% of this city's population.

Economic terrorism indeed. Here's what economic terrorism is. It is the building of a football stadium with taxpayer dollars that provided little or no opportunities to Blacks in Cincinnati. It is the same thing happening all over again with yet another stadium for the baseball team. Economic terrorism is the denial of an opportunity for Black developers to even bid for a piece of the $800 million riverfront project called The Banks. Talk about terrorism. How about the use of so-called Black pass-through and front companies for economic development projects?   Who are the real terrorists in those scenarios?

Economic problems require economic solutions.   The Mayor knows that just as well as the boycotters know it.   The big difference is that the Mayor can make the changes needed to end the sanctions.   The boycotters can only react to their plight and to what the Mayor decides to do.   The groups supporting the sanctions are fighting with the only weapons they have: Their dollars.

The Mayor, a Democrat, has the political bully pulpit, the business clout, and six more members of a nine-member city council on his side.   Check out the statistics for Black people in Cincinnati and you will not only see economic terrorism, but you will also find out who the real terrorists are and against whom this terrorism is perpetrated.

Cincinnati in Black, White, and Green

"It would be a terrible irony to have the [National Underground Railroad]
Freedom Center in a city that isn't moving forward."
... **John Pepper**, *Chairman of Procter & Gamble Co. March 4, 2001*

Mark Twain is often quoted as saying if he knew the world were coming to an end he would move to Cincinnati, because everything happens ten years later there. If that's true, and from all indications it is, it means Black people will have to wait ten more years for justice as it relates to the latest in a long string of ridiculous events in this town. It also means that white people are ten years ahead when it comes to the same things.

Want some examples? How about these? A couple of years ago, a white police officer, Steven Roach, killed a 19 year-old Black man, Timothy Thomas. The Black man was wanted for misdemeanors but received death. The officer committed a felony but received misdemeanor charges, for which he was subsequently told by a white judge, "You are free to go."

Last year, the second highest-ranking police officer in Cincinnati, a Black man named Ron Twitty, was indicted by a "special" grand jury for lying about a dent in his police car. He was charged with two misdemeanors and two felonies, which carried penalties greater than those of all three of the white cops who killed Timothy Thomas and another Black man, Roger Owensby, who was choked to death, despite not even being wanted by police when he was stopped.

There are several other incidents I could cite, especially things like a blind man being given a jaywalking ticket for crossing against the light, and the grandmother being cited because she put a quarter in someone's expired parking meter, but I am sure you get the picture.

Cincinnati's latest in-your-face-injustice inspired me to write this particular article. During a recent so-called "celebration" some college students decided to start invading private homes (Breaking and Entering, in police parlance), setting fires (Arson), overturning automobiles (Destruction of

Private Property and Vandalism), throwing rocks and bottles at police officers (Assault on Police Officers), and causing fear and panic among neighborhood residents (Disturbing the Peace, Intimidation, and Inducing Panic).

The local media gave it very little coverage and some attributed it to "a few college kids getting out of line." Several residents called 911 Operators but it took the police more than thirty minutes to react. Despite the same thing happening last year at the same event, the police were ill-prepared to take charge this year. According to the Chief of Police, their "intelligence" failed to advise them of the event. He also said they did not have enough officers to deal with that kind of situation. I reiterate, the same thing happened last year at the same time and at the same place!

Juxtapose that scene against the scene at City Hall a few weeks prior, when a few hundred Black supporters of Black attorney, Kenneth L. Lawson, rallied to let city officials know we would not stand by and allow Mr. Lawson to be vilified. (Ken Lawson is the attorney who brought and won the racial profiling lawsuit against the City of Cincinnati.) The cops assembled for that peaceful event were in vans, on horseback, in cars, on bicycles, on foot, hiding in alleys, on rooftops, and undercover in city council chambers, waiting for an outbreak that never occurred. Double standard? You bet.

Also compare the white youth who turned over the cars to the Black youth who turned over some hot dog stands in the aftermath of the Timothy Thomas killing. The white group was just a "little out of hand," while the Black group was immediately called "rioters" some of who received a year or more in jail. Compare the high-ranking Black officer, who lost his job after 29 years of unblemished service, to the cop who killed Thomas and received a new job.

That's the Black and White of it; now let's get to the Green. Two stadiums totaling nearly $1 billion have been built with taxpayer dollars, with around 5% of the aggregate economic benefits, both short term and long term, going to African Americans. A 30% "minority" allocation was included in a $200 million highway construction project a couple of years ago; white contractors filed suit and the 30% requirement was abandoned.

We are building a $110 million National Underground Railroad Freedom Center, and have allocated around 25% of the benefits to "minorities." We just cut the ribbon at our convention center, which will be expanded at a cost of $160 million. We are told, "This time it will be different."

And finally, we have a $1 billion school building construction project in the works. The good thing about this project is the bold move by the Cincinnati Board of Education in mandating a "race-conscious" program, unlike the "race-neutral" program approved by our "black" (small "b") city council members and city administrators. Please keep in mind that Blacks comprise nearly 50% of Cincinnati's population and 70% of our school district's population. (Update: As of March 2004, the Cincinnati Public Schools has yet to implement its resolution that calls for specific percentages of the construction work to go to African Americans.)

Maybe old Mark Twain was right about Cincinnati, at least when it comes Black folks' rights. In a city where you can turn over a hot dog stand and get a year in jail, but turn over a car and get nothing. In a city where you can kill a car and lose your job, but kill a Black man and get promoted. In a city where you can hold a brick and get killed by police, but throw bricks and bottles at police and get police "restraint." In a city such as this, Cincinnati, Ohio, when it comes to the Black, White, and the Green, it looks like we will never catch up.

Update:
The quote from John Pepper at the beginning of this article was absolutely right. It is a sad irony to have the National Underground Railroad Freedom Center located in a city that is STILL not moving forward.

Diversity or Adversity? That is the question.

Image campaign, lawsuit aim to turn back boycott
*Cincinnati's tourism industry and city officials hope that the campaign, called
"Cincinnati - We're on the Move!" - will bolster a national reputation battered
by the boycotts. The campaign includes a glossy color brochure promoting
events and attractions such as the Black Family Reunion and the National
Underground Railroad Freedom Center. Of the about five dozen faces on the
brochure, the only white one is [Mayor] Luken's. March 19, 2002.*

According to the dictionary I have, the definitions given
for "diversity" are: 1.) The condition of being different: variety;
and, 2.) An instance or a point of difference. I had to look that
word up because of what is currently taking place in my
hometown of Cincinnati, Ohio. In case you have not heard, we
are experiencing a few problems, or should I say, "Challenges,"
here in the river city that some refer to as, "Up South." One of
those problems is the economic boycott that has been called by
activist groups against this city's travel, tourism, and
entertainment industries. The city's first return salvo is a nice
glossy brochure with a picture of our Mayor, who is white,
surrounded by four Blacks who occupy various top level
positions within our city.

The public relations campaign that has ensued is based
on getting the word out to the country, especially Black people,
that Cincinnati is a city of diversity. Diversity? Yes,
Cincinnati does have diversity. In addition to the two
dominant groups, Blacks (43%) and whites, it has some 150
different ethnic groups, albeit in far fewer numbers.
Nevertheless, the city is definitely diverse. You can simply go
to the Census Bureau and learn that. But our city is spending
thousands of dollars to inform you of that very obvious fact.

The last time I checked, those who called for the
sanctions against this city did not do so because there is no
diversity here. Thus, I am puzzled as to why our Mayor chose
an anti-boycott strategy that simply says, "We have diversity in
Cincinnati, and we can prove it. Just look at the four Black
people seated around me on the cover of this brochure; they are
smiling, they have important positions, and they are happy to

be here. But that's not all, folks. Look inside and see all of the other Black people we have here. Look at the fun they are having. We have diversity here in Cincinnati, and we are on the move." Yes, we are on the move in Cincinnati. But just where are we going?

What we have here is a juxtaposition of "pictures" of diversity against a backdrop of "realities" of adversity. Now let's look at the definition for adversity. My dictionary defines it as: 1) A condition of suffering, destitution, or affliction. 2) A calamitous or disastrous experience. Now that sounds more like what is going on in Cincinnati, as well as the fact that diversity exists here. Adversity also brings to mind some of the things about which the activists are complaining. They are certainly not complaining about the lack of diversity.

Despite the tremendous difference between the two terms, in addition to the reasons for the sanctions being called against this city, the Mayor and his supporters have chosen to address this problem of adversity with a solution called diversity. In and of itself, diversity cannot solve very many problems; it is just an in-vogue term that is hauled out when racial problems arise. To suggest to the world that because Cincinnati has diversity in its population visitors should come and spend their money here is, quite simply, insulting to any educated consumer, especially an educated and conscious Black consumer.

The illness that plagues Cincinnati, not just since last April when the civil unrest took place but for many years prior, is deeper and more serious than for anyone to think a brochure or public relations campaign can cure it. Yet, some people think that's the answer, and many of those same persons wonder why Blacks are raising so much hell in this town.

Two things are obvious to me. One: The Mayor assumes he can make this rancor disappear by acting like it does not exist; therefore, he refuses to negotiate with the protesters. Two: Some Black people would allow themselves to be used in a flawed PR effort to encourage other Blacks to come and spend their dollars in a city that treats their brothers and sisters unfairly.

I will be the first to say everyone must make his own decision on whether to support the sanctions or not, but it seems to me that most, if not all, Black folks would see the value of not allowing themselves to be put in a position that smacks of collaboration with their brothers' and sisters' adversary. But, maybe I am too idealistic, and I could be wrong.

Bottom line, this city is on the verge of imploding, and I fear that will result in a wound that will take years to heal. We recently held an election to change Cincinnati's form of government to that of Strong Mayor, as in other cities. Our Mayor was elected not only to get things done politically, but also to help this city with its monumental racial and inequity problems. The only way he can take advantage of our *diversity* is by decreasing our *adversity*. His refusal to negotiate with those who called the boycott will only bring about his demise – and, more importantly, Cincinnati's as well. That would be a sad day for our city.

Diversity simply means differences. Adversity means suffering, and there is a lot of that going on in Cincinnati. Brochures will not solve it; negotiation followed by progressive action will.

Even before April's riots, community leaders ranked poor race relations as a top problem. Some of their comments, after a four-hour meeting held by the [Cincinnati] Enquirer in February 2001, were startlingly prophetic:

"There's a potential for violence. I hate to raise that issue, but I think there is."
... ***Karla Irvine***, *executive director of Housing Opportunities Made Equal*

"The racial issue has been central to virtually every major social problem that this community faces."
... ***Nathaniel Jones***, *federal judge, U.S. Court of Appeals*

"The future of this city depends more on our ability to treat one another fairly than on any single economic issue, and I think we have a long way to go."
... ***Mayor Charlie Luken***

Source: The Cincinnati Enquirer, March 4, 2001 "Divided by Race" report

The $30 Million Rip-off

"Defend the cause of the weak and fatherless; maintain the rights of the poor and oppressed. Rescue the weak and needy; deliver them from the hand of the wicked." **Psalms 82:3-4**

Here's a fantastic deal. Steal $30 million, and move on to the next project to steal millions more. What a country! More specifically, what a city! And once again this fiasco, this obvious, in-your-face, we can do whatever we want, rip-off, happened in none other than Cincinnati, Ohio. The latest public relations nightmare for this city is centered on the largest unsubsidized housing complex, Huntington Meadows, the 640 families who reside or resided there, and how they have been and are being treated like herds of unwanted animals. Of course 99% of the persons living there are Black, and they have been intimidated, coerced, and threatened in an effort to get them to move off these 65 acres of prime land in the middle of the city. And some still ask, "Why is there a boycott of Cincinnati?"

I don't know if you heard about the runaway cow that caused the authorities to expend hundreds of hours and numerous resources to capture after it obstinately eluded police in a park for a week or so. That cow, when finally caught, was named, celebrated, given a free pass from the slaughterhouse, and sent out of town to spend the rest of its life on someone's farm in New York. Well, the folks at Huntington Meadows have not been treated even half as well as that cow was treated by this city's authorities – and, dare I say, "Leaders."

The residents at Huntington Meadows, despite the media and others preferring to divert our attention away from them, represent another aspect of this city's lack of strong leadership. They have been caught in a vice being turned by greedy, non-caring, dishonest, malevolent, land barons, politicians (and others, I'm sure) who only want to recapture prime land now occupied by Black people.

I am very concerned about the fact that our politicians, especially the Black ones, are not speaking out on what many consider to be the biggest heist in Cincinnati's history – a $30 million heist.   The owners and managers of Huntington Meadows have received millions in subsidies and tax credits since 1997. They concocted a scheme to get the residents out, first through mass evictions, which was fought and won by the residents in January 2002. Then they came up with another scare tactic by calling in their own consultant to do a "health check" of the property.

After determining there were problems with mold and asbestos in some of the buildings, problems that can be fixed of course, the company put hazardous warning signs on the doors and windows of the complex, scaring the residents, the postal workers, and the utility meter readers who, in turn, refused to come on the property.

The Cincinnati Health Department came in after that and did its own study and, while it found a few problems, its report said those problems did not rise to the level that would call for evacuation of the property. Of the 1100 apartments, only six had real health problems. The plot thickens.

Then there was a court hearing and an agreement decided upon without the consent of the residents.   That "agreement" called for the residents to move out by September 3, 2002 and receive $500.00. Remember, the residents were being evicted for no fault of their own and yet were not allowed to give their input on the decision that was made on their behalf.

Here's the catch, as there is always a catch.   The residents, by taking the $500.00 would have to sign an agreement that waived their rights to file lawsuits "forever" in case something comes up in the future with their or their children's health. The residents, by signing the document, also waived their rights to go to court to plead their individual cases for adequate relocation assistance, which cost much more than a measly $500.00. By the way, the checks bounced when some of the residents cashed them. Crazy, isn't it?

There is too much to disclose in this one article, but suffice to say that the $30 million given to the companies has not been accounted for through audit, the same company has a history of doing the same thing in other Ohio cities, and only one politician, a white County Commissioner named Todd

Portune, has called for an investigation. He has since been silenced. Hmmm. You would think that if this city is willing to expend some 1200 hours investigating a one-car accident, if the sheriff's department is willing to assign 12 investigators to find out how that automobile was damaged, and if the Prosecutor is willing to convene a special grand jury to indict the highest ranking Black police officer for alleged lying about the damage to that car, then surely you would think they would waste no time investigating a $30 million rip-off.

And some still wonder why there is a boycott in my hometown, Cincinnati, Ohio.

Update:

After getting rid of the residents and turning down an offer of more than $2 million to redevelop the property, The Mayor and city council gave the property in question to two Black churches for redevelopment. That sweetheart of a deal comprised a $13.5 million subsidy, which included $10 million to purchase the land. (In less than a year the price mysteriously escalated by $8 million) The City is now being sued for conspiring to take the land and get rid of the residents under false pretenses. What did the two Black churches do? They went out and partnered with a white developer and friend of the Mayor, of course, instead of a Black developer, to receive a share of the windfall profits that will be gained from this under-the-table deal. Even when we get put in charge of a project, some of us still don't treat one another right. As Claud Anderson says, "Black folks can't even do wrong right."

Boycott Bustin' Black Folks

Friday the 13th was true to form for the groups that called the economic sanctions against the City of Cincinnati. Namely the weekend that began on Friday, September 13, 2002, was the kick-off of the Procter and Gamble Riverfront Classic, a football game between Morgan State and Florida A&M, and other associated activities. Despite the boycotters' many attempts to persuade the schools and the promoter to cancel or relocate the game, it came nevertheless and brought with it thousands of Black folks. It was indeed a boycott buster – at least for that weekend.

The Classic also brought with it something else. As the lead story on the local news that Saturday evening after the game informed us, "Football game brings $20 million in economic impact to the city." Talk about a boycott buster, the game is what Cincinnati had been waiting for all year long. The boycott has cost the city at least $60 million in tourism revenue, but the Black football game made a huge dent in that number.

The promoters said it was an effort to afford Black youth an opportunity to attend a Black college. They said it was an effort to help "heal" our city. They said it was not about a football game but about education. They said it kept Black businesses in business. They said the game should not be considered in opposition to the boycott, even though it was played in a stadium that ripped-off Black people when it was built (some call it the River-Fraud stadium) and in the downtown "boycott zone." They said Black youth needed the opportunity to see Black colleges in action and to be exposed to the kinds of activities they could expect if they attended a Black college.

There was a considerable amount of sponsorship money provided to the promoters of the game as well. Procter and Gamble, Fifth-Third Bank, and Hamilton County (a surprising first time that had been done) all chipped in. Surely there were others, but those three contributed nearly a half-million to the cause. A few white folks on a local news show were even touting the game as a "multicultural" event rather than a Black football game.

Because of the game Morgan State and FAMU will share $400,000; at least that's what the newspaper stated. In addition to that, Black vendors probably made a few thousand each, maybe even $100,000 collectively. There were the other promotional revenues that were generated by the Black media, certainly a good thing, and the promoters' income too. Who knows, maybe they made a couple of hundred thousand dollars.

Now, let's look at the stadium, which by the way belongs to Mike Brown. You know him; he runs the lousiest team in the NFL, the Cincinnati "Ben-gals." That's right, we built a stadium for him with our tax dollars, a $575 million stadium with no roof on it, so it's not even in use most of the time. In addition, Mikey-boy gets the concessions, that is, food and drinks; he gets the parking rights too. He also gets the County to pay for empty seats just in case the Bengals don't sell out. Is this guy shrewd or what? He managed to get a public entity to use tax dollars to guarantee his business success by making up the costs for not-so-well attended games. What a genius! I wonder how he knew the Bengals would not sell out. And add $6.00 hotdogs to all of this.

Back to the Black football game. The hotels made their usual 49% on every dollar the Black folks spent, and I am sure the restaurants, only two of which are Black owned in the downtown area, made their share as well. I remind you that the news reported a $20 million economic impact on the city. If my numbers are anywhere near correct, in the aggregate Black folks did not even get 10% of that.

But that's all right. They had a great time and the game showed us the good side of Cincinnati, according to Cincinnati's newly crowned Black leader, former federal judge, Nathaniel Jones. He was the one the television news media just happened to find on the streets and the one the print media sought out for comments. He is also the same person who threatened to resign from a position with the local Community Action Agency because the agency moved its annual dinner away from downtown in recognition of the boycott. He said he would not be associated with a group that would "capitulate" to boycotters' demands.

Jones is also the same person who sits on the $7.8 billion Toyota Diversity Advisory Board, formed after Toyota "capitulated" to the threat of Jesse Jackson's boycott. Finally, he is the one who caused the "capitulation" of that same social service agency to reverse its decision and go back downtown to have its dinner. What power! What hypocrisy!

Yes, the boycott did not survive Black folks on Friday the 13th. You know how it is; we have to *get our party on* some time, even if it means giving up $18 million in the process. Here's a thought: Once a year, every Black person send a check to a Black college. Maybe then we won't have such a pressing need to beg white folks for money to support us, nor will we have to turn over control of our events to them.

Does Marvin Lewis have the power to heal?

The power of public relations is amazing. In case you have not heard, Mike Brown, General Manager of the Cincinnati Bengals, recently hired Marvin Lewis to coach his miserable football team. Even before Lewis gets to call his first practice session, the local paper says, "Civil Rights Leaders Applaud Decision – Not just a hiring but some healing." Say what? The last time I checked, football coaches were hired to win games, and with a 2-14 record, the Bengals can surely use a lot of that. The last thing Marvin Lewis needs is more weight on his back in the form of healing the huge racial divide that exists in Cincinnati. It is unfair to him, and it is naive (maybe, maybe not) on the parts of so-called civil rights leaders to think Lewis will be about the business of healing this city.

Despite the past hope of "healing" by the likes of a Black college football game known as the Procter and Gamble Riverfront Classic, nationally known minister, Billy Graham, gospel singer Kirk Franklin, a Black (or should I say minority?) City Manager, and a host of other Black (or should I say minority?) city administrators, despite all of those "healers" Cincinnati has remained entrenched in the muck and mire of racial discord and at loggerheads when it comes to settling the racially-oriented economic issues that keep the city from moving forward.

But the Public Relations machine has cranked up and is at it once again, desperately trying to soothe our senses and lull us into the sweet slumber of apathy. It's been done before, many times, and it's being done now. That's why I call this city "Cincinn-apathy."

Another aspect of the hiring of Marvin Lewis is the "First Negro Syndrome." If you recall Albert Cleage's writing in the 1970's regarding this phenomenon, you should be insulted that we are still *counting to one* in 2003. The Bengals could have hired a Black coach 20 years ago if they wanted. Black men have been qualified to coach professional football for years (someone told me there was professional Black football coach in 1920), but it's just now that they are being given their shot, Johnnie Cochran's efforts notwithstanding. But here in the town that has the worst football team in history, a Black man is hired, and all of a sudden he has the "racial healing" mantle placed upon his shoulders.

Ex-footballer turned television announcer, Chris Collinsworth, commented, "How ironic would it be if Mike Brown and his family help heal this city?" Give me a break, Chris, and please hold the platitudes for rip-off artist, Mike Brown. And Cincinnati's own retired judge, Nathaniel Jones, in his inimitable way, offered his usual *calm-down-the-Black-folks* and *say-what-the-white-folks-want* rhetoric, lauded team president Mike Brown as having followed in his father's footsteps with the hiring of Lewis.

According to the article in the Cincinnati Enquirer, Jones recalled how the late Paul Brown broke the color barrier in high school football by "allowing" black players on his Massillon teams. Jones went on to say, "The timing is wonderful, and I have to applaud Mike Brown for stepping up to the plate." Unlike Jones, rather than applaud brown, I applaud Marvin Lewis for taking the worse coaching job in the NFL. I understand Mike Brown resisted the hiring, and were it not for Brown's daughter Lewis would still be in DC.

I wonder if Nate Jones also applauds Mike Brown for ripping off this city's taxpayers for a $500 million stadium and a long-term lease that is now being contested with a lawsuit by the Hamilton County Commissioners. Stepping up to the plate is easy; getting a hit is something else again. Mike Brown has been *whiffing* for a decade or more. And if timing is everything, as Jones says, what does the hiring of Lewis suggest beyond his ability to win football games?

We could assume, quite reasonably, that the timing of this hiring could be a mere public relations stunt and an effort to divert our attention away from the real problems in Cincinnati, using Lewis, of course, as the scapegoat. After all, he certainly cannot do any worse and has nowhere to go but up when it comes to winning football games. However, if he fails to heal the city, what are they going do? Fire him?

You know, it's about time we stop playing games (pardon the pun) with one another and stop letting others play games on us. God bless Marvin Lewis and his family as he makes his move to Cincinn-apathy, Ohio. I am proud of his accomplishments. Thanks to those who are continuing to push for more Black people in the top echelons of sports teams. But, please, let's stop accepting this "first Black" condescension and the empty rhetoric that follows an event that should be second nature in 2003.

This hiring is all about the money for Mike Brown; you can count on that. If more Blacks folks go to the stadium, that's also a good thing for him. (I thought fans went to see the players, not the coach.) Unfortunately, most of our children cannot afford the price of a ticket.

While it's fine to celebrate the Lewis hiring, we must always look beyond the P.R. hype, stay on the course for justice in all areas of our society, and not confine our concentration on economic justice to the sports arenas.

Marvin Lewis might have what it takes to "heal" the Bengals from their losing ways, but as to his ability to bring racial "healing" power to Cincinnati, I kinda doubt it. If putting more money into the pockets of football team owners was the answer to racial healing, we would have been healed a long time ago.

Susan Taylor - "Tailor-Made" for Cincinnati

I had the distinct pleasure, once again, to see and hear one of this country's true treasures, Susan Taylor, the *essence* of Essence Magazine. The last time I was in her company, in 1995, she spoke at the Cincinnati Black Expo. I interviewed her, not in a huge banquet hall or public venue, but in her hotel room during which time she impressed me as a truly genuine and special person, so much so that I wrote a dedication to her called, Susan's Song (Thanks for the title, Al Jarreau). From that day on I see Susan everyday; there is a picture of her, my wife, and me on a table in our home that constantly reminds me of how special she has been and continues to be.

Susan came back to Cincinnati to serve as keynote speaker for the Sankofa Educational Enrichment Program's Fourth Nguzo Saba Awards Ceremony, and she was just what the doctor ordered for this town. As a matter of fact, she said some things to us that are applicable to everyone, no matter where you live. But, at least for now, I am going to claim what she said as a special message just for us.

She talked about the power of the spirit, the power of prayer, the power of self-reliance, the power of persistence, the power of endurance, and the power of collective work. She took us on a trip back in history, both on our way to this country and during our early days on these shores. She took us with her to the Motherland, and made us feel the pain of our ancestors as they languished in the slave dungeons. She reminded us of our glorious past and encouraged us regarding our bright future. She was a blessing to us.

Ms. Taylor then said something to us that made me do the *church thang*. She was referring to our responsibilities toward one another and admonished us that we are our brother's keeper and there are things we should – and must do for ourselves and for one another. She used the Sankofa School as the example and cited the fact that Sankofa, like similar schools and programs around the country, is run by volunteers and struggles each day to survive, despite doing great work for Black youth of high school age. She reminded us of Sankofa's continuous work in our community, the results of which have been hundreds of youngsters traveling to Africa, during Sankofa's relatively short existence.

Oh yes, she laid it on us. She opened closed eyes and closed minds; she swept in and left a piece of herself, a piece that would elevate us to a higher level of mutual support. How? Well, here's the best part, the part that I screamed about. She told the crowd it is up to us to see that Sankofa not only survives but thrives.

Susan told us that Sankofa is our responsibility, just as our children are our responsibility. She said, "What you should do tonight is pass the collection baskets and raise some money for Sankofa." All of a sudden a couple of sisters grabbed some baskets and the money started to flow. I was as proud as I was when we did the same thing at the Million Man March.

Here's the crux of the matter. In my book, *Economic Empowerment or Economic Enslavement, We have a choice,* there is a chapter titled, "A Case for a Black Tax," in which I discuss exactly what Ms. Taylor asked us to do for Sankofa. I suggest that every time Black people get together for our banquets, our breakfasts, our music festivals, our football games, and all of our other events and occasions, we should make it a point to collect some money. We should start common funds in our various cities and neighborhoods that can be used to assist the many worthwhile efforts we conduct.

There are many Sankofa Schools across this country that need a financial lift to keep going. There are other programs that have little or no money in their treasuries and could stand a little help from time to time. There are people among us everyday who need assistance with emergencies, funerals, food, and other necessities of life. If your city is like mine, you always wait for a crisis before acting. Instead of *"laying by in store,"* as we were instructed to do in First Corinthians 16:2, we react.

A few years ago I started a fund here in Cincinnati. I asked everyone to make it a habit to deposit a few dollars every week or two. At first a few people made deposits, and we were able to help several folks. But that did not last very long. If we had continued to make those small deposits, Susan Taylor would not have felt compelled to ask us to pass the basket for

Sankofa because that school would have been financially secure long before she graced us with her presence.

Remember that commercial that said, "Thanks, I needed that"? Well, thank you, Susan Taylor, for reminding us of our obligation and responsibility toward one another. Thank you for being "Tailor-Made" for our people.

"Politricks" – It's that time again.

A commentary on Cincinnati Politics – November 2003
Published in the Citizens Report, Cincinnati, Ohio

It's that time once again. The politicians are making their rounds, raising their money, and looking for issues they can champion. They are busy putting the finishing touches on their campaign speeches and we, the proletariat, the lemmings, and the sycophants, anxiously await their appearances at our events, our churches, and in our neighborhoods, even if it is only once every two years. We are also heavily engrossed in the what-if scenarios, vis-à-vis who will get in and what he or she will do as a councilperson. We can't wait for this election because this is the one that's going to turn things around – for real – this time – no kidding, this is the one.

Aside from the fact that Black people have been duped by politicians for years and persuaded to vote even for those who have not and will not do one thing on behalf of their Black constituents, we always get *geeked-up* for the next election. Sometimes our giddiness lasts even until voting day, but soon wanes as we find excuses for not going to the polls that day. I think we just love the prelude to voting rather than the voting itself. But every election seems to be "the" one, and we keep doing the same thing over and over expecting a different result. The only way we are going to get what we say we want is to change the way we play *politricks.*

Cincinnati once again, for the *umteenth* time, is facing another watershed election. Black people and poor people, especially, say they want change; they want new blood; they want – and need – representation on council that will stand up for them and get something done on their behalf, something that will result in economic benefits similar to those that accrue to the affluent, many of whom do not even live in Cincinnati. That's what we say, but what are we willing to do to get what we want?

Are you willing to just stand on what has been said in the past? Are you willing to do a repeat performance of 2001 and put the same folks back into office – some of whom who have done just the opposite of what you want and need? Are you willing to continue to accept or at least turn your head to the lies, the deceit, the broken campaign promises, the gross in-your-face economic disparity, and the disrespect of council members toward the people for whom they work? If so, you can stop reading this right now. If not, please continue.

Those who vote in the city council election will have nine votes at their disposal. You do not, I repeat, <u>do not</u> have to use all nine of those votes. If you can find four or five persons you would like to see on council, four or five who will do the things you want and need done by your representatives, then vote for those four or five and for those only! There is no law that says you have to use all nine votes. Had we voted that way in 1999, as we were advised by the Smart Vote Project, I probably would not be writing this article today. When are we going to learn?

During the past two years we have witnessed many acts by our *vaunty* city council that would turn the stomachs of the most hardened politicians, not to mention ordinary citizens. We saw our council sit back and allow more that 500 families be treated like a bunch of stray dogs, forced out of their homes, into the streets in some cases, under the guise of trumped-up health issues that were later discounted by the city's own health department. We have seen this council capitulate to corporate pirates who come calling, making threats to leave the city if they don't get their millions in city support.

We have seen our council do everything it could to affect the poor, the homeless, and 43% of this city's population, Black people, in a negative manner. We watched as this council always found money to spend on out-of-town consultants and lawyers, metal detectors in city hall, and other "pet" projects, but could not find the money (or would not issue it) to fund safe streets in the West End, pay local attorneys for the city's coveted Collaborative Agreement, support neighborhood business development, or even build a new facility for the homeless. Remember them, the homeless, the *"least of these"*?

We have seen it all in the last two years, but what will we do about it, that is, if we want change? My immediate and admittedly pessimistic answer to that question is "absolutely nothing." We will go into the voting booth, those who decide to vote, and give our valuable votes to some of those same persons on council who have hurt us the most. We will rationalize and justify in our minds why we should "give them another chance." We will go through the motions of yet another election, only to start complaining all over again in January 2004 about what our council is not doing and how we are going to vote them out the next time. Give me a break!

The *politricksters* will only change when YOU change. Those you elect will control the destiny of this city for the next two years, and some of those asking for your votes are only in the running for selfish reasons rather than to help you. Carter G. Woodson said, *"If [a man or woman] goes into office, it should be as a sacrifice, because his valuable time is required elsewhere. From such a [person], then, we may expect sound advice, intelligent guidance, and constructive effort for the good of all elements of our population."* Carter G. also warned, *"Any people who will vote in the same way for three generations without thereby obtaining results ought to be ignored and disenfranchised."*

Select your candidates with Woodson's words in mind. Vote smart this time and move this city from business as usual to *business unusual*, which for Cincinnati would be a wonderful thing.

A parting note on business as usual in Cincinnati when it comes to the economic foolishness and disparity that exist in this town:

"Cincinnati taxpayers: Sure, City Council approved up to $6.6 million for Saks Fifth Avenue to renovate its downtown store. So yes, the $176,036 bill for interior designers can be justified - maybe even the $99,448 for mannequins. But $27,609 for executives' travel, hotel, meals and cell phone bills is hardly the kind of 'public improvement' specified in the 2002 subsidy pact. Can you say corporate welfare?"

Cincinnati Enquirer Editorial – December 5, 2003

Section XII

Action-Based Solutions
It's Time to Move Forward

...I still find in far too many of our people a 'scarcity mentality' versus an 'abundance mentality'. Those with a scarcity mentality believe that the resources, be it ideas, money, or opportunity, will disappear if they share them with others.... The abundance mentality provides us with a psychological confidence that says there is plenty for all of us; therefore, if we share and enrich one another today, we will all flourish and be continually enriched by the totality of our knowledge.
George Fraser, *Success Runs in Our Race*

I cannot imagine you reading this far and not having asked yourself, "What can I do?" "What can we do?" Following are several things that you, and we, can do right now. The key step to any economic empowerment strategy is ACTION. Let's get started.
Jim Clingman

Economic Solutions

As I travel around this country, speaking to brothers and sisters, I get the inevitable questions regarding solutions to our problems. Although I always deal with solutions in my speeches, noting economic power movements such as MATAH, Powernomics, and Recycling Black Dollars, there is still a need for more information on what we can and should do, as individuals, to gain our true freedom.

This column is solely dedicated to offering things we can do, right now, to solve our economic problems. .

- Instead of buying that $150 pair of gym shoes for your children, buy a less expensive pair and put some or all of the savings into a cooperative fund for new business development – or put it into your child's college fund.

- Discourage our children from being walking advertisements and billboards for people they don't even know. Rather, encourage them to explore their own talents and create their own brands to sell to one another – and to the world.

- Cut back on your cable and satellite services. Who watches 200 channels anyway?

- Consider giving up that cell phone, pager, and palm pilot, you know, those things you think you can't live without. Hey, maybe you can.

- Teach entrepreneurship classes in our public schools systems, elementary and high school, and if it is not offered in the local university or college, insist that a course be offered there as well.

- Stop complaining about others moving into our neighborhoods and setting up businesses; let's open our own businesses instead.

- Be producers and distributors of goods and services in industries such as Black hair care products and food (restaurants, grocery stores, and supermarkets).

- Stop giving your money away to the "Looteries' in your state. You have as much chance of winning as you do of getting hit by an asteroid. This is one of the biggest boondoggles in history.

- Buy and open hotels, the biggest beneficiary of tourism dollars, and consider other business that can take advantage of what is forecasted to be a trillion dollar industry by 2010.
- Do what Dr. Rosie Milligan does in L.A. Start a "Get on the bus" campaign and take Black folks to Black owned businesses for day-long shopping sprees.
- Establish additional financial institutions, pharmacies, small retail shops, computer stores, bookstores, and every other kind of business – and support them!
- Increase our support of Black owned media by advertising on our radio stations and in our Black newspapers in addition to just using them as Public Service Announcement vehicles.
- Start small and micro-business associations among similar business types, i.e., beauty shops, barber shops, grocery stores, book stores, and leverage their collective clout to obtain various concessions and considerations.
- Form cooperative buying clubs among consumers and cooperative purchasing programs among businesses, and leverage the collective clout to gain lower prices and better service.
- Support Black causes, Black institutions, Black programs, and Black people in their righteous endeavors and movements.
- Love and trust one another much more and stop selling your people out. It is not worth it and it does nothing to move us forward economically.
- Stop spending millions of dollars to smoke and drink yourself to death.
- Invest in and support Black-oriented media with advertising dollars, and stress to the owners of Black radio stations, magazines, and other channels of communication the importance of action-based progressive information in addition to the music, comedy, and gossip.
- Take the time to really consider what you drive and how many vehicles you must have. Aren't two enough? Besides, gasoline prices are ridiculous, so cut down on unnecessary trips.

- Support these practices with a strong spiritual foundation, and there will be no stopping us in our collective endeavors, because:

It's not what you drive; it's what drives you.

It's not what you live in; it's what lives inside of you.

It's not how you act; it's what acts upon you.

It's not where you've been; it's where you're going.

It's not how high you rise; it's how low you reach down to pull someone else up.

It's not what's on your back; it's what's in your head.

It's not how much you have; it's how much you do with how much you have.

It's not who you are; it's whose you are.

It's not about you; it's not about me; it's about God.

Now, here are some things you can do on a national level to gain your true freedom. Support the MATAH Network. Brothers and sisters, this is a Black owned and operated true freedom movement; this is an African centered economic solidarity movement; this is a Black distribution channel through which Black manufactured products flow throughout this country. Even more important, the people who are MATAH are true freedom fighters, running for freedom 24/7. The least you can do is purchase the products.

Finally, you can support the Powernomics Program, which calls for the development of vertically integrated business development, Black owned I might add, across this nation. Buy the book and get started working the Powernomics National Plan to empower Black America.

A side note to all of you well-to-do brothers and sisters who have millions of dollars at your disposal: Why don't you put some of your money into the Powernomics Program, via the Harvest Institute, and set the example that some of our less fortunate brothers and sisters need to see? It's tax deductible.

There are things all of us can do right now; we don't have to wait for someone to do for us. We don't have to wait for a plan to be written; it's already done. We can all participate in these and other efforts right now. In addition, we can start to do some or all of the things listed in this article. Let's get busy, Black folks. Add to the above list and start running for true freedom before it's too late – too late for our children.

Abundance or Scarcity?

City Paper, a Nashville publication, carried an article discussing a situation reminiscent of George Fraser's words regarding abundance versus scarcity.

The article titled, "Businesswoman, Black Chamber Clash Over Directory," discloses an aspect within the Black community that often divides us and keeps us from gaining true economic freedom: competition. The businesswoman cited in the article says, "[The Black Chamber] is in business to ... assist minority businesses, not to compete [with] or run them out of business." She went on to suggest that the Chamber would contradict its principles by publishing a directory that will compete with hers.

First of all, the businesswoman started her directory 12 years ago, according to the article, and second, the Black Chamber was founded in 1998. I would assume a directory that has been around for 12 years has a loyal following when it comes to advertisements and readers. I would also assume there is a white Chamber of Commerce in Nashville that has its traditional "minority" division that publishes a directory of "minority" businesses, as well as several other organizations that publish directories of minority businesses, all of which are "competing" for advertising dollars from a finite number of businesses.

To suggest the Black Chamber of Commerce is somehow encroaching upon the current Black business directory's turf is a reach that only points out our scarcity mentality and zero-sum thinking when it comes to doing business with one another. We must understand, as George Fraser points out, that there is enough for all of us. I would venture to guess that many Black businesses in Nashville do not advertise in any medium. That's one of our problems when it comes to issues such as this one. The other problem is our reluctance to share and to be open to the possibility of someone else doing the same thing we do, notwithstanding that in this case the Black

Chamber directory is for its members and serves a very narrow business segment in the Black community.

When a businessperson raises the specter of competition in this context, some people may perceive fear or inferiority on the part of the person who is sounding the alarm about competition. My answer is: Simply make your product better and intensify and broaden your sales effort. Don't get into a shouting match about what the Black Chamber is doing; support the Black Chamber and encourage all Black businesses to support it. Who knows, many Black businesses, and maybe a few White and Hispanic one too, may place ads in both publications. A business cannot advertise too much you know.

I speak from the personal experience of having founded and managed a Black Chamber of Commerce. We used current publications, both Black and White, to find and solicit new members, and we printed a directory in conjunction with the local Black newspaper. We never received a complaint from the two or three other directory publishers; as a matter of fact, they were members of our Chamber.

We must find ways to work together and to share the wealth of our people. Believe me, there is plenty of it. Scarcity thinking is a function of the very successful programming to which we have been subjected and continue to pass down from generation to generation; it must be changed to abundance thinking. Two Black business entities getting into a fight about a directory, the basis of that argument being the fear of competition is exactly where we must not go as a people.

We must work together, in support of one another, just as the co-founder of the Nashville Black Chamber, Rosetta Miller-Perry, suggested in the article. She said she wants the other directory to continue to be printed. We must find ways to collaborate and grow our businesses via strategic partnerships and other alliances, and Black Chambers of Commerce, if they are doing their jobs for Black people, will be the ultimate force to make that happen.

What kind of a thinker are you? Abundance or scarcity? George Fraser, at the end of his book, talks about "Getting together to get it together" and "Networking for the success of all." He passionately and eloquently states, "Our thinking and values must embrace the Afrocentric principles of cooperation, not competition; community, not just the individual." I pray that all Black businesses and individuals will support the Nashville Black Chamber; and I pray for the continued success of the business directory, the Black Yellow Pages. May both parties enjoy even more advertisements and may you both work together in support of each other.

The Collective Banking Group

I recently had the pleasure of interviewing Pastor Jonathan Weaver, Greater Mount Nebo AME Church, Upper Marlboro, Maryland, on my weekly radio program. Our conversation centered on an organization that Pastor Weaver and several other ministers founded a few years ago: The Collective Banking Group (CBG). The ministers who started the CBG were literally fed up with being mistreated and discriminated against by the very banks in which their churches deposited millions of dollars annually. The ministers decided they would work together to change their relationship with banking institutions, and did they ever change it.

After paying off a thirty-year, $250,000 mortgage loan in just seven years, Pastor Weaver, on behalf of Greater Mt. Nebo AME Church, applied for a loan of $50,000. They were denied. After assessing the situation and dealing with the fact that he and his congregation had been insulted by the bank they had supported for years, Weaver decided to take a stand. Even though he eventually received the loan for the church, Weaver knew he had to do more and had to put an end to the practice that has haunted Black folks for years. He was tired of going *hat-in-hand* to bank officers and being treated unfairly, despite the support he and the church rendered to the bank.

Weaver's actions led to the formation of the CBG in 1996. Today the group comprises some 260 churches representing more than 300,000 members who, when they go to the bank to do business, now get first-class treatment and fair consideration for their loan requests. In essence, Pastor Weaver and the founding group of ministers created their own Community Reinvestment Act (CRA). They did not want to continue to wait for the government to "force" banks to treat Blacks and other minority groups equitably. They took things into their own hands and have accomplished – by collective and cooperative action – what the government and other organizations have tried to do since the 1980's when the Community Reinvestment Act was passed by Congress.

The Collective Banking Group has been the catalyst for hundreds of business, mortgage, and personal loans for CBG members since its inception. It has taken a pass on the chicken dinner banquet sponsorships, the small donations, and the condescending programs developed and promoted by various banks. CBG has taken control of its future by sending the word out to area banks that inequity and discrimination will not be tolerated, and if it persists the members will simply withdraw their support of the bank guilty of such practices. I love it.

Back in 1993, I wrote an article in the Cincinnati Herald asking the churches to consider forming a consortium of some kind through which they would deposit their church funds into common banks. They would then be able to leverage their collective deposits into real power to effect change in the way their members were being treated. While we heard the whining and complaining about mistreatment and disparity, we never saw a logical action step to make significant change in the situation here in Cincinnati. We are hearing the same complaining to this day.

The CBG was a breath of fresh air to me, and I hope it will be as well to our religious community when we move to organize a chapter of the CBG here. That's right. Pastor Weaver and the Board and staff of CBG are actively spreading the gospel of cooperation, collective activity, and financial leverage to other cities. New chapters are being formed along the east coast and this economic movement is now moving west. I hope and pray now that our words back in 1993 will be transformed into reality through the establishment of a Collective Banking Group chapter in my hometown. God knows we could certainly use one.

Kudos to Pastor Weaver for his vision and his positive action to bring our people out of financial bondage. It makes no sense for Black people to stay in our current position vis-à-vis the lack of reciprocity from banking institutions. We have complained long enough. We have waited for the government long enough. We have provided a windfall to the banks long enough. We have done absolutely nothing long enough – too long! It's time for a change, folks. The CBG has shown and continues to show the way to economic freedom and fair play. Will we follow?

As our dear Brother Amos Wilson said in his book, **Afrikan-Centered Consciousness Versus the New World Order**, "...we don't have to spend a great deal of time always appealing to [whites] and analyzing them. We can better appeal to our sense of self and our own consciousness. We waste a lot of time trying to transform them when through transforming ourselves they will be transformed automatically. The power is in our hands." Brother Wilson strongly and rightly suggested that when Black people change the relationship in which we find ourselves, be it economic, political, social, or otherwise, the nature of the system that governs that relationship will change.

The Collective Banking Group has done exactly that. It changed its relationship with banks, and the rest is history – beautiful history. That history continues to be made everyday by the CBG.

Distribution is the Question – MATAH is the Answer (Part One)

You know, it's one thing to make a product; it's another thing to get it to the marketplace. Have you ever heard the saying, "Production minus sales equals scrap"? It is so true, and a major part of the economic empowerment solution for Black people – and any other people – is distribution. Since we own very few retail outlets, i.e., supermarkets, pharmacies, warehouses, etc., the products we make are at the mercy of those who own and control the distribution outlets. We must change that scenario.

There are two important aspects of commerce on which Black people must work: Business development and industry impact. Of course we must have more businesses, but that alone will not alleviate our economic problems. We must carve out niches in various industries and develop vertically integrated chains within those industries, from natural resource to retail, thus creating job and business opportunities for our people. For example, Dr. Claud Anderson's effort to increase our control of industry-specific entities such as fish and seafood, leather, and tourism is essential to our economic uplift.

Key to those two aspects of commerce is distribution – the means to get our products and services to the market. If we do not also control that step, we will continue to be at the mercy of those who do. The most glaring example is the Black hair care industry, but there are many more examples of either limited shelf space allocated to Black products or just plain old "boycotting" of Black owned products from the main channels of distribution.

Does anyone remember seeing Dick Gregory's Bahamian Diet Drink on the shelves of their local supermarket shortly after it was introduced? Ken Bridges, who was responsible for the marketing of this Black product, says the large chains and distribution channels simply said "No" we are not going to carry it. That was that. Case closed. If there had been a Black owned and managed distribution channel, that scenario would have been quite different.

In this country today, as in years past, Black people are producing goods and services that are better than those we purchase everyday, but they have great difficulty getting their goods to us. Black brothers and sisters are using their intellect to invent household items and other products that, if they had access to a distribution system, would generate millions of dollars in wealth for our people. Instead, many times their products simply become fond memories and paperweights.

Brother Athan Gibbs, of Nashville, Tennessee, has designed a voting machine that, if adopted by local precincts, will revolutionize the voting process, especially as it relates to voter fraud and the kinds of things we witnessed in Florida during the presidential "selection." What chance do you give Brother Gibbs to get his machine on the market? By the way, I hope you will investigate his invention and support its use by voting precincts across this country.

The bottom line is this: We must have a distribution system that we own and control. Distribution is the lynchpin of a sound economy and the key to wealth-building and business development for Black people. Can you imagine Black-manufactured products flowing through a Black owned and operated distribution system to Black customers and retail outlets? Can you imagine Black manufactured products going to the general marketplace via a Black controlled distribution system? I can. As a matter of fact, that system already exists. It's called the MATAH network.

MATAH is a Black owned and operated distribution system, and it stands ready for us – Black people – to access its tremendous reach. Comprising thousands of individuals across this country, with the potential to expand to Africa and the Caribbean, MATAH is a "no-brainer" for conscious Black consumers, business owners, organizations, and churches. Just check out what MATAH brothers and sisters are doing in Los Angeles, Atlanta, and even little Toledo, Ohio. They are organized around a very basic economic principle: Buying Black. Unfortunately, many of our people simple find those words to be a nice sounding slogan they can throw out when it's convenient.

Within MATAH is a program called One Church – One Channel (OCOC), introduced by the internationally renowned innovator, Father George Clements, who also brought us the One Church – One Child program, which led to the adoption of over 100,000 Black children. OCOC is designed especially for Black church members to participate in the "Black Channel" of distribution by purchasing Black manufactured products and services. You should check out the One Church – One Channel program and get involved in it.

I think we can all agree that distribution is a key aspect of our economic freedom. There is no way around this fact. Therefore, it is incumbent upon us to support our own channel of distribution, and we should explore more outlets to get our products to the marketplace, e.g., beauty and barber shops, grocery stores, etc.

Update:
Brother Athan Gibbs, whom I mentioned in this article, was killed in an auto accident in his hometown of Nashville, Tennessee on March 12, 2004. Athan was 57 years of age. Pray that his dream of providing the voters of this country with his TruVote System will be actualized. May he rest in peace.

Distribution is the Question – MATAH is the Answer (Part Two)

The channel of distribution is mostly acknowledged by Black consumers as supermarkets, drugstores, and mega-department stores. While retail outlets play an important role in distribution, they do not comprise the entire channel. There are several other links in the distribution chain that affect not only the price at retail but also the very life (or death) of certain products. Distribution is more important than the product itself!

As we noted in Part One of this article, someone can make the best product in the world, but if that product cannot be distributed and put where people can easily purchase it, the producer of that product will fail. The Bahamian Diet is one example, but let's revisit Black hair care manufacturers in the mid-1980's. These companies were mixing all the right chemicals to produce excellent products for the Black consumer. Is it not conceivable that they could have also mixed the right chemicals to produce laundry detergent or dishwashing liquid or multi-purpose cleaner? Of course they could have made excellent products, but since they could not get distribution, their manufacturing abilities did not matter.

Here is another issue that many of us are not aware of. Obtaining retail distribution in supermarkets and drugstores requires expensive "slotting allowances," thus, even if Black producers would be accepted in conventional channels of distribution, it would cost millions of dollars just to place their products in those stores. This is one of the reasons we see very few Black manufactured items sitting on the shelves of the supermarkets and drugstores. All you need to do is compare the shelf space occupied by Black products to the shelf space of other products and you will see exactly what I mean.

So what is the solution to the distribution problem faced by Black manufacturers? The answer is simple. Create a Black channel of distribution. Why should we continue to complain about someone else not allowing our products into their channel and not make any effort to create our own channel? Well, I reiterate, MATAH is one step ahead of us. We must have a Black channel of distribution if we want to become real competitors on the new battlefield: the marketplace.

Creating and supporting a Black channel of distribution are the most important things Black people can do to build and support a Black economic infrastructure. It will provide the vehicle for us to consistently and persistently redirect our spending toward one another. Our incentive to produce for ourselves will always be stymied if we do not have a channel of distribution that is controlled by people of African descent. Additionally, if we do not produce many of the products we consume, we will forever be economically dependent on others to provide for us -- and for our children.

Now don't go off thinking this so difficult and Black people will never be able to accomplish such a lofty goal of creating and managing a Black channel of distribution. Since we know that MATAH has already done the hardest task of creating the channel, the next step is up to us, conscious and conscientious Black consumers. We must make the channel work to our own benefit, you know, like the Koreans do with Black hair care products, like the Jewish people do in the music and film industry, like the East Indian people do with their motels, and like the Arabs have done with their convenient stores and gas stations.

How do we do that? Very easily. We must start now to gain control of at least one product that we all consume on a regular basis. How about detergent? Don't get scared. Remember, I did say "conscious and conscientious" Black consumers; no wimps allowed in this game. Let's produce, sell, and distribute MATAH Laundry Detergent, which is made by and providing jobs for people of African descent. Let's make it the number one selling detergent among Black people. Don't you think Black folks can make soap? Your great-grandmother made it. Don't you think Black folks can make all of the household products you now use? The more important question is: Would you purchase these and other items made by your people?

Well, try these numbers on for size and then answer those questions. Black consumption spending exceeds $600 billion per year. Nearly all of that money goes away from our people via retail outlets that are not owned by us or distribution channels that we do not own and control. The other glaring number you should consider is the $1.4 billion Black people spend on home care products per year. If you are looking for an economic opportunity in an industry, it is staring us in our collective face right in our kitchens, bathrooms, and laundry rooms everyday!

We are always seeking solutions to the economic problems we face, and I always try to present at least one in my weekly column. Now, having read about this solution, you have a responsibility. You can shirk your responsibility to your people and your children's future by doing nothing, or you can do your individual part in our run for true economic freedom by supporting the MATAH Network. In the inimitable words of Jim Brown, as told by Richard Pryor, "What choo gon do?"

Getting Our Dollars To Make More Sense.

"Our Black dollars don't make sense!" Those are the words of a man who has worked for more than fifty years to get Black people to understand the very basic principles of economic empowerment. Those are the words of Bishop Luke Edwards, founder of R.E.A.C.H., which is an acronym for Research, Education, and Community Hope, headquartered in Eutaw, Alabama.

In my personal visits with Bishop Edwards, in sessions the MATAH calls "Sitting at the Feet of Our Elders," I was taken on a trip that began on a sharecropping farm in Florence, Alabama, to the big cities of Detroit and Ypsilanti, Michigan, through a stint in the U.S. Navy, to the Black Political Convention held in Gary, Indiana in 1972, and finally to a small congregation of welfare recipients in Mississippi. But the story did not end there. On the contrary, it was just the beginning of an amazing chronicle of one man's resolve, determination, ingenuity, and love for his people. It was also an account of Black men, women, and children dedicated and committed to the fruition of the vision of one man, Bishop Luke Edwards. Quite simply, it was a Love Story.

Daily episodes of this love story take place everyday in Livingston, Eutaw, Tuscaloosa, Demopolis, and Emelle, Alabama, and in Meridian, Mississippi when the seventy-six year-old Edwards awakens at 1:30 A.M. to make his rounds. By the time most of us get to work Bishop Edwards has already put in a full day! A tireless champion of hard work and dedication, Edwards, along with his team, has built one of the most admirable examples of economic empowerment in this country.

As he travels from county to county, in the wee hours of the morning, he surveys all he and his people have accomplished. He proudly visits the three Western Inn Motels, the several restaurants, the convenient stores and service stations, the huge department store fully stocked with clothing, shoes, house wares, tools, and thousands of other items. He checks out the hog and cattle farms, the processing plants and the computerized feed lots he is so proud of, the land they have set aside for the amusement park, the area where the annual rodeo is held. Bishop Edwards makes sure the fishponds under construction are just the right size and depth, and sees that all the equipment necessary to maintain and process the fish is ready to go. He assures the R.E.A.C.H. K-12 school is well equipped and supplied for the coming school year, and he considers a couple of pieces of land owned by R.E.A.C.H. as possible locations for truck stops. (That land is just off the main expressway, I-59, and will make excellent locations for rest stops and service stations for truckers.)

After the Bishop finishes his "morning chores" he goes to Eutaw, the headquarters for R.E.A.C.H., and strolls down the street where on both sides there are spacious brick homes, a beautiful church building, and the jewel of the development, "The Mansion," where the elderly reside and are taken care of by R.E.A.C.H. He also sees children at play in an environment built and owned by their parents. "How proud they must be of their fathers and mothers," the Bishop muses. You will not see those children throwing trash on their street or writing graffiti on their walls, or disrespecting their elders. They have an ownership stake in their community, and they take care of it.

The REACH Program evolved from an idea that Brother Edwards had for many years prior to its implementation. He attempted to actualize his economic plan during his years in Michigan where there was (and still is) enormous Black wealth-building potential. His plan fell on deaf ears for the most part (that sounds familiar). While his northern brothers and sisters were so enthralled with gaining political clout, Edwards was constantly preaching the economic gospel of ownership and self-determination via the attainment of income-producing assets and good stewardship of those assets. "The Bishop," as most people call him, did not let his detractors deter him from his plan and from doing what he knew would propel his people to heights never envisioned prior to the formation of R.E.A.C.H.

Edwards drew upon his childhood in Florence, Alabama, having witnessed his father sharecrop for a white farmer, and decided he should have his own farm instead of working on a farm that belonged to someone else. He determined the way to economic freedom, especially for those of limited means, was to pool those limited resources and create businesses that would lead to self-sufficiency.

With that vision Bishop Edwards decided to say to his congregation one Sunday morning, "We are not going to shout today; we are not going to dance today; we are simply going to talk." He proceeded to ask each of the members to write down the amount of food stamps they received each month. He compiled the aggregate amount and showed the members how much "money" they had collectively. They pooled their food stamps, bought their groceries cooperatively, and received discounts, the money from which they saved for the next month. Their monthly savings eventually allowed them to be able to buy their own grocery store, and the rest is history, as they say. Collective and cooperative economics – Ujamaa at work – are now manifested in an economic power movement unsurpassed in this country. It's called R.E.A.C.H.

A short list of the assets accumulated by R.E.A.C.H. includes 5000 acres of prime property in five counties, thousands of grain-fed cattle and hogs, a meat processing and packing plant, an elementary and high school complex with separate dormitories for boys and girls, motels and restaurants, Greyhound bus stops that create a captive market for his restaurants, Western Union outlets, Citgo convenient stores and gas stations, an Ostrich farm, a tire store, a shoe manufacturing company, tractor-trailer trucks, and all of the heavy equipment necessary for clearing land and building homes.

Understanding that ownership of income-producing assets is the key to economic empowerment, Bishop Edwards has surrounded himself with a team of experts, twelve brothers and sisters who comprise the R.E.A.C.H. Board of Directors. He understands that he cannot do everything and needs people with experience in computer technology, law, accounting, business development, finance, and real estate. He is a shrewd businessman who is well ahead of the curve when it comes to "doing" in addition to just "talking."

As most people know, job creation is vital to the economic uplift of a people, and the best way to create jobs for your people is to open and grow businesses. Another Bishop with whom we are very familiar, T.D. Jakes, was quoted by *Moneywise,* saying, "You have to learn how to open your own business. You are supposed to have your own. Nobody gets wealthy working for somebody else." We shudder to think what impact Jakes could have if he were to take on the practices of Bishop Luke Edwards. Jakes' financial resources and his ability to rally Black people could turn us around by making R.E.A.C.H., The MATAH Network, and the Visions 2000 Black-owned hotel project the models for gaining true freedom for people of African descent. Both Edwards and Jakes have the right idea, but Edwards has three decades of experience doing what Jakes and others are preaching these days. Wouldn't it be wonderful if they – and other "leaders" got together?

But let's get back to Luke Edwards. What are his plans for the future? Well, for a seventy-six year-old man, he has many plans, and he works on them everyday. R.E.A.C.H. is planning to build an amusement park and a convention center. All he needs are a few commitments from groups like the N.A.A.C.P., Urban League, Masons, and sororities and fraternities to convene their meetings at the R.E.A.C.H. convention center and the work on the center will begin. He is exploring opportunities with Texaco and other companies for rights to locate their gas stations and truck stops on R.E.A.C.H. property. And he is digging fishponds in preparation for supplying fresh fish to Wallace D. Muhammad and his followers. This is the kind of commerce we should be engaged in with one another. All we need, according to Bishop Edwards, is "trust." R.E.A.C.H. has also supplied fruits and vegetables to groups around the country as well.

Doesn't it make sense that we use our resources to help one another and to empower one another the way Bishop Edwards is doing from his Alabama and Mississippi locations? Wouldn't our dollars "make more sense" if they circulated among our people more than they do presently? R.E.A.C.H. is showing the way and continues to show the way. Shouldn't we follow?

Needless to say, Bishop Luke Edwards is busy and plans to stay busy until he leaves this earth. "I have a lot of work left to do for my people," says The Bishop, as he gets up from our meeting to continue his busy schedule. He continually says, "I pray for you, Brother Clingman. I pray for your strength and I pray that you really see this thing I am trying to do." I assure him I do understand and will continue to spread the economic gospel. I will also continue to work on and work for projects and programs that lead to true freedom for our people – just like Bishop Edwards has done for most of his life.

As we celebrate the 30th anniversary of the Black Political Convention, a meeting that Bishop Edwards attended, and wonder what we should do to commemorate that auspicious occasion, as well as ponder our continued lack of real political power after thirty years, Bishop Edwards continues to preach the economic gospel. He reflects on what could have been if only some of the convention delegates had followed economic empowering principles in addition to the political paths they chose. "I want what we have done down here in Alabama to be emulated all over this country," says the Bishop. "This is just a small portion of what we can do as a people for ourselves. All it takes is love, trust, determination, and a willingness to share. We have the dollars, but do our dollars have any sense?" That is the question," he smiled.

Bishop Luke Edwards and the R.E.A.C.H. organization continue to gather even more economic resources, such as small businesses, land, and housing. They are creating more jobs than they can fill, and they are building a firm economic foundation for future generations.

We can learn a great deal from R.E.A.C.H. Our ministers, community leaders, and all Black people, especially those promoting economic empowerment, should find out more about R.E.A.C.H., and support it in any way we can. We should emulate its programs and its efforts and work closer together to leave a firm economic foundation for our children. Bishop Edwards and R.E.A.C.H. are doing what most of us are just talking about and feeling good about. Remember: there is a big difference between feeling good and doing good.

Pardon my grammar, but when it comes to economic empowerment, R.E.A.C.H. is doing good.

Section XIII

The Source of Our Resources

Well done my good and faithful servant. You have been faithful over a few things, I will make you ruler over many things.
Matthew 25:21

Who then is that faithful and wise steward...?
Luke 12:42

Now he who supplies seed to the sower and bread for food will also supply and increase your store of seed and will enlarge the harvest of your righteousness.
2 Corinthians 9:10

The earth is the Lord's and everything in it, the world, and all who live in it.
Psalms 24:1

You may say to yourself, "My power and the strength of my hands have provided this wealth for me." But remember the Lord your God, for it is He who gives you the ability to produce wealth..."
Deuteronomy 8:17-18

Stewardship

If we do not take care of what we have, we will surely
lose it. If you believe that, and I am sure you do, "Can we
talk?" There is a parody in my book, Blackonomics, titled "The
Parable of the Talents, 1990's Style," which points out the
value of good stewardship. It deals, in what some have called a
comical way, with the fact that Black folks do not take good
care of what we have been given. Instead of using what we
have to gain more, we simply turn over our resources to others
and create tremendous wealth for them and their children. As
we move through 2003, and our collective income rapidly grows
toward $700 billion, the trend continues. This is a call to our
people to stop the madness!

Brothers and sisters, we cannot continue to think it is a
privilege to spend our money at the businesses of others. Sure,
it is a right, but certainly not a privilege. In addition, we
cannot continue to squander the resources we have been given
and think our economic situation will change for the better.
Good stewardship demands that we use our resources wisely; it
also suggests that by doing so we will obtain new resources.

Those of you who read the **Basic Instructions Before
Leaving the Earth** (The Bible) should be aware of the
stewardship principles therein. We are taught to multiply
what we have been given, to help others with our blessings,
and to make sure that we leave an inheritance not only for our
children but also for our children's children. Are we doing
those things with our billions per year income? What role are
you playing in that regard?

Our very existence in this country depends upon how
well we manage our resources. We must not get hung-up on
what others have and what we do not have. We must
concentrate on our resources and do everything we can to
multiply them. Good stewardship demands no less of us than
it did in the case of the person to who received only one talent.
It's not what you have – It's what you do with what you have.

Black consumers have become more than mere purchasers of necessities and a few desirables. We, through our conspicuous consumption of every trinket and bauble developed by anyone else, have been transformed into salivating dogs, as national newspaper columnist, Junious Stanton suggested in one of his articles titled, "Your consciousness is showing." He referred to us as Pavlovian consumers, and I certainly agree with his assessment. We buy everything from $2,000 rims for our cars, to $10,000 (and more) Rolex watches (when a watch from Black-owned Wittnauer will do), to gold-plated sunglasses, to diamond-studded medallions, to $1,500 shoes made of some exotic or endangered animal.

We must have three, four, or five different cars and trucks, all the latest video game machines, and of course, designer labels must be draped across our chests. We make rap videos about "My Truck" that features a Cadillac Escalade and another in which the rapper is constantly shown in front of a Bentley. I would venture to guess there is no advertisement contract attached to those videos, and if there is, I bet the car companies are getting off dirt-cheap.

As I said in the opening paragraph, "Stop the madness," because that is exactly what it is. From a spiritual perspective, we are called upon to take care what we have been given. We have dominion over this earth and we are its stewards; we must watch over everything that is here. From an earthly perspective, we must turn our spending habits around; we must redirect a greater portion of our consumption dollars toward one another; and we must understand that *we get by giving*.

You've heard the saying, "Waste not, want not." Well, the situation in which Black people find ourselves today typifies the need for such an axiom. We want more, and we complain about not having certain things because we waste what we have. We literally throw our money at others for anything they make or do, all the while denying those same dollars to our own brothers and sisters who make or do the very same things.

We waste our intellectual resources by failing to use even a portion of them for the benefit of our own people. In what Brother George Subira calls, "The Black Brain Drain," we cannot wait to get that job in that huge corporation, make those large salaries, and obtain the best training in the world, only to use that talent to create wealth for the very folks we complain about not accepting us as equals in corporate America. Instead of bringing some of that knowledge back to our brothers and sisters, we do the opposite of what W.E.B. DuBois suggested in his Talented Tenth prescription for the uplift of Black people. We allow our selfishness to override and dominate our willingness to sacrifice.

I implore you to be a good steward. Multiply what you have; use what you have to help your people – and your children. Believe me, when the owner of ALL resources returns, He will hold us accountable.

"In the final analysis, how you lived your life will be determined by your ability to hold yourself up to the light and like what you see. It will come at that final moment when all of us assess what we accomplished with what we had and whose lives we touched as we passed through this world. The final measure of your life will not be found in the question, "What did I have?" You will know what your life was worth when you answer the question, "What did I do with what I had?"

--James E. Clingman
Economic Empowerment or Economic Enslavement – *We have a choice*

Room at the Inn

There are many areas of economic empowerment available to African Americans in this country, the sad part of which is the fact that brothers and sisters for more than 100 years have told us over and over about their importance. They have given the clarion calls to generation after generation, much of which has fallen on deaf ears.

One area of economic empowerment exists in an industry to which Black people contribute hundreds of millions of dollars every year. That industry is tourism. Tony Brown, one of our economic empowerment sages, gave us an economic empowerment strategy to claim a portion of this industry back in 1990, when he told our organizations to cancel their meetings for one year, pool their money, and build hotels in which they could hold their annual meetings. Apparently that fell on deaf ears as well. I guess many of us just cannot do without our annual meetings from which hotel owners reap huge economic benefits.

Now there is another wise sister who has come up with a plan for Black people to gain collective and individual ownership and control over the venues in which we conduct our meetings and conventions. Her name is Ernestine Henning, founder of Visions 2000, an Inglewood, California foundation whose mission is to empower Black people via ownership of hotels. She continues to beat the drum for economic empowerment through pooling our funds and our intellectual resources to build and leave an economic foundation for our children.

Tourism is a burgeoning industry. Black people play a major role in this industry. Black people own very few hotels across this country. Black people spend hundreds of millions of dollars on travel and accommodations. Should we not own hotels and other venues through which we can pay ourselves when we travel? Should we not pool our money to purchase these venues and create investment opportunities for our own people? Should we not put ourselves in the position to establish other businesses that take advantage of the tourism industry?

Mrs. Henning has been developing these opportunities and more by establishing Visions 2000. She is busy traveling around the country, holding her meetings in Black owned hotels such as those owned by the R.E.A.C.H. Program in Mississippi and Alabama, those owned and operated by Mabra Holeyfield in Memphis, Tennessee, Black owned bed and breakfasts like Claudia's Manor in Savannah, Georgia, Rockland Farm Retreat in Bumpass, Virginia, and other Black owned venues like the Dudley Complex in Greensboro, North Carolina. She is practicing what she preaches by seeking out Black owned businesses to support while, at the same time, building an economic infrastructure that will spawn even more opportunities for our people.

Hotel ownership and investment in these properties by Black people will truly empower us in an area where our dollars play a major role. We must move to the supply side of the tourism economy and away from the demand side. Ownership of income producing assets, especially hotels, will assure our people and our children of having a valuable stake in an industry that is growing faster than all others worldwide.

Visions 2000 is the vehicle that will take us to the tourism promise land. Of course we need to do more, explore more opportunities in other industries, and work on other economic fronts. But we cannot and must overlook the tourism industry. Y'all know how we like to have fun, how we love to party, how we love our Black football games, especially the marching bands. But after the party is over, what do we have besides empty pockets? The managers of those hotels in which we stay go to the bank; in most cases, we go back to the planning table to get started on next year's event.

The bottom line in all of this is stewardship, a tenet to which we can all relate. We have been given tremendous collective resources. It is our obligation to be responsible with those resources, both intellectually and financially, and to build a base from which we can increase the resources we have, just like the Parable of the Talents indicates. For those of you who believe in Jesus Christ, if He came back to visit Black people in the vast majority of our cities, we would not even be able to offer Him a luxury hotel suite. He had no room at the inn when He was born, and His relatives do not even have inns some 2000 years later. Of course, we would not be able to take Him to a nice sit-down restaurant in many of our cities, or provide transportation for Him, or purchase oil for His feet from one our own pharmacies, or take Him to one of our supermarkets to buy Him some groceries. But I digress.

The source from which our resources flow must be shaking His head in sadness and disappointment at our slothfulness when it comes to what we have been given. We should be ashamed of ourselves, and we should repent from the insanity of wasting our resources instead of using them to produce even more resources for ourselves and our children. One way to do that is through ownership of hotels. Please commit to being a Founding Sponsor in the Visions 2000 Program. We must be able to say, in every city in which we live, "There is room at the inn – our inn."

The Business of the Black Church

One thing I am sure we can agree upon is the fact that the greatest example of pooling our resources is demonstrated every Sunday in our churches. People work collectively for common goals, and they pool their dollars to support their church and its programs. That's simple economic empowerment. Churches do it every Sunday. Why can't we do it on the other six days of the week?

As long as I have been writing about and studying this phenomenon I still have not figured that one out yet, but let's concentrate on the following positive notion of economics in our churches. Every church probably has men and women who own businesses. Each church more than likely has members who have talents or hobbies through which they could create some level of income for themselves. If the members of our churches made it a practice to utilize the goods and services of their fellow members, the church would be stronger collectively, and the individuals in the church would have more to give back to the church.

Makes a lot of sense doesn't it? So why don't we see more churches promoting this brand of empowerment? It is a known fact that the Black church is, as Willie Sutton said, "Where the money is." It is common knowledge that Black churches deposit millions of dollars into banks every Monday morning. It is also common knowledge that many of those same church members cannot go to those same banks and get loans for which they qualify. We also know that many of the individual members of churches are struggling everyday to make ends meet. This in spite of all the financial resources within the church they attend.

Now I am not saying churches should, willy-nilly, give collected resources to members, some of who may simply be taking advantage of a particular church's benevolence. I am saying that our church leadership should rethink their mission by revisiting the procedures of the first century church and getting back to the principles of *Koinonia*.

A very practical agenda for Black churches should include stewardship seminars, business forums for members who have their own businesses and for those who may want to become entrepreneurs, and our church leaders should always do everything they can to empower the members collectively.

In my hometown, *Cincinn-apathy,* Ohio, I hear a great deal of complaining from our brothers and sisters about banks not lending to us fairly and so on and so forth. You know the story. Well, I say our churches should do what Jonathan Weaver did with the Collective Banking Group. Form a group of churches and take advantage of our leverage when it comes to bank loans and other services offered by banks. Assure, via the thousands of members in the collective, that our people are treated fairly by an industry that makes billions of dollars from Black consumers. That's what economic empowerment is all about. And what better place to accomplish it than in our Black churches?

Additionally, when we build these churches let's seek out and use Black developers, contractors, insurance agents, and other Black professionals. (Why do I have to even say that? It should be a no-brainer) Let's get to know who attends our churches and what they do, even if it's a hobby, and let's support these members in their business endeavors. By circulating our dollars among our fellow members first, we all become empowered through the empowerment of the church. Because the more we have as individuals, the more we have as a collective body – the church.

Is this making any sense? Maybe I'm missing something, but it seems so simple to me. I know, I know, there are a lot of egos in the church, a lot of jealousy, and a lot of other "issues," which are completely contrary to what church is about anyway. But, as Dr. Michael Grant once told me, "E.G.O. is an acronym for Ease God Out." We had better change those kinds of attitudes in our churches and get on with taking care of our business, after we take care of God's business, of course.

Let the Churches Say, Amen. Please!

That's a phrase we hear a lot during our church services, isn't it? Well, I am saying it now in this column because of an article I read by Bishop Noel Jones. The Jones' article is published in the 2nd quarter 2003 edition of the One Hundred Magazine, the Official Publication of the 100 Black Men of America, Inc. Titled, *Our Late Summer Should Be Their Spring*, this outstanding article not only laid out what we must do for the future of our children, it also delineated how we can do those things – via our churches.

Brother Jones attended the symposium hosted by Tavis Smiley in Detroit, at which a panel of ministers from across the country discussed the relevance of the Black Church in today's society. By the way, one obvious absentee was Pastor Jonathan Weaver, Greater Mt. Nebo A.M.E. Church, the Harvard educated, progressive, action-oriented brother who founded the Collective Banking Group (CBG). I called Pastor Weaver and asked if he had been invited to participate; he said, "No." What a shame, I thought. Here is a man who is doing what many on the panel and in the audience talk about, but he was not there to share the CBG's success with the world.

Jones' article cited the "alarming but revealing statistic" shared by Economist, Dr. E. Lance McCarty. "There are 65,000 [Black] churches, 25 million members which deposit $50 million a week; therefore depositing $2 billion annually, with the members having a spending power of $300 billion annually, yet 70 percent of these same churches cannot get a loan." In my book, Economic Empowerment or Economic Enslavement, We have a choice, I cite a similar scenario, which was written in 1994!

Obviously we are still in the same shape when it comes to our lack of cooperation, our reluctance to move our egos aside, our unwillingness to pool our resources and leverage our so-called spending power, and make even the slightest dent in our horrendous situation. We continue to create wealth for everyone else and neglect doing the same for ourselves. We continue to carry money, by the sack-full, to someone else's bank instead of establishing our own banks. Is that "good and faithful" stewardship? Are we using our "talents" wisely?

We continue to allow discrimination, insulting and disrespectful treatment from bankers, when it comes to obtaining loans. And, we continue to gather at forums to discuss our plight on national television, talk for two days and leave without a plan – just like the first forum of national Black leaders, during which, at the end of the two-day discussion, Kweisi Mfume said, "We don't have a plan."

I don't know what note the pastors' symposium ended on, and I don't know if they resolved to really do something about the situation Noel Jones described in his article. But I do know that Jonathan Weaver has already done, and continues to do, what Brother Jones said we must do. I do know that Weaver had the same problem of not being able to get a loan for his church and decided to put an end to that kind of treatment from his bank. I do know he formed the CBG and now has more than 250 Black churches and more than 300,000 members involved in the Maryland Chapter. I do know that Weaver has started other chapters across the country and is moving now toward the establishment of a national Black bank. I do know that Weaver is quite willing to share the information he has and will come to your city and show you how to start a local chapter of the CBG.

I also know that even though he was not invited to the symposium, Weaver's message to our churches and his example of what we can do when we work together should have been there. And I know that once again the call has gone out for leadership, by Bishop Noel Jones, for commitment, for collective and cooperative work among Black churches, especially when it comes to economic empowerment, and a call has gone out for action.

Noel Jones challenged the "...intellectuals and the church leaders to a summit, where we implement a plan to network, share and merge." He says, "Presently we are too splintered to leverage the resources that we currently have... this reveals a prevailing plight of [B]lack individualism" Man! I hope all the ministerial *muckety-mucks*, and their congregations, read Jones' article – and I hope they read this article too.

"'In closing" (to borrow another phrase from the pulpit), we do not need to reinvent the wheel. Black folks have already done all the basic things we say we need to do. The prime example is the CBG. We must simply learn from the past, take the models that work, and replicate them. We must put our egos in check and not allow our personal quest for recognition to overshadow what is truly important. And, we must not let our egos prevent us from doing the things we simply "discuss" at our forums.

Noel Jones says, "We are power broke, not power brokers." We have too many resources to settle for less than a bright future for our children and a permanent seat at the economic table of this country. I hope and pray the words of Noel Jones and the actions of Jonathan Weaver, and those of other less known Black ministers across this country, will be heeded. Let all the churches say, "Amen," and mean it.

Black Churches Funding Black Colleges

On October 15, 2002, I sat in a Philadelphia sanctuary, along with more than 1,000 other mourners, to celebrate the life of Kenneth Bridges, a modern-day Marcus Garvey and co-founder of the MATAH Network. As you know, Ken was one of the persons killed during the 23 days of terror in the Washington, DC area. Exactly one year later on October 15, 2003, I sat in a Winston-Salem, North Carolina sanctuary to celebrate the legacy of Ken Bridges. I watched and listened as no fewer than forty Black church leaders and Black College Presidents publicly announced a self-empowering strategy to fund North Carolina's eleven Black colleges; the name of this new organization is **North Carolina Black Churches for North Carolina Black Colleges**, or **NCBC²**.

This is truly an economic movement we can all relate to, get excited about, and one in which we can participate as well. Here we have churches from all of the major cities in North Carolina, representing the entire state, collaborating in an effort to add $11 million to the coffers of Black colleges and universities, not just for one year but perpetually.

To make it even more exciting these church officials are not asking their members to ante up more money; they are simply asking them to "redirect" a small portion of their everyday spending to a Black owned business – The MATAH Network.

MATAH, a people, a business, and a movement, creates opportunities for Black manufacturers and producers to get their products out to the market. MATAH also helps create employment opportunities and serves as a vehicle through which entrepreneurs not only build wealth but retain it as well.

The churches, working within MATAH's One Church – One Channel Program, devised by Father George Clements, have crossed denominational lines to embark on a mission that will go down in history the same way Black churches of the 1700's and 1800's made history by establishing and supporting Black colleges. These churches have taken up the gauntlet thrown down by their predecessors by, once again, doing what is necessary for the benefit our progeny.

The schools to receive the funds are Barber Scotia, Bennett, Elizabeth City State, Fayetteville State, Johnson C. Smith, Livingstone, A&T State, North Carolina Central, Saint Augustine, Shaw, and Winston-Salem State. While $1 million per school is the initial goal, **NCBC²** has the potential to expand its funding capacity exponentially. As church members continue to purchase MATAH-distributed laundry detergent, dishwashing liquid, body lotions and oils, Grenada Nutmeg Oil for topical pain relief, Mariandina nutritional products, and other MATAH products, the **NCBC²** fund increases and perpetuates.

There's more: North Carolina is just one state; this group of Black churches comprises only a small percentage of our churches in this country; in addition to church organizations, there are hundreds of Black organizations in this country that could, if they would just act on this very practical and simple strategy, create a revenue source that will allow them to move away from being mired in the fund-raising mode, and spend more time fulfilling their missions.

I am proud to have been among those strong, committed, and resolute brothers and sisters who stood up publicly and proclaimed their love and concern for our youth and for our revered educational institutions. I am proud to have witnessed, just one year after the transition of our dear brother Ken Bridges, men and women acting in the tradition that Ken left behind.

It made me feel so good to hear the president of Bennett College, Johnetta Cole, speak so eloquently about the MATAH – Church partnership. It was fantastic to hear Dr. Carlton Eversley, executive director of the **NCBC²**, discuss how this "new" money would be raised through the MATAH network as church members redirect their everyday spending via MATAH's Autoship Program. It was touching to see Al Wellington, Ken's longtime partner and dear friend, as he quietly smiled; no doubt rejoicing at what was taking place. And, it was indeed an honor, once again, to be in the company of Jocelyn Bridges, Ken's "Queen," as she proudly watched the realization of one of her husband's goals.

Dr. John Mendez, President of the Ministers' Conference of Winston-Salem and Vicinity, said, "There is no logic to having millions of so-called 'educated' people (most from HBCU's) and thousands of churches that have enlightened and 'saved' millions of Black people, and yet we stand by and allow our colleges and universities to suffer and close their doors for financial reasons."

But, Rev. William S. Fails, pastor of the Greater First United Baptist Church, and originator of **NCBC²**, put it best by saying, "Judging by the fruits that our efforts bear, we would have to question the relevance of our own 'education' and the role of the church in our community, if we do not immediately take steps to provide greater financial security for our ... Black colleges and universities." Amen, my brother!

Let Pharaoh Go!

Do you ever think about the similarities between the Children of Israel and Black people in America today? I make the comparison often in my speeches and in my classroom discussions on economic enslavement versus economic freedom. And we don't need to revisit slavery in America to find those common attributes that exist in both groups. We need only look at what has taken place among the great-grandchildren of former slaves since 1965.

When the Israelites were freed, in Exodus 12 we see the first case of reparations in history when God told them to go back and get gold and other valuables from their former captors. He knew they would need some "money" to do what He wanted them to do.

The Israelites were "free at last" after over 400 years of captivity. They were certainly physically free, but they were still psychologically enslaved. How do we know that? Well, some wanted to go back to Egypt. Many of them complained about what they didn't have. Others, even after seeing the miracles in the desert and on the banks of the Red Sea, rebelled and did not believe they could accomplish what they had set out to do. They did not believe they could "possess" the land that had been given to them. They felt inferior to the inhabitants of the land. They called them "giants" and referred to themselves as lowly "grasshoppers."

Because of their rebelliousness, their murmuring, their complaining, and their ungratefulness at what they had been given, they were made to wander in the desert for 40 years, only a short distance from their destination. They had to wander the desert until all except two of those in the original group that left Egypt had died. Caleb and Joshua, both brave and willing men, were the only ones of the original group to make it to the promise land.

Although these freed slaves walked in shoes that did not wear out, drank water from a rock, ate manna from heaven, were given more quail to eat than they could consume, and saw the work of God almighty, first hand, they were still psychologically enslaved. They still believed Pharaoh's "ice was colder." They paid a high price for their disbelief and their reluctance to possess their land.

In 1964 and 1965 two important freedom documents were signed for Black Americans by President Lyndon Johnson: The Civil Rights Act and the Voting Right Act, respectively. Black folks were "really" free *this time*. So we ran out and started spending our money in everyone else's business, abandoning our own in the process.

This is similar to what the Children of Israel did when they were set free. On their first occasion to "spend" their "money" they "bought" a golden calf and began to worship it, much akin to the things we spend our money on these days and how we worship all the "stuff" we have, especially our cars. But, the Israelites' dollars started *making sense* after the Israelites had been severely disciplined for their outlandish behavior. Thus, the next time they had the opportunity to spend their money, they pooled their resources and "spent" it on the Tabernacle. I told you God knew they would need some money at some point on their journey.

After Black people in America had secured the right to spend our money wherever we wanted, we bought a lot of golden calves and we went to work on our voting rights and elected 12,000 Black politicians across this country. Unfortunately, just like the Israelites with all of their resources, we were still not psychologically free. Consequently, we have been wandering around this desert we call the United States of America since 1965, nearly 40 years now, complaining about what we don't have and what "the man" won't let us do, some of us even wanting to stay in Egypt with Pharaoh, and some of us in complete and utter disobedience and rebellion.

Just as the Israelites did when told to take only as much manna as they needed, that it would be there on the next day, today's Black folks think scarcity and overstuff their pockets with all they can carry, not believing in sharing and abundance, as well as the fact that there is enough for all of us.

What parallels there are between us and the Children of Israel. Both groups were given all of the resources, financial and intellectual, necessary to achieve psychological and economic freedom. Both groups, at least in the relative short term, failed to do so. The sad thing is that we, the modern generation, the most educated Black folks on the face of the earth, the most affluent Blacks in the world, did not learn the lesson provided to us by the Children of Israel. Many of us study their history; we hear sermons about them; and some of us look back at what they went through and how disobedient they were, and we ask, "How could the Israelites have been so misled?" Well, we now have to ask that same question of ourselves because we have virtually duplicated the plight of our progenitors.

What must we do to change the situation in which we find ourselves? Some would say pray. Others would say nothing will change until we "submit" to the will of the Almighty and be obedient to His word. Still others would say we must "come together." All of these responses have some validity; however, any one of them alone will not take us where we need to go. Millions of Black folks pray everyday. Millions of us have submitted. And millions of us have worked together, and still do, on various projects and programs all over this country. There is a missing ingredient though: Sacrifice.

When it comes to making the sacrifices necessary for collective economic empowerment, too many of our people back up and mimic DuBois' Talented Tenth, who he said held on to selfishness and would not embrace sacrifice to lift up their people.

Praying is good and it is right, but after we pray, aren't we supposed to do something? When Saul was praying, after his road to Damascus conversion experience, Ananias told him to get up and go be baptized. He told him to take some action.

Isn't obedient submission to God's will grounded in doing some work? If not, where is the proof of your obedience? Is it merely in your belief and your faith? James says "Faith without works is dead. So if you are not willing to do some work to show your faith, then your faith is dead. And since faith gives access to God's grace, maybe that's why we are still so far behind and find ourselves lacking in the things we need.

Finally, once we "come together" shouldn't we work collectively to build something? Shouldn't we put our resources together for the benefit of the group? Shouldn't we stop spending our billions on golden calves to worship? When we come together shouldn't we be eager to rip the gold earrings from our ears (and gold chains from our necks) for the building of our modern-day tabernacles? And I am not talking about multi-million dollar edifices; I would rather see us build and own "performing assets" like malls, hotels, housing, and other necessities of this life in the desert. We are not lacking for grandiose church buildings, especially those that are not utilized to exhibit our "works." There's nothing wrong with having a comfortable church building; but do we really need monuments to men and women? The people comprise the church; so what then should the work of the church (the people) be? Come together? Yes. Do some real work? Absolutely yes!

Achieving economic empowerment, something our leaders say is the most important goal in the 21st century, albeit, after squandering nearly 40 years directing us down other paths and neglecting this most important aspect of our freedom, will only be realized through the "work of our own hands," as Martin Delany told us. We have much work to do.

In 2005 we will have seen our 40 years in the desert, that is, if we do nothing to change our situation before then. And for those of you who believe we are being chastised for our disobedience and will have to do our 40-year penitence, just as the Israelites were made to, I say let's at least start getting ready for our release from captivity. How about that?

We cannot do the work nor can we even prepare to work for our future until we are willing to let go of our past enslavement and our enslavers. By that I mean we must decide once and for all to let Pharaoh go. After all, he let us go a long time ago when he no longer needed us to care for his possessions, to take care of his children, to clean his house, and to work in his fields. The only things he needs us for now are to fight in his wars, to occupy his prisons, and to spend our money in all of his businesses. And we have been, and continue to be, willing accomplices in this diabolical plan of continued economic enslavement of Black Americans, by financing our own oppression.

"Let Pharaoh go," and we will finally be free.

Stand! And Move Your "S" to the Front!

"When a cause comes along and you know in your bones that it is just, yet refuse to defend it--at that moment you begin to die. And I have never seen so many corpses walking around talking about justice." - **Mumia Abu-Jamal**

Every now and then my minister asks me to offer a sermon to our congregation and, even though I am not a preacher, I do it, but only after I have made every effort to prepare myself with thorough research, prayer, and resolve to give it all I have and to do my best. It is an awesome and very serious responsibility to stand and speak to God's people, so I take it quite seriously.

Two of the several topics I have spoken on have to do with our obligation to take a stand and our responsibility to turn our words into action. I suggested we stand up for four things: The truth; what is right; justice; and the rights of others. There are other things we must stand up for as well but those were the ones I chose for that particular message. I also suggested we turn our words into action by moving the "S" at the end of "words" to the front, thus, changing it to "sword," which always implies some kind of action.

Some of us like to quote biblical scripture, but we don't like it as much when we have to follow it. Take the subject of standing up. We love to hear Donnie McClurkin and BeBe Winans sing the song, "Stand," and we love the part in Ephesians 6 where it talks about the armor we need to fight against those "principalities" and "rulers of darkness." We especially like the part that tells us after we have done all we can do, still stand. Sounds good, doesn't it? Do we stand when the times get rough?

As far as the action goes, we love what the Book tells us about faith being dead without works. We love to read and recite the great stories of strength and courage and resolve among the men and women of old. We get riled up on Sunday mornings all over this country when we hear about Joshua and

Gideon and all of the others who changed their words into action by moving their "S" to the front.

I can hear you now saying, "But God was with those persons back then. God told them what to do and He was there with them when they did those things." Well, don't we believe that God is with us today, talking to us, and telling us what to do through His divine Word? What is wrong with us today? Are we so afraid of the consequences of doing what's right, and taking some righteous action against the disparities we face, that we are willing to remain in our cocoons refusing to stand and to act?

Just where is our faith anyway? Better yet, in what or whom do we have faith? Black people in America have been blessed with everything we need to fight the battles we face daily. Why do we cower and crouch at even the thought of having to stand and fight? Suppose Marcus, Medgar, Malcolm, and Martin had been so afraid of standing up and taking action that they decided to sit out the battles they faced – the battles we faced. Where would we be today?

Where would the Children of Israel have been if Joshua and Caleb had also been afraid like the other spies were and decided they could not possess the land God had already given to them? The people would have had to continue to walk around that desert for, who knows, maybe another forty years.

Black people have been walking around this desert called the United States of America for nearly forty years now, as Brother Shy du Reaux of Nashville, Tennessee, once told me. We may still be walking forty years from now if we continue to sit down and refuse to take the appropriate action necessary for our collective economic survival and growth. I don't know about you, but I do not want to eclipse the record set by the Israelites.

Stand up against injustice; stand up for what is right; stand up for the truth; and stand up for the rights of others. And, stop being tepid; stop being bland; stop being stoic; and stop being apathetic. Move your "S" to the front and take action, understanding and always acknowledging the Source of your resources and your strength. We can do no less for our people, for our children, and for the world.

Epilogue

My passion for economic empowerment and my compassion for our people continue to inspire me to write my weekly newspaper column, Blackonomics. But I too must move to an even higher level. A great deal more of my work will now be concentrated on the actualization of the economic principles and goals I espouse in my writings.

It is one thing to continue to talk about our problems, but it's another thing to stand up and do something about them. I have been heavily involved in all aspects economic empowerment, the teaching, writing, reading, studying, the talking, and the implementation of economic empowerment strategies. Now, with all of the information we have, we must be more action-oriented in our approach to our economic problems.

That action begins with me, so I will continue to "walk the talk." I will continue to teach entrepreneurship; I will continue to support Black owned businesses; I will offer whatever information I have to help in the maintenance and growth of our businesses; I will continue to help raise funds for our institutions.

I will continue to stand against economic injustice; I will follow the instructions found in Psalms 82:3-4, which says, "Defend the cause of the weak and fatherless; maintain the rights of the poor and oppressed. Rescue the weak and needy; deliver them from the hand of the wicked;" and I will not be afraid to claim who I am and whose I am.

As I commit to doing my part, I will be looking for you to do your part as well. I will encourage you to do more than merely talk about economic empowerment; I will stress the importance of you holding your "leaders" accountable for where they lead you; I will seek your support of projects like the Piney Woods School $5.00 campaign, the Blackonomics Million Dollar Club, and other worthwhile causes.

I will encourage you to put into action the principles of Dr. Claud Anderson's Powernomics. Our elder has laid out a complete plan for our economic salvation, and all we have to do is implement that plan to obtain the freedom we seek. What are we waiting for?

I will continue to solicit your support of Jackie Mayfield's Compro-Tax companies throughout this country. I will continue to ask you to join the MATAH Network and to give and buy Black. How can we successfully strive for economic empowerment and not utilize the economic resources we already have in our midst? Supporting Compro-Tax and the MATAH Network, on some level, should be automatic for Black people. Please start now!

I will also continue to ask you to love and trust your brothers and sisters; and I will always be your cheerleader, because I love you all and I will always do whatever I can to help build a strong and everlasting economic foundation for our children and their children.

If you act upon the concepts, strategies, and solutions contained in this book, we will be successful. Knowledge is power only if we use it, and only if we share it. Knowledge can only benefit us if we do not reject it. Please use the information in this book – this Black-o-Knowledge – to make a better life and a better world for us all.

Peace, love, and blessings.

BOOK AVAILABLE THROUGH

Milligan Books, Inc.

Black-o-knowledge $16.95

Order Form

Milligan Books, Inc.

1425 W. Manchester Ave., Suite C, Los Angeles, CA 90047

(323) 750-3592

Name_____ Date _____

Address _____

City_____ State____ Zip Code _____

Day Telephone _____

Evening Telephone_____

Book Title_____

Number of books ordered___ Total ....$ _____

Sales Taxes (CA Add 8.25%) ....$ _____

Shipping & Handling $4.90 for one book..$ _____

Add $1.00 for each additional book...........$ _____

Total Amount Due.....................................$ _____

☐ Check   ☐ Money Order ☐ Other Cards _____

☐ Visa   ☐ MasterCard Expiration Date _____

Credit Card No. _____

Driver License No. _____

Make check payable to Milligan Books, Inc.

_____   _____

Signature   Date